THE
UNBOUGHT GRACE OF LIFE:
Essays in Honor of Russell Kirk

THE

UNBOUGHT GRACE OF LIFE:

Essays in Honor of Russell Kirk

Edited by James E. Person

Sherwood Sugden & Company

PUBLISHERS

315 5th Street, Peru, Illinois 61354

ISBN 0-89385-043-8

Sherwood Sugden & Company
P U B L I S H E R S
315 5th Street, Peru, Illinois 61354

CONTENTS

I. The Man and His Works

II. Redeeming the Time: Essays by Divers Hands

Additional commentary by:

Ray Bradbury, 170 • *William F. Buckley, Jr., viii* • *Roy Campbell, 54* • *Whittaker Chambers, 86* • *Eugene V. Clark, 268* • *John Dos Passos, 266* • *Jude P. Dougherty, 18* • *John P. East, 267* • *Lee Edwards, 12* • *T. S. Eliot, 183* • *Joanne Emmons, 65* • *John Engler, 92* • *Edwin J. Feulner, Jr., 268* • *Madeleine L'Engle, 65* • *Wyndham Lewis, 69* • *W. Wesley McDonald, 246* • *Malcolm Muggeridge, 105* • *George H. Nash, 198* • *Richard John Neuhaus, 222* • *Flannery O'Connor, 69* • *Ronald Reagan, vii* • *Wilhelm Roepke, 266* • *William A. Rusher, 50* • *David L. Schindler, 222* • *Ernest van den Haag, 170.*

"It is ideas that truly rule our world, that govern our lives and values, and move men to action. Indeed, Russell Kirk's life work reflects his conviction and ours that ideas do have consequences.

"Dr. Kirk has helped renew a generation's interest and knowledge of these 'true ideas', these 'permanent things', which are the underpinnings and the intellectual infrastructure of the conservative revival in our nation. He has guided Americans in finding the meanings of the political world around them and in dealing with the universal problems of the human experience. The values and ancient truths of our civilization have been the focus of his powerful intellect in such major works as The Conservative Mind and The Roots of American Order. . . .

"We look to the future with anticipation that his work will continue to exert a profound influence in the defense of our values and our cherished civilization."

— Ronald Reagan, in a letter read
at a testimonial dinner for
Russell Kirk at the Mayflower
Hotel, Washington, D.C.,
October 1, 1981.

"*In 1954, I flew to Michigan. I had a single objective, and I greatly feared that I would fail in it. I desired that Professor Kirk would consent, beginning with the opening issue, to contribute a regular column to* National Review *on doings of the academic world.*

"*I confess I was very nervous. Although he was only a few years older, at 28 I felt that an entire world lay between us, and this is so today as, with dismay, I contemplate how very much he knows, that I shall never know — that ever-widening gulf between his learning, and my own. He was then a bachelor, and shortly after I arrived he took me to dinner at a neighborhood restaurant, where he ordered Tom Collinses for both of us. Emboldened by that warm aloofness which is his trademark, I put it to him directly, and his reply was instantaneous: Yes, he would be glad to write a regular column for my prospective magazine. I was so elated . . . that I took to ordering more Tom Collinses, but in every case, one for each of us. The evening proceeded toward a pitch of such hilarity that, at midnight, I barely was able to drive the car back to Russell's house. On arriving, he led me to my bedroom, bade me goodnight only a second before I collapsed into my bed, to rise seven hours later and bump into Russell only then emerging from his study. He had, in the interval since dinner, written a chapter of his history of St. Andrews College, and would be catching a little sleep after he served me breakfast. . . .*

"*Reflecting on his formidable work one's mind rests principally, I think, on Russell's knowledge of the critical importance of what came before, of the intellectual treasures of the past. His perspective on the matter is so clear that he recognizes that every generation is dependent on what came earlier, to which insight he devoted the epigraph of* A Program for Conservatives, *published by Henry Regnery in 1954. 'Long before our time,' Cicero wrote in his* De Re Publica, *'the customs of our ancestors molded admirable men, and in turn these eminent men upheld the ways and institutions of their forebears. Our age, however, inherited the Republic like some beautiful painting of bygone days, its colors already fading through great age; and not only has our time neglected to freshen the colors of the picture, but we have failed to preserve its form and outlines.'*

"*But, applied to America, that is less true today than it was 25 years ago when Russell adduced it, as an epigraph fitting not only for Rome, but prospectively for America. And the difference, between then and now, is substantially of his own doing.*"

— *William F. Buckley, Jr.,
from remarks read at a testimonial
dinner for Russell Kirk at the
Mayflower Hotel, Washington, D.C.,
October 1, 1981 (and reprinted
in his* Right Reason, *1985)*

Introduction

"The unbought grace of life, the cheap defence of nations, the nurse of manly sentiment and heroic enterprise, is gone!" wrote Edmund Burke in one of the more often-quoted sections of his *Reflections on the Revolution in France* (1790). Seeing well the folly and brutality into which revolutionary France was sinking, Burke realized that what Cicero termed "the unbought grace of life"—honor—faced a season of being trodden beneath the feet of ruthless expediency. He reasoned far better than the *philosophes* that much more than the dead hand of the past was being lost by the disposal of all custom, convention, and prescription by the French nation. Having disposed of a king and deified themselves, the French gained an emperor within a short time. Thus was the cautionary wisdom of Cupid's curse borne out: "They that do change old loves for new,/Pray gods they change for worse"—lines quoted in a fitting context on the final page of Russell Kirk's *The Conservative Mind*.

Truly, Kirk embodies "the unbought grace of life," a fact attested to by his family, his friends, and by many who have made his acquaintance over the years. He is a quiet, dignified, good-humored man, but he is also a passionate defender of the roots of American order. He has been honored by presidents, governors, fellow scholars, and his students for his work in shoring up that which makes for the noble and enduring in American culture. For this and for the professionalism he has demonstrated in performing this labor, he has been likened by William F. Buckley, Jr. to Samuel Johnson and G. K. Chesterton. What Michael Henry once wrote of Gerhart Niemeyer can also be said confidently of Kirk: "Like Richard Hooker he has labored 'for no other cause but for this; that posterity may know we have not loosely through silence permitted things to pass away as in a dream.'"

1

Although called by admirers the American Cicero, the Sage of Mecosta, and other titles, Kirk has retained the stamp of his upbringing in the small railroad town of Plymouth, Michigan and in the village of Mecosta in Michigan's upstate "stump country." By happy coincidence I too have grown up in Plymouth, and I have walked the railroad line with my son, looked upon the house in which Kirk was born and raised, and skated upon the millpond he adapted and described in his ghost story "An Encounter at Mortstone Pond." To those of us who came of age in Plymouth or any other such small town where the people are generous and neighborly — while knowing how to mind their own business — it was a wonderful place to live. Each in its own way, Plymouth and Mecosta are what Thornton Wilder had in mind as the setting of *Our Town.*

"We are people to whom the past is forever speaking," wrote Kirk's fellow Michiganian, Bruce Catton. "We listen to it because we cannot help ourselves, for the past speaks to us with many voices." Among the voices from the past whose writings shaped Kirk's thought early on were Marcus Aurelius, Dr. Johnson, Sir Walter Scott, James Fenimore Cooper, Nathaniel Hawthorne — and Edmund Burke. These stirred his imagination as he grew up beside the railroad tracks in the lower end of Plymouth, even as the chuff and rumble of trains accompanied his readings; and perhaps the voices of trains in the night, evoking thoughts of long journeys and the brevity of mortal life, helped in their small way to whet the sword of his imagination.

Leaving Plymouth to pursue higher education, Kirk took his B.A. at Michigan State College (now Michigan State University), his M.A. at Duke University, and his doctorate at the University of St. Andrews. During a career as a nationally respected man of letters, which began in earnest with the publication of *The Conservative Mind* in 1953, he has been on friendly terms with the likes of Wyndham Lewis, Roy Campbell, Whittaker Chambers, Ronald Reagan, Flannery O'Connor, Richard M. Weaver, Ray Bradbury, T. S. Eliot, and Barry Goldwater (who is, to my knowledge, the only person in the world who addresses Kirk as "Russ"). In 1964 he married Annette Courtemanche, who deserves a *Festschrift* of her own for the encouragement and assistance she has provided Russell over the years, for her efforts on behalf of excellence in education, and for the vitality she instills in others by her words and example. The Kirks have lived for many years now in his ancestral home, Piety Hill, in Mecosta,

2

where they have raised four daughters. The "Mecosta Mission," as one writer has called their house, has also served as a refuge for homeless immigrants in need of job and language skills, half-reformed burglars in need of shelter and work, unwed mothers in need of acceptance and help, and students seeking answers to the essential questions of life. At present, while maintaining a busy schedule of speaking engagements, Kirk is preparing for the publication of his autobiography, which bears the title *The Sword of Imagination.*

In this short sketch of the life of Russell Kirk, I have deliberately presented only the barest outline of his writing career and related accomplishments, believing that this aspect of the story can be best told by the first ten contributors to this collection. It is enough to say here, though, that Kirk's name appears on virtually every list of those who revitalized conservatism. Lee Edwards has identified the three progenitors of modern conservatism as Kirk, Buckley, and Goldwater. Edwin Feulner, on the other hand, has cited conservatism's three prime movers as Kirk, Friedrich von Hayek, and Milton Friedman. William A. Rusher, former publisher of *National Review*, considers Hayek's *The Road to Serfdom*, Chambers's *Witness*, and *The Conservative Mind* the three most powerful philosophical contributions to the conservative movement that awakened in the 1950s. Even *American Spectator* editor R. Emmett Tyrell, Jr., who otherwise has little favorable to say of the man from Mecosta, has named Buckley, Friedman, and Kirk as "superb role models" for the conservative movement as he encountered it during the 1960s. Whichever group of influential conservatives is named, then, it seems Russell Kirk is the constant. Indeed, as Buckley has written, "It is . . . inconceivable to imagine an important, let alone hope for a dominant, conservative movement in America, without his labor."

Following in this frame of thought, Forrest McDonald opens the first section of this *Festschrift* with an introductory overview of Kirk's significance to the conservative movement. Next, in the first biographical essay in the collection, the distinguished Burke scholar Peter J. Stanlis recounts the milestones of nearly 40 years of close friendship with Kirk, recalling moments of shared laughter, battles against intolerant opponents, memorable conversations, and other events. John Lukacs and Irving Horowitz follow with their own memories of long friendships with Kirk, positing the salient features of his outlook, personality, and accomplishment. Next, Cecilia Kirk,

Russell and Annette's second-oldest daughter, recounts her father's influence as a reader and storyteller during her childhood and young adulthood. *The Conservative Mind's* original publisher, Henry Regnery, then offers a survey of Kirk's career. Assessments of key works among Kirk's canon then follow. Jeffrey Hart writes of Kirk's importance as the author of two key works, *The Conservative Mind* and *Prospects for Conservatives*. M. E. Bradford, a longtime admirer of Kirk, though not an uncritical one, discusses *The Roots of American Order*, while M. D. Aeschliman, the noted C. S. Lewis scholar, expresses admiration for *The Wise Men Know What Wicked Things Are Written on the Sky*. The first section of the collection closes with commentary by the ageless Agrarian Andrew Lytle upon Kirk's collection of ghost stories, *Watchers at the Strait Gate*.

With one exception, the following section contains essays in disciplines to which Kirk has contributed. The distinguished literary scholar Cleanth Brooks begins with an essay on the value of poetry to mankind. Another literary essayist, Louis Filler, then assays the value of Helen Hooven Santmyer's novel *". . . And Ladies of the Club"* as an example of regenerate small-town fiction. Claes G. Ryn discourses on virtue, determining that it can be inherited, taught, and possessed, but not coerced or legislated into existence: a common-sense conclusion, but one that is curiously unfashionable today. On a related note, but in a field outside Kirks' expertise, social anthropologist Grace E. Goodell offers a convincing study of the damaging effects of governmental paternalism upon its recipients. Next, Paul Gottfried provides an overview of classical assessments of the value of history. Gerhart Niemeyer then surveys the history of a revolutionary doctrine, millenarianism, and its culmination in Marxism, itself truly the god that failed, as recent events testify. Attorney William Bentley Ball traces legal decisions that bode ill for people of faith in America. An expert on the life and work of one unintimidated man of faith, Ian Boyd relates Chesterton's journalism — itself long derided by commentators as a distraction to GKC's true literary destiny — to the rest of his canon, finding it integral. (Curiously, Kirk's own journalism has been subjected to the same judgments.) Anne Husted Burleigh ruminates on the significance of the Adamses of Massachusetts — a family whose thought was masterfully limned in *The Conservative Mind* — and their relevance to America today. Robert Nisbet examines the relationship between Alexis de Tocqueville and Lamennais, concluding that the pluralistic world-view of the two was considerably indebted to the form of liberal Catholicism founded in the 1820s as a middle ground between the conservatism and the egalitarian individualism of their age. Finally, Otto von Habsburg closes the volume with a view to recent events in Eastern Europe; he offers, as his essay title states, "a strategy for freedom."

Additional commentary on Kirk's life and works by T. S. Eliot, Wyndham Lewis, and Flannery O'Connor, among many others, rounds out the volume. Just before a bibliography of Kirk's major works, John Dos Passos has the final word, scoring the neglect of history and its lessons by many Americans and urging that in order to face the social and political issues of today and the future, we need to listen to those voices of the past that are forever speaking. Thus informed, we will then need "all the verve, all the refusal to accept things as they are, all the brains the new generation has to offer."

All in all, then, the essays collected here form a fitting tribute to this remarkable man who grew up in an old Midwestern railroad town. Like George Willard in Anderson's *Winesburg*, Russell Kirk eventually left his home in the town of his youth, but he never left small-town living and values behind. He and all of us are a people to whom the past is forever speaking. But unlike so many moderns, Kirk chose to listen to its wisdom. Just now as I write, I can hear the whistle of locomotives in the night. Just outside nearby Plymouth Township, one of them is rumbling around the long curve near the Beck Road crossing and heading northwest toward Michigan's stump country, home of one of the wisest and noblest souls this Republic has produced.

James E. Person, Jr.
Canton, Michigan
February, 1993

Acknowledgments

Many people are due thanks for their roles in bringing this book into existence. I wish to thank Father Ian Boyd for contributing his essay, which was originally published in a different form in *The Chesterton Review* XVIII, May 1992 (©1992 *The Chesterton Review*. Reprinted by permission of the publisher); Mr. Ray Bradbury for granting permission to reprint his letter of 16 September 1974; Mr. John Chambers for allowing us to reprint a portion of a letter from his father, Whittaker Chambers; the University of Chicago Press for permission to reprint an essay (©1985 by the Wenner-Gren Foundation for Anthropological Research. Reprinted by permission of the publisher) from *Current Anthropology* 26 (April 1985); Dr. William Bedford Clark, Mrs. Charlene Clark, and the Friends of the Sterling C. Evans Library for permission to reprint an edited version of Cleanth Brooks's essay "Poetry and Prophecy," which was originally a lecture delivered before the Friends of the Sterling C. Evans Library at Texas A&M University at their April 23, 1988, meeting in Winedale, Texas; The Educational Reviewer, Inc., for permission to reprint Andrew Lytle's "The Terrors of the Soul," which first appeared in a slightly different form in *The University Bookman* 25 (Spring 1985); Mrs. T. S. Eliot for kindly authorizing me to quote from one of her husband's previously unpublished letters, to which correspondence she retains copyright; and the Intercollegiate Studies Institute for granting permission to reprint two essays: M. E. Bradford's "A Proper Patrimony: Russell Kirk and America's Moral Genealogy" (copyright © 1976 by the Intercollegiate Studies Institute, Inc. Reprinted by permission of the publisher), which first appeared in a slightly different form in *The Intercollegiate Review* 12 (Fall 1976); and "The Family Adams" (copyright © 1981 by the Intercollegiate Studies Institute, Inc. Reprinted by permission of the publisher), which originally appeared in an altered form in *Modern Age* 25 (Spring 1981). I would also like to thank *National Review* for permission to reprint an essay from the December 31, 1985 issue (©1985 by *National Review*, Inc., 150 East 35th Street, New York, NY 10016. Reprinted by permission); Mr. Omar S. Pound for granting permission to quote from Wyndham Lewis's letter of 29 August 1955 (copyright The Wyndham Lewis Memorial Trust, by permission) and The Honorable Ronald W. Reagan for permission to quote from his letter of 1 October 1981. A short item from *The Religion & Society Report* 6 (September 1988) is reprinted by permission of The Rockford Institute.

I would also like to thank my wife, Lista, for her patience and help throughout the production of this *Festschrift*, Mr. Edward V. Giles and Mr. Jeffrey O. Nelson for their enthusiasm for this project from the beginning, and Mr. Gerard J. Senick and Mr. Arthur Single for their insights. Finally, I would like to thank Mr. Robert Kamphuis, who conceived the idea for this collection, made initial contact with many of the contributors, and otherwise conducted much of the difficult planning and legwork at the beginning that set this worthy enterprise in motion.

THE CONTRIBUTORS

M. D. Aeschliman was, until recently, Lecturer in English literature at the University of Virginia. He holds B.A., M.A., M.Phil., and Ph.D. degrees from Columbia University, and taught there as well as in Switzerland for seven years. He is the author of *The Restitution of Man: C. S. Lewis and the Case against Scientism* (1983). Dr. Aeschliman also wrote the introduction to a new edition of Malcolm Muggeridge's 1934 novel *Winter in Moscow* (1987). His essays and reviews have appeared in a dozen journals on both sides of the Atlantic.

William Bentley Ball is a constitutional lawyer and member of the law firm of Ball, Skelly, Murren & Connell, Harrisburg. At one time a teacher of constitutional law, he now frequently writes and lectures on issues pertaining to religious liberty, in which field his practice has basically concentrated. Since 1960 Mr. Ball has been active in litigation both at the trial and appellate level. His cases have taken him to the courts of twenty-two states — and eight times to the Supreme Court of the United States, where he argued in the landmark cases of *Wisconsin v. Yoder, Lemon v. Kurtzman,* and *Bob Jones University v. United States.* Over the years, Mr. Ball has been counsel to the Pennsylvania Catholic Conference, the Association of Christian Schools International, and the National Committee for Amish Religious Freedom. Out of this has grown his strong interest in the common public concerns of evangelicals and Catholics, an interest reflected in the book he has edited, *In Search of a National Morality: A Christian Manifesto* (1992).

Ian Boyd is the editor of and frequent contributor to *The Chesterton Review,* which is published at St. Thomas More College in Saskatoon, Saskatchewan. He is the author of *The Novels of G. K. Chesterton: A Study in Art and Propaganda* (1975). Father Boyd belongs to the Congregation of Priests of St. Basil, in which order he was ordained in 1963.

M. E. Bradford was an essayist, editor, and professor of English at the University of Dallas whose main interests were American literature, history, and political philosophy. As he once wrote, "The particular emphasis of my work is on the continuity of Anglo-American culture and on the importance of rhetoric to the study of politics and literature. Much of my literary criticism concerns the literature of the American South." He was the author of such works as *Generations of the Faithful Heart: On the Literature of the South* (1983), *Remembering Who We Are: Reflections of a Southern Conservative* (1985), *The Reactionary Imperative: Essays Literary and Political* (1990), *Against the Barbarians and Other Reflections on Familiar Themes* (1992), and *Original Intentions: On the Making and Ratification of the U.S. Constitution* (forthcoming).

Cleanth Brooks, Gray professor of Rhetoric emeritus at Yale University, is among the foremost American literary scholars. He is distinguished for his achievements in literary theory and for his skills in explicating poetry, drama, and fiction. Dr. Brooks introduced the New Criticism into the teaching of poetry with his textbook *Understanding Poetry* (1938; 4th ed'n. 1975), written with Robert Penn Warren. He also contributed to the study of William Faulkner's works with such widely respected studies as *William Faulkner: The Yoknapatawpha Country* (1963), and *On the Prejudices, Predilections and Firm Beliefs of William Faulkner* (1987).

Anne Husted Burleigh is the author of *John Adams* (1969), a biography with emphasis upon Adams's political thought. She earned her B.A. from DePauw University and the M.A. in history from Indiana University. Mrs. Burleigh is the editor of *Education in a Free Society* (1973) and a contributing editor of *Crisis*, a periodical of lay Catholic opinion to which she contributes a regular column. Other essays and book reviews have appeared in *Modern Age* and *The Intercollegiate Review*.

Louis Filler, a widely travelled academic and author, has long valued continuity from past to present; and maintenance — recovery, in some cases — of vital traditions. His books *Randolph Bourne* (1943), *The Muckrakers* (1976), *Appointment at Armageddon* (1976), and *Vanguards and Followers: Youth in the American Tradition* (1978) examine aspects of several key national developments. He notes that dictionaries on American social reform and on American conservatism have argued, in effect, for their relationship; in support of this, Dr. Filler often cites the friendship in old age of Thomas Jefferson and John Adams.

Grace E. Goodell is Director of the Program in Social Change and Development at The Johns Hopkins University School of Advanced International Studies, Washington, D.C. She has taught anthropology at Wellesley College, been Visiting Scholar at the Harvard Law School and the Harvard Institute for International Development, and served as Rockefeller Foundation anthropologist at the International Rice Research Institute, the Philippines. Dr. Goodell has conducted field research on problems of economic development for several United Nations and U.S. government agencies, and on Andean and Middle Eastern indigenous crafts for the American Museum of Natural History. She is currently conducting a long research project on "the non-economic factors contributing to the remarkable development of East Asias's 'Four Little Dragons' ": Taiwan, South Korea, Singapore, and Hong Kong.

Paul Gottfried is a professor of political science at Elizabethtown College, where he specializes in European social and intellectual history. His essays have appeared in such periodicals as *Thought, Journal of the History of Ideas, Telos, Church History, Modern Age,* and *Review of Politics.* A former senior editor of *The World and I* and the former editor-in-chief of *Continuity: A Journal of History,* he is the author of *Conservative Millenarians* (1980), *The Search for Historical Meaning* (1987), and (with Thomas Fleming) *The Conservative Movement* (1988; second ed'n., without a coauthor, 1992). Dr. Gottfried is currently the editor of *This World.*

Otto von Habsburg, son of the Emperor Karl and head of the house of Habsburg-Lothringen, renounced his claim to the throne in 1961 and became president of the Paneuropa Union twelve years later. In 1979 he assumed his present position as a member of the European Parliament. In addition to his political responsibilities, Dr. von Habsburg is a writer who has contributed to scholarly periodicals throughout the Western world. His publications include *Politik für das Jahr 2000* (1968), *Rudolph v. Habsburg* (1973), *Ein europäischer Friedensfürst* (1978), and 24 other books on history and political science. He has received the Bavarian Order of Merit, the Ordre du Lion d'Or, the Europäischer Karlspreis der Sudentendeutschen Landsmannschaft, and the 1977 Adenauer Prize. Dr. von Habsburg resides in Bavaria.

Jeffrey Hart is a professor of English at Dartmouth College, a syndicated columnist, and a senior editor at *National Review.* He is the author of *Political Writers of Eighteenth-Century England* (1964), *The American Dissent* (1966), *When the Going Was Good: American Life in the Fifties* (1982), and *Acts of Recovery: Essays on Culture and Politics* (1989), among other works.

Irving Louis Horowitz, Hannah Arendt Distinguished Professor of Sociology and Political Science at Rutgers University, has lectured widely on hemispheric and developmental themes. His writings include *Cuban Com-*

munism (1970; seventh rev. ed'n. 1991) and *Beyond Empire and Revolution: Militarization and Consolidation in the Third World* (1982).

Cecilia Kirk, one of Russell and Annette Kirk's four daughters, earned the B.A. in English at Hillsdale College and the M.Phil. in Modern History at the University of St. Andrews. She is program director at the Young America's Foundation, a conservative educational group, in Herndon, Virginia.

John Lukacs is an historian and professor at Chestnut Hill College, in Philadelphia. Some reviewers of his 17 books have been led to call him a "philosophical historian." His works include *The Great Powers and Eastern Europe* (1953), *A History of the Cold War* (1961; 3rd edition published as *A New History of the Cold War*, 1966), *The Passing of the Modern Age* (1970), *Outgrowing Democracy: A History of the United States in the Twentieth Century* (1984), and *The Duel* (1991).

Andrew Lytle is the surviving member of the Agrarians and contributor to their manifesto, *I'll Take My Stand* (1930). A farmer, novelist, former friend of the individual Fugitives and Agrarians, editor of *The Sewanee Review*, and professor of English at the University of the South and Vanderbilt (among other institutions), he has been a prominent figure in American literature for over sixty years. Retired now, Dr. Lytle lives in Monteagle, Tennessee.

Forrest McDonald is Distinguished Research Professor at the University of Alabama. His most recent books are *Novus Ordo Seclorum: The Intellectual Origins of the Constitution* (1985) and *Requiem: Variations on Eighteenth-Century Themes* (1988).

Gerhart Niemeyer is Professor Emeritus of Government at the University of Notre Dame, where he still serves in a part-time capacity as an educator. A longtime associate editor of *Modern Age*, he is the author of *Deceitful Peace* (1971) and *Aftersight and Foresight* (1988), among other works. In his introduction to *Aftersight and Foresight*, Michael Henry wrote, "Gerhart Niemeyer's work, in his writing and his teaching, has been the recovery of order and wholeness, the conservation of the tradition, and the awakening of reason and the life of the mind." In addition to being an educator and essayist, Dr. Niemeyer also serves as Canon of the Episcopal Cathedral of St. James in South Bend, Indiana.

Robert Nisbet is Albert Schwietzer Professor Emeritus at Columbia University. He is the recent recipient of the Ingersoll Prize in scholarly letters and in

1988 became seventeenth Jefferson Lecturer under the auspices of the National Endowment for the Humanities. Among his two dozen books are *The Quest for Community* (1953), *The Sociological Tradition* (1967), *Twilight of Authority* (1975), and *History of the Idea of Progress* (1980). He and his wife live in Washington, D.C.

Henry Regnery, conservative publisher, founded the Henry Regnery Company (forerunner of present-day Regnery Gateway Inc.) in Chicago in 1947. Pledging to "publish good books, wherever we find them," he published William F. Buckley's first book, *God and Man at Yale* (1951), and works by many other distinguished authors, including Wyndham Lewis, Ezra Pound, William Henry Chamberlin, and James J. Kilpatrick. Regnery considers his publication of Kirk's *The Conservative Mind* in 1953 as one of his most significant contributions to publishing. He is the author of *Wyndham Lewis: A Man against His Time* (1969) and *Memoirs of a Dissident Publisher* (1979); he also edited *Viva Vivas!* (1976) and has contributed articles to such periodicals as *National Review*, *The American Spectator*, and *Modern Age*.

Claes G. Ryn is Professor of Politics at The Catholic University of America. He served as chairman of his department and is currently Chairman of the National Humanities Institute. Among his books are *Democracy and the Ethical Life* (1978; second ed'n. 1990) and *Will, Imagination and Reason* (1986). Co-editor of the journal *Humanitas*, Dr. Ryn is the author of numerous articles and chapters in scholarly journals and collective volumes published in the United States and abroad.

Peter J. Stanlis, Distinguished Professor Emeritus of Humanities at Rockford College, is the author or editor of ten books and more than 100 articles and reviews on political, legal, historical, and literary subjects. He has taught at numerous colleges and universities in the United States and Europe, including the universities of Michigan, Detroit, Heidelberg, St. Andrews, Salzburg, and Stockholm, among others. Dr. Stanlis was a founder of the American Society for Eighteenth Century Studies, served as its national treasurer, and was president of its Midwestern branch. The recipient of numerous grants, academic awards, literary prizes, and honors, Dr. Stanlis was appointed to the National Council for the Humanities for a six-year term by President Ronald Reagan in 1982. Five years later, he was appointed a British Academy Research Fellow. Dr. Stanlis was a personal friend of Robert Frost for 23 years and is currently writing a book on the poet's philosophy. His most recent book is entitled *Edmund Burke: Enlightenment and Revolution* (1992).

Also included are excerpts pertinent to the accomplishment of Russell Kirk from the published and unpublished writings of *Ronald Reagan*, former President of the United States; *William F. Buckley, Jr.*, editor, novelist, and commentator; *Whittaker Chambers*, autobiographer and essayist; *Jude P. Dougherty*, Dean of the Department of Philosophy, The Catholic University of America; *W. Wesley McDonald*, American educator; *Flannery O'Connor*, short story writer and novelist; *Wyndham Lewis*, artist and man of letters; *Roy Campbell*, poet and adventurer; *William A. Rusher*, former publisher, director, and vice president of *National Review* and syndicated columnist; *Malcolm Muggeridge*, man of letters; *Lee Edwards*, biographer and essayist; *Edwin J. Feulner, Jr.*, President of the Heritage Foundation; *Madeleine L'Engle*, essayist and author of young-adult fiction; *Richard John Neuhaus*, Roman Catholic priest, editor, and essayist; *Jeanne Emmons*, Michigan State Senator; *John P. East*, lawyer, essayist, educator, and U.S. Senator from North Carolina; *John Engler*, Governor of Michigan; *T. S. Eliot*, man of letters; *Ray Bradbury*, short-story writer, novelist, and screenwriter; *Ernest van den Haag*, scholar and authority on psychology, sociology, and criminal justice; *George H. Nash*, historian and biographer of Herbert Hoover; *Wilhelm Roepke*, economist; *John Dos Passos*, man of letters; *David L. Schindler*, theological scholar and editor of *Communio*; and *Eugene V. Clark*, Vice President and Secretary of the Homeland Foundation as well as Priest of the Archdiocese of New York.

*   *   *

"There are many reasons for the emergence of modern American conservatism. . . . I believe that the political impact of the post-World War II conservative movement can be traced essentially to three men — Russell Kirk, William F. Buckley, Jr., and Barry Goldwater. First came the man of ideas, the intellectual, the philosopher; then the man of interpretation, the journalist, the popularizer; and finally the man of action, the politician, the presidential candidate. . . .

"Robert Nisbet wrote to Kirk that [with The Conservative Mind*] he had done the impossible: he had broken 'the cake of intellectual opposition to the conservative tradition in the United States.'* The New York Times *favorably reviewed* The Conservative Mind *as did* Time*, one of its senior editors going so far as to call it the most important book of the 20th century. . . .*

"In a word, Russell Kirk made conservatism intellectually respectable. Before Kirk, conservatism and extremism were one and the same to most liberal intellectuals."

— Lee Edwards, from his essay
"The Other Sixties: A Flag-Waver's
Memoir" in Policy Review,
Fall 1988.

I.

THE MAN AND HIS WORKS

Russell Kirk:
The American Cicero

by Forrest McDonald

Russell Kirk's contributions to the conservative intellectual movement have scarcely gone unheralded. His founding of *Modern Age* and of *The University Bookman*, his long-running "From the Academy" column in *National Review*, his syndicated column, his foundation activities, his private philanthropies, his personal University of Mecosta, and, above all, his books have been justly celebrated. "The American Cicero," M. E. Bradford has called him, and the appellation seems entirely fitting.

Yet there is one truly impressive aspect of Kirk's career that, as far as I am aware, has gone virtually unremarked: I refer to his capacity for continuing to grow, despite his age and attainments. To the not inconsiderable number of his admirers who, since the first publication of *The Conservative Mind* in 1953, have regarded Kirk as a veritable demigod, the observation may appear presumptuous. From another point of view it may appear to be almost a contradiction. Growth necessarily entails change, and Kirk's subject matter is immutable truths. Moreover, in his writing as well as in the way he has chosen to live his life, he has adhered undeviatingly to the principles he proclaimed to the world in that book. Nonetheless, there has been a continuous evolution in his thinking that has broadened and deepened it and, into the bargain, made possible the resolution of a grave problem that plagued the conservative revival from the outset.

The problem lay in the apparently irreconcilable tension between traditionalism and classical liberalism. As is well known, the spectacular success of *The Conservative Mind* had been preceded and in fact exceeded by that of F. A. Hayek's *The Road to Serfdom*. Kirk explicitly rejected liberalism; indeed, he treated Benthamites and Manchesterians no less harshly than he treated the eighteenth-century French ideologues. He became engaged in a running controversy with Frank Meyer on the subject that went on throughout the 1950s, and in 1960 the continuing debate moved Hayek to write an article renouncing conservatism. The American Left, which embraced neither position, declared that if conservatism meant a Burkean reverence for history and tradition, as Kirk insisted, then American conservatives must be liberals, for liberalism was the American tradition. Conservatives who embraced both positions were (according to John Roche, Arthur Schlesinger Jr., et al.) therefore "schizophrenic."

Now I seriously doubt that Kirk deliberately set out to find a middle ground. Both temperament and experience (including hitches in the Army and a Ford assembly plant) led him to question the value of the economic achievements of the liberal way. Moreover, unlike some agrarian conservatives who denounce industrialism but hunger for its fruits, Kirk has never been particularly attracted to the creature comforts and gadgetry that capitalism makes abundantly available. And as late as 1974, when his monumental *Roots of American Order* was published, he was citing with warm approval Orestes Brownson's dictum that a regime based upon the pursuit of individual interests is inherently self-defeating, for it "promotes the growth of selfishness, and therefore increases the very evil from which government is primarily needed to protect us."

Careful comparison, however reveals some subtle but profound differences between *The Conservative Mind* and *The Roots of American Order*. Somewhat surprisingly, considering that Kirk did most of the work on the earlier book while studying for his doctorate at St. Andrews, he pays almost no attention in it to Scottish thinkers. He mentions Adam Smith only in passing (and somewhat disparagingly), and his few comments on Hume are emphatically negative. But in *Roots* he was obliged to give Hume closer scrutiny because of Hume's obvious influence on Madison, Hamilton, and other Framers; and he discovered that beyond Hume's skepticism and seeming impiety lay a deep and powerfully persuasive understanding of the force of prescriptive order in shaping society.

Then in 1976 Liberty Fund published its elegant new edition of Smith's *Theory of Moral Sentiments*, and at some time during the next five years Kirk devoted a great deal of study to that work. He thereby came to perceive, what only a handful of specialists had been aware of, that there is far more to Smith than *The Wealth of Nations*. Indeed, in an article published in *Modern Age* in 1981, Kirk pointed out that various of John Adams's ideas that he had long admired and thought "original" with Adams were "borrowed—almost plagiarized—from Smith's *Theory of Moral Sentiments*," and Kirk now grouped Smith together with Burke and Johnson as "Three Pillars of Order."

To bring the Scots into the pantheon was to give conservatism an even broader and firmer intellectual foundation than Kirk had provided before. Hume and Smith shared Kirk's (and Burke's) belief in a transcendent moral order, in social continuity, in the principle of prescription, in prudential and natural change as opposed to forced change on the basis of abstract theoretical systems, in variety and inequality, and in the imperfectibility of man; but they went further. Rejecting the mechanistic model of society that was so fashionable in the eighteenth century, they viewed it instead as a living organism. From that premise it followed that society could not be tampered with or improved as an engineer might work with a machine, except at its mortal peril. It also followed—and this is crucial—that in the absence of coercion by government, society would heal its own ailments.

Formulating this as an additional conservative principle to the six that Kirk brilliantly described in the introduction to his *Portable Conservative Reader* (1982), one might say that Hume and Smith teach that society spontaneously and repeatedly generates its own order, and does so through the self-interested activities of the members who compose it at a given time. The principle is most obviously operative in the workings of the Invisible Hand, but the same process is at work in every aspect of society—provided that government allows it to work. Thus, the incorporation of the Scottish thinkers into the conservative tradition enables liberty and tradition to be reconciled: They are not antithetical but complementary.

Kirk's mission, over the years, has been to enrich the conservative intellectual tradition by searching for and reporting to us the wisdom of our ancestors. Every additional finding moves us closer toward a whole from which internal contradictions and tensions are entirely absent. We shall never get there, of course, for what Kirk is seeking, ultimately, is the Truth; and it is inherent in the conservative way of viewing things that the Truth is not for man to know. But he continues to search and to find, and we continue to be enriched.

* * *

"At a time when the West seems to be in a period of moral and cultural decline, and that in spite of its awesome material achievements, it is prudent to turn to the past for guidance. Ours is by no means a unique period. The first-century Roman historian, Titus Livius (59 B.C.–A.D. 17), better known as Livy, recommended to a failing Rome: 'I invite the reader's attention to the much more serious consideration of the kind of lives our ancestors lived, of who were the men and what the means, both in politics and war, by which Rome's power was first acquired and subsequently expanded. I would have him trace the processes of our moral decline, to watch first the sinking of the foundations of morality as the old teaching was allowed to lapse, then the final collapse of the whole edifice, and the dark dawning of our modern day when we can neither endure our vices nor face the remedies needed to cure them.'

"Though all would admit that the present is necessarily shaped by the past, attitudes toward the inherited vary, and those attitudes in turn govern behavior. Respect for ancestry, heritage, or tradition determines concretely the emphasis placed on the study of history, languages, and art, and on the observance of religious and civic ritual.

"Cicero, reflecting on qualifications for leadership in the commonwealth, made a knowledge of and respect for tradition a prime requisite for office. Such knowledge is required of those who would assume positions of leadership for without it they will have no framework from which to judge. For to judge is to measure, to compare, to assess. Judging requires a standard against which a measure is taken.

"For more than one generation Russell Kirk has been both a Livy and a Cicero leading his readers to an appreciation of the time-transcendent. Kirk has taught us that cognitive claims cannot always be directly adjudicated, that the process of judging can be complicated, that if standards are not to be trivial they will have to transcend the present and rest upon the best judgments available to man. His conservative mind is really a Greek mind convinced that nature is intelligible, that the human mind is capable of ferreting out the secrets of nature, and that standards can be adduced and employed. It is a mind to be emulated."

— *Jude P. Dougherty, 1992*

Russell Kirk: An Appraisal

by Henry Regnery

"**H**e doesn't say much—about as communicative as a turtle—but a formidable intelligence, and when he gets behind a typewriter, the results are *most* impressive." So, approximately, was Russell Kirk first described to me by a mutual friend, Sidney Gair, who went on to say that this young instructor in history at Michigan State College (today Michigan State University) had recently finished a manuscript which he, Sidney, thought was of the greatest importance and would interest me. The manuscript—at first entitled "The Conservatives' Rout"—was published a year later, in May 1953, as *The Conservative Mind*. The jacket asserted, in the way of jackets, "This book is a landmark," but so it proved to be. Almost overnight it catapulted the author from the obscurity of East Lansing, Michigan, into national prominence, and restored the word "conservative" from an adjective of opprobrium reserved for members of the Liberty League to respectability—with the publication of *The Conservative Mind* one could call oneself a conservative without apology. The book received a major and carefully written review by Gordon Chalmers in *The New York Times*, *Time* magazine devoted its entire book-review section to it and mentioned it in the feature article of the same edition, which was devoted to George Washington (it was the July 4th issue), it was discussed and reviewed in almost every major newspaper and magazine in the country, even the scholarly publications considered it, often, it seemed, somewhat reluctantly and keeping their distance—who, after all, was this young instructor from Michigan State?—and groups of students in several universities read it together. The appearance of *The Conservative Mind*, in short, was a major intellectual event.

How was it possible that a book which took a position in direct opposition to the orthodoxy that had dominated American intellectual life for more than a generation should have been given so much, and generally favorable attention? What was it about this book by an unknown instructor at a university of no great distinction that should have put it in the very center of discussion? Although a prominent New York publisher had rejected the manuscript before it came to me, the timing was perfect: after years of the pale, self-righteous egalitarianism of liberalism, its adulation of the "common man," its faith in mechanistic solutions to all human problems and its rejection of the tragic and heroic aspects of life, such concepts as "a natural aristocracy," "the unbought grace of life," a view of politics as "the art of apprehending and applying the Justice which is above nature" came like rain after a long drouth. Then, as now, the younger generation was looking for something more inspiring than a guaranteed annual wage and a monthly social security check upon retirement. As August Heckscher remarked in his review in the *New York Herald-Tribune*, Kirk's "proud justification" of the term conservative was "to be welcome." The Goddess Fortuna also played a part: Gordon Keith Chalmers, who was then President of Kenyon College, knew and admired Kirk; when he offered to review the book for the *Times* he could hardly be refused, and Whittaker Chambers, whom I knew and to whom I had sent a set of galleys, suggested to *Time*, where his judgment was still much respected, that *The Conservative Mind* might well be the most important book they would ever have a chance to review, but all this was possible only because it was a book of great quality and substance, written in a clear, vigorous style, skillfully organized, and of sound scholarship.

In the first letter I had from Russell Kirk, written from St. Andrews in Scotland and in reply to mine inquiring if we might have an opportunity to consider his manuscript, he described his new book as " . . . my contribution to our endeavor to conserve the spiritual and intellectual and political tradition of our civilization; and if we are to rescue the modern mind we must do it very soon. . . . The struggle will be decided in the minds of the rising generation — and within that generation, substantially by the minority who have the gift of reason. I do not think we need much fear the decaying 'liberalism' of the retiring generation. . . . But we do need to state some certitudes for the benefit of the groping new masters of society." The book is not, he tells

20

us at the beginning, a history of conservative parties, but a prolonged essay in definition. In the first chapter, therefore, he sets before us the principles of conservatism as they were developed by Edmund Burke in opposition to the three great disintegrating influences of his time: the romantic sentimentalism of Rousseau, the utilitarianism of Bentham, and the rationalism of the French *philosophes*. A sentence from this chapter, which, in a way, contains the essence of Kirk's position is worth quoting. "Now and again Burke praises two great virtues, the keys to private contentment and public peace: they are prudence and humility, the first pre-eminently an attainment of classical philosophy, the second pre-eminently a triumph of Christian discipline. Without them, man must be miserable; and man destitute of piety hardly can perceive either of these rare and blessed qualities."

Having laid down the basic principles of conservatism Kirk goes on to follow the development of conservative ideas and their influence through such men as John Adams, Alexander Hamilton, Walter Scott, John Randolph of Roanoke, John Calhoun, James Fenimore Cooper, Macaulay, Tocqueville, Disraeli, and Cardinal Newman, and so down to Paul Elmer More, Irving Babbitt, George Santayana and T. S. Eliot. The first edition of the book had the sub-title "From Burke to Santayana." In the second revised edition, in which the last chapter was extensively re-written, the sub-title became "From Burke to Eliot." However much the last chapter may have been changed in various editions of the book, all end with the same somber admonition: "They that do change old loves for new,/Pray gods they change for worse."

Russell Kirk was in his late twenties and still a graduate student at St. Andrews University when he began his book — it grew out of his doctoral studies — and in his early thirties when it was finished. It is the work, therefore, of a young man; one senses the freshness of discovery, the immense pleasure of a man, searching for his way in a confused and confusing age, who has discovered a view of life that gives him direction and seems to answer his most pressing questions. For all its maturity and sound scholarship, Kirk is able to maintain throughout the book the quality of discovery that is evident in the first chapter; he writes not only with profound knowledge of his subject, but also with the passion of a man who has discovered a great truth and wishes to communicate his discovery to others. It may well be this quality of the freshness of discovery that carried the day for *The Conser-*

vative Mind and made it one of the most influential books of the post-war period.

The influence of *The Conservative Mind* was not confined to this country. There were two extended essays about the book in German publications, one by the historian Golo Mann and the other by the economist Wilhelm Roepke, which were followed by a German translation, published by Eugen Rentsch in Zurich; there was a Spanish translation, published in Madrid, and through the influence of T. S. Eliot, Faber & Faber published a separate English edition. The seriousness with which the book was taken in England may be judged by the fact that D. W. Brogan reviewed it in the *Manchester Guardian*, R. H. S. Crossman in *The New Statesman*, Michael Oakeshott in *The Spectator*, and Colin Clark in a four-part essay in *The Tablet*.

The Conservative Mind was followed a year later by *A Program for Conservatives*. Having successfully re-established conservatism as a viable and responsible body of ideas, it seemed appropriate to bring out a book which would relate those principles to the problems and issues which confront modern man. *A Program for Conservatives*, however, was not at all intended to be a guide through the political thickets of our time, nor does Mr. Kirk endeavor to offer ready-made solutions to our troubles; rather, he describes "the awful gravity" of the problems which confront us, knowing full well that such problems are not susceptible to easy solutions, if they are susceptible to solutions at all; he then undertakes to help us to acquire the wisdom, patience and understanding to accept the fate that is meted out to us, to learn to get along with our fellow man, and to believe in the wisdom of Providence. The first two chapters of the book give us an account of the essential nature of conservatism: the conservative believes, he tells us, that "Men are put into this world . . . to struggle, to suffer, to contend against the evil that is in their neighbors and in themselves, and to aspire toward the triumph of Love. They are put into this world to live like men and to die like men." The remaining chapters of the book are indeed concerned with problems, but not with the problems certain politicians love to talk about and to "solve" for us — poverty, unemployment, racial discrimination, etc. — but the problems of the heart, of community, of justice, of order, of loyalty. An abridged and revised edition was later published, in paperback, as *Prospects for Conservatives*; then, in 1962, another revised, paperback edition was published under the original title.

Many of the chapters of *The Conservative Mind* had appeared in one form or another in various journals, many in England, before the book itself was published, and the material gathered together on John Randolph of Roanoke, an American follower of Edmund Burke, arch conservative and wonderfully eccentric, became the substance of a small book published in 1951 by the University of Chicago Press. This was Russell Kirk's first book. A much enlarged edition, which contained a selection of Randolph's speeches and letters, was published in 1964 by Henry Regnery Company and then reissued in 1978 by Liberty Press. Another small book, Kirk's *St. Andrews*, a history of the town and university, was published by Batsford in 1954.

The next major book of Russell Kirk was *Academic Freedom*, which appeared in 1955. The sub-title of *Academic Freedom* is "An Essay in Definition." It will be remembered that Kirk also described *The Conservative Mind* as "a prolonged essay in definition." In Ezra Pound's translation of Confucius's *The Great Digest* we are told: "The men of old . . . wanting good government in their states . . . first established order in their own families, wanting order in the home, they first disciplined themselves; desiring self-discipline, they rectified their own hearts; and wanting to rectify their hearts, they sought precise verbal definitions. . . . " Order begins, therefore, with the precise use of words, and no word, in the 1950s, was in greater need of precise definition than academic freedom, which, in the confusion of the time, had become a cloak for arrogance, cowardice, and irresponsibility. As Kirk pointed out in his book, "academic freedom is a 'natural right', and is expressed in custom, not in statute." It docs not mean "complete autonomy for teachers, or the licentious toleration of a bewildering congeries of private fancies," but properly understood, provides a form of protection which is necessary if the university is to perform its high moral and intellectual purpose. Kirk's objective, therefore, by defining academic freedom rigorously and clearly was to protect the university, largely, it must be said, from itself. Furthermore, he maintains, the university will survive only so long as it remains true to the high purpose which is the basis and only reason for its own form of freedom.

Although it was not specifically described as such, there was another "essay in definition": *The American Cause*, published in 1957. The book was written following the disclosure of the dismal performance of many of the American soldiers taken prisoner by the Communists during the Korean War. The fact that a high proportion of these young men, all products of the American educational system, had little or no knowledge of their country's history, its traditions or achievement made them an easy prey to Communist indoctrination. It was Kirk's purpose in writing *The American Cause* to define the higher purpose of American society, and, thereby, to fill a gap in the education of a whole generation of Americans. One reviewer, Thomas Molnar, remarked that it combined the qualities of the philosopher's grasp of ideas with the pamphleteer's singleness of purpose.

There are four collections of essays among the books of Russell Kirk: *Beyond the Dreams of Avarice* (1956), *Confessions of a Bohemian Tory* (1963), *The Intemperate Professor* (1965), and *Enemies of the Permanent Things* (1969). Publishers are notoriously wary of such books: made up as they nearly always are of previously published pieces on various, often fleeting subjects, they usually lack coherence and are difficult to sell. These four collections do not conform to this not invariable rule, although their publishers, unfortunately, were probably not overwhelmed by orders. Each is a work in its own right and holds together. *Confessions of a Bohemian Tory* probably comes closest to what a publisher fears in such a book: it is not well titled, is somewhat uneven, many of the pieces included are rather ephemeral and several could have been omitted, but many are well worth reading and pleasant to turn back to — "The Valor of Virginia," for example, an amusing short piece; "The Class Struggle in Jos," describing the effect — unexpected and violent — of the showing of the American film "Death of a Salesman" in an outdoor movie in Nigeria; or "A House on Mountjoy Square," on the charm and contradictions of modern Dublin. *The Intemperate Professor* has a tighter, more unifying theme — Kirk describes the essays collected in it as "studies in the afflictions of modern culture [which] are meant as diagnoses of certain present intellectual and social discontents." A particularly perceptive essay on the American private college proposes a drastic, radical reform, that the college turn its back on "relevance" and revert to its original purpose, in Kirk's words to "produce a body of high-principled and literate men" and "then send them into the world with a cast of character and mind fitted for ethical and intellectual leadership."

Most, if not all, of the essays included in *The Intemperate Professor*, *Beyond the Dreams of Avarice*, and *Enemies of the Permanent Things* take some topic of immediate interest as their starting point; their significance and quality of timelessness derive from Kirk's ability to relate a current subject to the principles and standards which are unchanging. An essay on censorship, for example, included in *Beyond the Dreams of Avarice* was written following the publication by the American Library Association of a pamphlet called "The Freedom to Read," concerning USIA libraries and Senator Joseph McCarthy. Kirk uses this contemporary incident to define and clarify the true meaning of censorship and to point out that every society has the right to protect itself from those who would destroy it, that in an encounter with falsehood truth does not necessarily arise triumphant, and that "the same freedom to read which elevates the character of one man may be employed to degrade the character of another." In a sympathetic essay on Woodrow Wilson in the part of *Enemies of the Permanent Things* called "The Norms of Politics" Kirk sets out to explain the failure of Wilson, who, as he said, may have been the last "of our literary statesmen." He brought to the presidential office "the humane and juridical disciplines," combined "a disposition to preserve with an ability to reform," and was head of a country at the peak of its power and world-wide influence in a prostrate world; why, in spite of all this, did he fail so miserably? He had not learned prudence, Kirk concluded, and in coming to that conclusion we are led to understand why prudence is one of the cardinal virtues.

The first edition of *The Conservative Mind* contains one rather long paragraph about T. S. Eliot, which begins: "Despite his hesitations and ambiguities, Mr. T. S. Eliot stands in the tradition of Burke and Coleridge. . . . " In the sixth revised edition, it is interesting to observe, Eliot is not only included in the sub-title, three full pages are devoted to him, he is referred to on five other pages, and rather than described as hesitant and ambiguous, Kirk refers to him as "the chief poet and critic of the century." In an essay, "T. S. Eliot's Permanent Things" (included in *Enemies of the Permanent Things*) Kirk does not hesitate to speak to Eliot as "the greatest man of letters of this century" and "to confess to writing in the spirit of Eliot." During the years following the publication of the book that made his reputation, Kirk not only became thoroughly familiar with the work of T. S. Eliot, he became his friend. It is probably true also that Eliot's respect for Kirk's work and his acceptance of him as a friend was a source of great encouragement to Kirk at a time when, his reputation made, he was seeking a place for himself in the world of letters. Kirk acknowledged his debt to Eliot with one of his best books, *Eliot and His Age*, published in 1971. Kirk did not attempt to write a detailed biography—Eliot was a private person and Kirk respected his privacy—what he has given us, rather, is a thorough and sympathetic account and evaluation of Eliot's achievement as a poet, critic, and man of his time, showing as well the relation of his work to his own era and its sources in the past. It is a work of great erudition—Kirk must have read every line Eliot ever published—and a fitting tribute to one of the most elusive and significant creative men of our century.

On the first page of *The Roots of American Order* (1974) Kirk tells us, "The human condition is insufferable unless we perceive a harmony, an order, in existence." Later, in the same book, we read, "our religion, our culture, and our political rights all are maintained by continuity: by our respect for the accomplishments of our forefathers, and by our concern for posterity's well-being." In this large, far-reaching book, one of Kirk's most impressive achievements, he traces the sources of the American view of morality, of individual and civic responsibility, of justice and law—the basis of order, therefore—in the long continuum of history. From the prophets of the Old Testament through the Greeks, the Romans, and the Christian revelation to the colonial experience and the Founding Fathers of our country is a long journey, a journey Kirk describes with enormous skill and erudition, never losing his way, or the reader, and, having arrived at his destination (his last chapter is called "Contending Against American Disorder"), one is well aware of the strong sense of purpose that motivated him in this difficult venture. The two men he refers to in the last chapter to characterize the struggle against American disorder are Abraham Lincoln and Orestes Brownson. "In a democratic society, as in every society, order must have primacy: that," Kirk says, "was the meaning of Lincoln's successful struggle to maintain the Union." But, Kirk goes on to say, Lincoln believed that "Man's order is subordinate to a providential order."

To express the purpose of American society, Kirk goes to Orestes Brownson, a man with whom, one senses, he feels a close affinity. Brownson, Kirk says, "courted no man's favor, and was as fierce against the Utilitarian intellectual and the money-obsessed entrepreneur as against the Marxist fanatic and the doctrinaire social revolutionary." Every living nation, Brownson wrote "has an idea given it by Providence to realize, and whose realization is its special work, mission, or destiny." The American mission is to reconcile liberty with law: " . . . its mission is not so much the realization of liberty as the realization of the true idea of the state, which secures at once the authority of the public and the freedom of the in-dividual — the sovereignty of the people without social despotism, and individual freedom without anarchy. . . . The American Republic has been instituted by Providence to realize the freedom of each with ad-vantage to the other." During those rough-and-tumble, over-confident years following the Civil War, Brownson did not hesitate to say, as Kirk puts it, "that simple popular opinion never can maintain justice." Then in Brownson's own words, "But we are told . . . the will of the people is the will of God. We deny it. The will of God is eternal and immutable justice, which the will of the people is not." Kirk concludes his reference to the work of Brownson with the words: "The reconcil-ing of authority and liberty, so that justice might be realized in the good state: that mission for America is not accomplished, a century later, but is not forgotten." That it helps us to remember this mission is one of the great achievements of *The Roots of American Order*.

One of Russell Kirk's more recent books of social criticism, or, perhaps more accurately, pleas for social renewal, is *Decadence and Renewal in the Higher Learning* (1978). The structure of the book is straightforward and clear: defining the aim of education, with Plato, as wisdom and virtue, and decadence, with C. E. M. Joad as "drop-ping the object," as losing sight of "real objectives, aims, or ends," and settling "instead for the gratification of mere 'experience'," Kirk pro-ceeds to describe the present state of college and university, and the prospects for better times. He is uniquely qualified for such a task: he has demonstrated by his achievement that he can qualify as an educated man, and having visited more than three hundred colleges and universities as guest lecturer and professor, often for extended periods, he writes with the supreme advantage of familiarity with his subject. His description of what passes for the higher learning on many American campuses, much of it ludicrous, some of it actually destructive, degenerate, and obscene, is not encouraging, but Kirk never misses the opportunity to single out administrators and teachers who have remained faithful to the ideals and aims of true education, so that the book is by no means a tale of woe merely. While there is less renewal than decadence, he makes us feel that in spite of ideological departments of education, bureaucratization, masses of "students" who, if they belong in a college or university at all, are being betrayed, teachers and professors who suffer from the arrogance of the half-educated, and much more besides — and he doesn't mince words — in spite of all this, that the cause of the higher learning is not entirely lost.

This is a powerful book, and has doubtless had, and will continue to have, a considerable influence, more, probably, as a guiding light and source of encouragement to those in the academy hoping and struggling for better days than as admonishment to the ideologues responsible for the present plight of education. If the book has a fault, it is the mass of evidence Kirk brings in to substantiate his case. He does indeed prove that the proper aim of education has largely been lost in the passion for bigness, "relevance," and giving the public what it wants, or thinks it wants (advanced degrees in such "disciplines" as packaging, physical education, "beautology," etc.) but in all this proliferation of horror stories there is danger that Kirk's eloquent and beautifully stated description of the true nature of education and the means by which it may be and sometimes is acquired will be lost sight of. His account, for example, of his own schooling in Plymouth, Michigan, a railroad town outside Detroit, is beautifully done, and gives us some idea of what we have lost at the hands of the educationist. After comparing a contemporary, much advertised and promoted series of books designed for the teaching of English in the schools, with great emphasis on relevance, of course, to the books used in his day in the schools of Plymouth, Michigan, he has this to say:

> Genuine relevance in literature . . . is relatedness to the permanent things: to the splendour and tragedy of the human condition, to constant moral insights, to the spectacle of human history, to love of community and country, to the achievement of right reason. Such a literary relevance confers upon the rising generation a sense of what it is to be fully human, and a knowledge of what great men and women of imagination have imparted to our civilization over the centuries. Let us be relevant in our teaching of literature, by all means — but relevant to the genuine ends of the literary discipline, not relevant merely to what will be thoroughly irrelevant tomorrow.

How wonderful it would be if the president or dean of one of our great universities, or the Secretary of Education, could write such a paragraph, but the fact that we have a man who can and does write such paragraphs gives us reason for gratitude and hope.

Of Russell Kirk's imaginative works, his ghost stories, his Gothic novel, his short stories and other work of fiction, I feel incompetent to say much. It is more fitting, instead, to quote what he has to say about imagery, and his method of writing fiction, this from *Decadence and Renewal in the Higher Learning*:

> The image, I repeat, can raise us on high, as did Dante's high dream; also it can draw us down the abyss. It is a matter of the truth or the falsity of images. If we study good images in religion, in literature, in music, in the visual arts — why, the spirit is uplifted, and in some sense liberated from the trammels of the flesh. But if we submit ourselves (which is easy to do nowadays) to evil images — why, we become what we admire. Within limits, the will is free.
>
> It is imagery, rather than some narrowly deductive and inductive process, which gives us great poetry and scientific insights. When I write fiction, I do not commence with a well-concerted formal plot. Rather, there occur to my imagination certain images, little scenes, snatches of conversation, strong lines of prose. I patch together these fragments, retaining and embellishing the sound images, discarding the unsound, finding a continuity to join them. Presently I have a coherent narration, with some point to it. Unless one has this sort of pictorial imagery — Walter Scott had it in a high degree — he never will become a writer of good fiction, whatever may be said of expository prose.

Shortly after the publication of *The Conservative Mind*, Russell told me that he had made up his mind to resign his teaching position at Michigan State, and thenceforth to make his way in the world as an independent man of letters. I took it upon myself to advise caution, pointing out the advantages of the regular salary of a university teacher as opposed to the uncertainties of living as a writer. To this he replied in his characteristic fashion, in a letter dated October 12, 1953:

> Poverty never bothered me; I can live on four hundred dollars cash per annum, if I must; time to think, and freedom of action, are much more important to me at present than any possible economic advantage. I have always had to make my own way, opposed rather than aided by the times and the men who run matters for us; and I don't mind continuing to do so.

As Charles Brown's bibliography (1981) of his work makes clear, Kirk has managed to make his way as an independent man of letters. From Plymouth to Mecosta in the Northern Michigan "stump country," where he has lived ever since resigning from Michigan State, is no great distance as distances go these days, but Russell Kirk has come a long way since he left the modest house of his parents to enter Michigan State College as a scholarship student. His work stands as one of the major intellectual achievements of our time: he has successfully challenged the reigning orthodoxy of liberalism, point by point, and, without the advantage of a prestigious university behind him and, as he remarked in the letter quoted above, more often opposed than aided by the times or the men who run matters for us, he has been largely responsible for replacing a tired, destructive liberalism with a vigorous, positive conservatism.

Mecosta, where he lives in a large, square brick house with his wife and daughters and does his work in a library fashioned from an abandoned wood-working shop, is not an impressive place—one could easily drive through it, in fact, hardly being aware of its existence—but in the intellectual life of our country it doubtless has a greater influence than the huge, sprawling university (it really does have an "Institute for Packaging" in a separate building) he left in its favor. Russell Kirk's career is a wonderful example of the power of ideas: his influence derives from the fact that he has fashioned a coherent position for himself which is based on established principles—the "permanent things" as he calls them—and has stood by it. His influence has been greatest, probably, among the younger generation "blessed with the gift of reason." He has tirelessly lectured at colleges and universities in all parts of the country, met with groups of students, welcomed young people seeking order in a disorderly world to his study. Every year a group of students spends a week with him, usually at Christmas time, to talk, listen, and learn. We listen to Russell Kirk because he knows where he stands and has tried to conduct his life in accordance with the high principles he espouses for all of us.

Russell Kirk:
Memoir of a Friendship

by Peter J. Stanlis

In the spring of 1951, while teaching English at Wayne State University in Detroit, I submitted my doctoral dissertation, *Burke's Politics and the Law of Nature*, to the graduate school of the University of Michigan. After receiving my degree in June I spent that summer organizing a conference on Edmund Burke for the December meeting in Detroit of the Modern Language Association of America. Since I planned to mine my dissertation for articles, and eventually to publish a book on the moral and legal foundations of Burke's political philosophy, I continued to read widely in Burke studies and political theory. Purely by chance I ran across a small book, recently published by the University of Chicago Press, called *Randolph of Roanoke*, by Russell Kirk. I knew little about Randolph of Roanoke and nothing about Russell Kirk, but my eye caught a statement on the flyleaf that the great "political exemplar" of Randolph of Roanoke was Edmund Burke. A glance through the index showed twenty-four references to Burke.

In writing my dissertation I had read the complete works, speeches, and correspondence of Burke, and had noted the cardinal principles and concerns in his political philosophy. These included the moral natural law, prudence, legal prescription, limited power under constitutional law, normative appeals to Providence and religion, appeals to history and tradition as preceptors of experience and prudence, a defense of private and corporate property as essential to civil liberty, and respect for party government. In his opposition to revolutionary innovations Burke had also expressed strong criticism of rationalist speculative ideologies based upon primitivist theories of the social contract and appeals to abstract "natural rights." On the basis of very extensive empirical evidence in Burke's writings, I had concluded that the ultimate basis of his political philosophy rested upon the moral natural law — a thesis which totally contradicted the over-whelming consensus of more than a century of scholarship on Burke. Utilitarian and positivist scholars claimed that Burke had rejected moral natural law and had adhered to the relativism and expediency of Utilitarianism. When I began to examine Russell Kirk's *Randolph of Roanoke* I fully expected to encounter yet one more of the countless commentaries on Burke filled with the usual errors of the utilitarians and positivists.

Although Kirk presented no sustained exposition of Burke's political thought, beyond a few paragraphs or brief statements, to my great surprise and joy I discovered that he was wholly on target in every important subject he dealt with, and frequently hit the bullseye. It was clear to me that Kirk had a far better understanding of Burke's politics than any of the many established experts on Burke that I had read during the past three years or more. Only Professor Ross J. S. Hoffman of Fordham University understood the importance of moral natural law in Burke, and he had not written on it. Unlike most eighteenth-century scholars, Kirk had even perceived that when Burke attacked revolutionary "natural rights" he did not thereby reject nature as a norm in favor of social customs, as practically all previous writers on Burke had assumed and argued. Although Kirk stressed legal prescription as most fundamental in Burke's politics, whereas I had argued that legal prescription was a vital derivative principle from natural law, nevertheless he was close to the essence of Burke's thought.

On October 30, 1951, I wrote to Kirk at his academic address at Michigan State College, inviting him to participate in my December conference on Burke. I noted that our assumptions, understanding, and reasons for admiring Burke were practically identical. Early in November he responded, not from East Lansing, but from St. Andrews, Scotland. He stated that since he would be in Scotland until September 1952 he regretted deeply having to miss the conference on Burke. He mentioned that he was "finishing a great fat book to be called *The Conservatives' Rout: An Account of Conservative Ideas from Burke to Santayana.*" He added that he had written three more articles on Burke that were about to appear, and that he would send off-print copies to me. This gesture of interested benevolence was to prove a dominant trait in Russell's character as a lifelong friend. Finally, he in turn invited me to attend a meeting in East Lansing of the George Ade Society of Michigan. He explained that he and some of his friends at Michigan State College had founded a sort of democratic Johnsonian club which met regularly for dinner and good talk, and had named their club in honor of George Ade, the great Hoosier humorist. He listed among the members "automobile executives, bartenders, professors, journalists, engineers, entrepreneurs, and Lord knows who all." He suggested that I might give a talk to the society, and in payment I would receive "a fine dinner, all you dare to drink, and overnight hospitality." Who could resist such a charming invitation? (The following fall, after Russell had returned from Scotland, I attended several meetings of the George Ade Society, and found the members perfectly delightful, their talk on a high level of intellectual excellence, and their social and aesthetic virtues such as Samuel Johnson would have approved.) Neither of us in our wildest imaginings ever dreamed that these first letters, exchanged late in 1951, were the beginning of a correspondence that over the next thirty-nine years would total over 400 lengthy letters on a wide range of personal and public subjects.

On November 30 I received a packet from Russell containing two off-prints and another letter. He asked whether I had "a publisher in prospect" for my doctoral dissertation, and suggested that his publisher, Henry Regnery, might be interested in it. Regarding his own writing he remarked: "I hope to have my big book done in not much more than a fortnight, to which end I am writing with desperate diligence." He said that he would spend Christmas in St. Andrews, even though "Scotland is probably the dreariest land at Christmas in all the Christian world," where "the Kirk-session no longer can confiscate the Christmas goose, but they'd like to." He also mentioned that he "wrote ghost stories," and had a contract with Batsford to write a history of St. Andrews for their British cities series.

From Russell's second letter I perceived four important impressions about his character, temperament, personality, and value system, which were to prove decisive over our long friendship, and which provide the substance of much that follows in this memoir. First, it was typical of Russell to give of himself much more than he had any reason to believe he would ever receive in return. It would take a small volume to describe the many kindnesses Russell extended to me over the next thirty-nine years, in helping me to secure grants for my various publications, in our joint enterprises in organizing and participating in conferences, lectures, panels, and various academic meetings in Detroit, Chicago, New York, Philadelphia, and many other cities, and on college and university campuses. We wrote articles for each other's journals, and book reviews galore. It is significant that Russell wrote the preface to my first book on Burke in 1958 and my sixth book on Burke in 1989. I sensed and appreciated his rare degree of unselfishness and benevolence in his second letter, and knew intuitively that he was the kind of man I would enjoy having as a friend

The second quality revealed in his second letter was the enormous reservoir of psychic energy, to go with his literary talent, that enabled him to produce two fine books so quickly, and to project active plans for a third book before the second was completed. It did not surprise me that by 1984 Russell had published twenty-four books, in a style of writing that was consistently excellent. Third, I sensed that any admirer of Burke who also wrote ghost stories could not be anything but critical of the abstract rationalism of the Enlightenment, and would have a strong affinity for the baroque culture of Europe, with its Gothic literary traditions. Russell's temperament and moral and aesthetic perspectives had their roots in the rich and varied cultural traditions of Medieval Europe. Fourth, his comments on the repressive Puritanism of the Kirk-session indicated that despite his own Hibernian background his spiritual affinities were with a much older and richer religious tradition and humanistic culture than the austere asceticism of Calvinism, and included an important place for the arts and the art of living.

Our letters during the spring and summer of 1952 soon took on a dimension of wide-ranging common interests and views on politics, education, literature, religion, travel, persons, and many other subjects. We were of one mind that the recovery of norms in every aspect of modern life should be the most essential objective of every good writer, and that this involved a restoration of sound religious and humanistic principles in the souls of individuals and in the external order of civil society. Therefore, in advancing our conservative views we made a strong and healthy culture the basis of our writing, and not merely any economic system, including the free-market economy that we defend against socialism. We believed that the moral order of a just society is reflected in the individual and corporate souls of its citizens and institutions, so that when the intellectual, moral, aesthetic, and social norms of a culture decay, or are corrupted by sophistry or ideology, the standards of the whole body politic of a nation suffers. These were the grand themes of Irving Babbitt and later of Eric Voegelin, in their critical strictures regarding the cultural decay in Europe and America. In this regard our correspondence soon became a kind of continuing dialogue on many of the most important cultural concerns of the last half of the twentieth century. Although Burke held for us the central place in the restoration of a just political order, we were aware that there was a great need of a renewal in the whole culture of Western civilization.

When Russell returned from Scotland in September 1952 we began to work in a close but unofficial collaboration to make the academic world in America (and later in Europe) aware of Burke's importance for the restoration of a well-ordered, free, and just society. Our common efforts extended over the next three decades. Between 1952 and 1982 Russell and I published fifty-six works on Burke (twenty-eight each), including eight books, many sections or chapters of books, articles, biographies, anthologies, translations, journals, and miscellaneous items. We organized and participated in conferences and programs on Burke at the University of Detroit, Seton Hall College, Georgetown University, and Carleton College. We lectured widely for the Intercollegiate Studies Institute and at their summer seminars. We discussed Burke at meetings of the Philadelphia Society and the Mont Pelerin Society. We held meetings on Burke at the regional and national meetings of the Modern Language Association, the American Historical Association, the Political Science Association of America, the American Society for Eighteenth Century Studies, and other academic and public organizations, including programs of the Liberty Fund. Our efforts were reinforced by the work of such Burke scholars as Ross J. S. Hoffman, Carl B. Cone, Francis Canavan, Jeffrey Hart, Charles Parkin, Louis I. Bredvold, Charles P. Ives, Thomas H. D. Mahoney, Thomas Copeland, Thomas Chaimowicz, and others. The revival of interest in Burke was also helped greatly by the publication of Copeland's edition of Burke's correspondence, in ten volumes, and by the availability of Burke's papers, which had been withheld from scholars for a century and a half. By the time I published *Edmund Burke: A Bibliography of Secondary Studies to 1982* (1983), we had achieved a counter-revolution on traditional grounds by firmly establishing Burke's principles as the basis of modern American political conservatism.

In the process of making America and Europe aware of Burke's politics we encountered many academic trials and financial problems. Much credit is due to the conservative foundations and publishers who came to our assistance at crucial times. Russell founded and was the first editor of the quarterly, *Modern Age*, launched in August 1957 with 700 subscribers. By the end of that year he had 4,000 subscribers and hoped to have 10,000 before long. Because of his connection with *National Review* Russell's other quarterly review, *The University Bookman*, had over 100,000 readers. My own journals, *The Burke Newsletter* and *Studies in Burke and His Time*, which I edited and published for thirteen years beginning in 1959, were much more specialized, aimed primarily at college teachers, so that they never had more than 1,000 subscribers. But in thirteen years they totalled over 4,500 pages of articles and reviews on Burke and his era, in the light of twentieth-century scholarship. These resources and others provided us with readily available means to make Burke's political philosophy widely known to teachers, students, and the public at large.

Our cultural foundations were based upon a much broader literary and political base than Burke, and included the better conservative writers in the whole Christian and humanistic tradition of Europe and America. During the spring of 1952 we discovered that we had a common strong enthusiasm for the poetry of Robert Frost. Russell was pleased to learn that I was a friend of Frost, having had many conversations with the poet in his cabin during six summers at Bread Loaf, Vermont. Frost was a political conservative, a pre-New Deal, "old-line" state's-rights Democrat, who detested what he called "the sweep to collectivism in our time," and the egalitarian levelling policies of the Roosevelt administration, which resulted in "a homogenized society." Also, Russell was pleased to know that Frost was a severe critic of John Dewey's theories of progressive education. The Gothic element in Frost also appealed to him; he considered the poet's "The Witch of Coös" "the best ghost story ever written in verse." In November 1962, I arranged for Frost to come for two days to the University of Detroit where he received an honorary degree and gave a poetry reading before almost 10,000 listeners in the university fieldhouse. Russell came down from his home in Mecosta, stayed with me in Trenton (one of southeastern Michigan's "Downriver" communities), met and talked with Frost, and later published an essay, "The Poet as Conservative," in his *National Review* column. In 1973 I published a little book, *Robert Frost: The Individual and Society*, and Russell used it as a text for a course he was teaching at Hillsdale College.

Another writer we both admired was Orestes Brownson (1803–1876), particularly for his greatest work, *The American Republic* (1866). As an account of the origins and nature of our federal republican system of government we considered Brownson's work vastly superior to the popular liberal versions based upon John Locke's political theory as taught in many American history texts. Russell published several articles on Brownson, and edited a Brownson reader. In May 1953 I organized a symposium on Brownson at the University of Detroit. It was attended by over 900 persons, including Elizabeth Brownson, who told me that Russell's paper was the best brief account of her grandfather's ideas that she had ever heard. Later Russell convinced his friend T. S. Eliot that Brownson was a badly neglected writer well worth knowing. For over two decades Russell made American academics aware of Brownson's importance as a conservative social and political thinker. In 1977 we each contributed an essay to the symposium on Brownson sponsored by Fordham University in New York City. These essays were later published in a book, *No Divided Allegiance* (1980).

With *The Conservative Mind* (1953), Russell commenced the firm establishment of Burke as the fountainhead of modern conservative politics. This, his second book, derived from his doctoral thesis at St. Andrews University, was a history-of-ideas study of over thirty writers, consisting of a series of highly condensed vignettes which identified, described, and summarized a continuous intellectual and political Burkean tradition in Britain and America, a tradition that had survived many vicissitudes and was still a vital force in the present. *The Conservative Mind* proved beyond question that the facile claims of such liberals as Lionel Trilling that there was no meaningful conservative cultural or political tradition in America was at best an illusion and at worst a lie. Burke's defense of the Christian commonwealth of Europe included a rich humanistic culture wholly at variance with the secular ideology of the Enlightenment, from which modern liberalism and ideological totalitarianism were descended. The rationalist ideology of the French Revolution, essentially atheistic or deistic, taught a materialist theory of man and society, and provided the basis of nineteenth-century Utilitarianism and Marxism. These in turn evolved into the liberal and totalitarian socialist ideologies of the twentieth century. Thus the political philosophy of Burke and the conservative tradition of culture were the best weapons to combat the collectivist tyrannies of our bloody era of wars and revolutions.

By defining conservatism as a philosophy of life, with specific normative moral and political principles, Russell's study destroyed the assumption of American liberals that conservatism was merely a defense of entrenched economic corporate interests, or of every *status quo* regime, regardless of its theoretical basis or behavior. Liberal journalists who have continued to assert this fallacy — either inadvertently, out of ignorance, or deliberately, as propaganda — can best be answered by the conservative principles defined in *The Conservative Mind*.

Within a few months of its appearance *The Conservative Mind* had established itself as one of the most important books on social, political, and cultural thought published in the twentieth century. This fact was confirmed by reviews in all of the important popular and academic publications in America and Britain. Even some liberal reviewers had to admit that Russell had presented a formidable case for the conservative philosophy. Very shortly there were British, Spanish, and German editions of the book. In less than a year it was in its third printing. By the spring and summer of 1954 the impact of Russell's book upon the American public and the academic world became so evident that Marxist and liberal critics felt obliged to launch an attack on both Russell and his book.

To underscore the importance of Russell's achievement, and to counterattack the smears of the liberal and Marxist press, I published a lengthy review article, "The Conservative Mind of Russell Kirk," in the December 1954 issue of *The Newman Review*. In the essay, I noted that "a whole literature of disillusionment has been created from the pieces of the fallen idol of dialectic materialism," of which Whittaker Chambers's *Witness* (1952) was the most notable recent example. I underscored the American public's "present disillusionment in secularism and liberalism," and suggested that Russell Kirk deserved to be the acknowledged intellectual leader in the emerging American conservative movement: "As the brilliant and acknowledged founder of modern conservatism, Edmund Burke is placed by Mr. Kirk at the fountainhead of a rich and impressive stream of Christian and humanist thought in American and British social philosophy and literature." I concluded that Kirk's book, "cast in an epic mold," was "one of the great intellectual achievements of the present decade," and that his thesis showed the moral bankruptcy of liberals who believed in "political and economic levelling carried through on utilitarian principles by a multi-functional, all-powerful and secular state." My whole strategy in defending *The Conservative Mind* against its Marxist and liberal detractors was to set Russell's book within the context of the battle that was then raging over the Chambers-Hiss trial.

To understand my motive and strategy it is necessary to review briefly the essential facts that brought about Alger Hiss's trial, the significance of that event, and how it involved American conservatives and liberals. On August 3, 1948, when Whittaker Chambers accused Alger Hiss of being a Soviet agent before the House Committee on Un-American Activities, he began an intense and protracted public controversy that was at its height when Russell published *The Conservative Mind*. As he noted in *Witness*, the harrowing account of his spiritual and political odyssey, Chambers had defected from Stalinist Communism in 1938, after a long struggle with his conscience, but *before* the Nazi-Soviet Pact of August 23, 1939, together with Stalin's purge trials, had converted many Stalinist Marxists into Trotskyite anti-Soviet Marxists. Even after abjuring Soviet Communism many convinced Marxists continued to carry an ideological wound that never healed, and lived out their lives within the dialectics of Marxism. But like Arthur Koestler, Ignatio Silone, and other former Communists, Chambers had come to believe that communism in all its partisan forms and allegiances was an evil ideology. After a decade of hiding his communist past—one year of which he spent literally hiding in fear of being "liquidated" by Soviet agents—he had concluded that informing on the Communist underground conspiracy to the American government was a moral duty.

But the anti-Stalinist American Trotskyite Marxists, and especially their liberal allies, regarded Chambers's testimony against Hiss as the betrayal of a cowardly and selfish turncoat. As Diana Trilling put it, when Hiss was convicted and sent to Lewisburg Penitentiary in March 1951, "Alger went to jail for all our sins." For the two years after Hiss was imprisoned and *The Conservative Mind* appeared, the liberals in the American academy, the press, and the American government continued to attack Chambers and defend Hiss.

The importance and great success of Russell's book was partly the result of good timing. Precisely one year before *The Conservative Mind* appeared, in May 1952, Chambers's *Witness* became the Book-of-the-Month selection. At that time Chambers was not so much a conservative as an anti-Communist counter revolutionist. (Probably he was a conservative of sorts when he died in July 1961.) His book had alerted Americans to the growing post-World-War-II conflict between American constitutional democracy and Soviet totalitarianism, most evident in the foreign policy and spy apparatus of the Soviet Union. But Chambers's book did not provide an adequate social and political philosophy, centered in the Judaeo-Christian religion and the humanistic culture of Western civilization, with which to combat the materialistic ideology of Marxism. *The Conservative Mind* provided the strongest weapons needed to make war upon Communism and its liberal supporters; it made clear that conservatism was in every way the antithesis of the brutal and dehumanized totalitarian system preached by Marx and practiced by the Soviet system. Thus Russell's book brought into sharper focus and gave body to the significance of the conflict in the Chambers-Hiss controversy. Readers of *The Conservative Mind* who had been misled by the propaganda and slogans of the Marxist and liberal left now had a positive alternative in the historic reality since Burke's time of the legal and political constitutional systems of the West, centered in governments with limited powers and full accountability.

The strategy in my review of *The Conservative Mind* was largely shaped four months before I wrote it. In September 1954 Russell wrote to me that he was to appear on October 17 in a television interview on "Author Meets Critic," with James Burnham and Sidney Hook as the critical commentators on his book. Russell knew that Burnham would be a friendly critic, because like Chambers he had turned against his former Marxism without making any distinction between Stalinists and Trotskyites. But the ambiguities in Hook's position were such that Russell asked me to send him whatever information I had that would provide him with knowledge or insights on how to deal with Hook during his interview. Fortunately, I had recently read a great deal about Hook, including his review of

Chambers's *Witness*, and Chambers's reply to it. It was plain to me that Hook's conflict with the Soviet Marxists was a jurisdictional, not a philosophical, difference. On October 3 I sent Russell all the materials I had on Hook, and summarized his position as a Trotskyite anti-Soviet Marxist. Two weeks later, in his television interview, Russell almost gleefully anticipated every critical point Hook made, and answered him with brilliant rejoinders that left his opponent bewildered and speechless.

After the great success of *The Conservative Mind* Russell realized that the philosophical principles of the writers he had described needed to be applied in practice in American politics. To this end, late in 1953 I arranged for him to give the Daly Lectures at the University of Detroit. In the winter and spring of 1953–54 Russell journeyed from Mecosta to Detroit every other week and gave a lecture at the university. Before each lecture we would have dinner together, either with his father in Highland Park, or at the London Chop House in downtown Detroit. His subjects included "The Problem of Community," "The Problem of Social Justice," "The Problem of Order," and other such subjects that we had discussed in our correspondence. He was too good a student of Burke to presume to make abstract recommendations on how to cure the ills of American society. The Daly Lectures, combined with others he gave throughout the Midwest, were published in 1954 as *A Program for Conservatives*. Together with *The Conservative Mind* this book firmly established Russell as one of the principal spokesmen for American political conservatism. It is noteworthy that his lectures stressed the need for a sense of community as the basis of a strong and practical conservative philosophy far more than economics. Russell believed then—as he believes now—that only culture, not wealth, can produce the greatness of mind and heart necessary for a sound civil order.

Thirty-five years later, when Russell came to Chicago to receive the Ingersoll Prize, we talked about the importance of *A Program for Conservatives* in his career. Russell mentioned that he was thinking of writing his memoirs, and on November 16, 1988 I noted that in our correspondence "We discussed just about every important subject that concerns reflective people in the modern era. It should be highly illuminating to review in capsule form how we perceived our age; the people in it, and the great events which have shaped our lives." The results of such a memoir would surely show the fruitful consequences of our frequent collaboration on various projects.

A case in point is the sustained and generous help Russell gave me in my revision and publication of *Edmund Burke and the Natural Law* (1958). He was aware that our studies in Burke supplemented each other to a great degree. In 1954 he recommended me for a Newberry Library Research Fellowship, and helped me to secure an Earhart Foundation grant. The great collection of eighteenth-century political literature in Chicago's Newberry Library, and several excellent law libraries, enabled me to enrich by several hundred new sources the political and natural law content of my original doctoral study, and to restructure and rewrite my book on Burke's politics.

During the spring of 1955, while I was working at the Newberry Library, I came to know Richard Weaver through Russell. I had dinner with Weaver several times, and we enjoyed much good talk together. I wrote to Russell that "Weaver is a fine fellow," but that he did not understand Burke. When Russell came to Chicago in April to see Henry Regnery, we had dinner with Weaver for what proved to be the last time I ever saw him. We discussed his *Ideas Have Consequences* (1948) and I sympathized with him over the vicious review of his book by Howard Mumford Jones of Harvard, in *The New York Times Book Review*. Weaver mentioned that Jones's negative review had hurt the sale of his book, and since he was feeling very depressed Russell and I decided not to attempt to correct his misunderstanding of Burke until later. In July I sent four chapters of my finished manuscript to Russell, and he responded enthusiastically: "I have read your chapters. What an important and really scholarly book! It would do Richard Weaver much good to read it, and read it he shall." Later I received a brief note from Weaver saying that Russell had let him see my manuscript and that it had enabled him to understand how Burke combined his general principles with appeals to concrete circumstances.

In December 1955 Russell wrote an excellent foreword to my book, and in February 1956 he sent the manuscript to the University of Michigan Press, recommending it for publication. Louis I. Bredvold, chairman of my doctoral committee at Michigan, added his support. In his foreword Russell emphasized what was to become the recurrent theme in over fifty reviews: "Dr. Stanlis' book does more than any other study of this century to define Burke's position as a philosopher, relating the convictions of Burke to the great traditions of Christian and classical civilization. . . . The grand Natural Law tradition of Cicero and the Schoolmen . . . reemerges in all its strength in Burke's reply to the French revolutionaries; and through Burke, in large part, it nourishes today whatever is healthy in our civil social order." His conviction that *Edmund Burke and the Natural Law* would reach beyond the academy into the public at large proved to be correct.

No one worked harder than Russell to make his conviction into a self-fulfilling prophecy. He wrote to me that he hoped my book would "establish your reputation nationally, and even internationally." He sent a copy to T. S. Eliot, urging that Faber and Faber (of which Eliot was a director) publish an English edition. He secured German translations of portions of the book in Austria, and I was able to do the same in Italy and Japan. Much of the success of the book is owing to the efforts of Russell.

Conservatives accepted my thesis, shared by Russell, that the philosophical roots of modern political conservatism extend back over many generations through Burke and the natural law to the Middle Ages and classical antiquity. This meant that in every historical epoch in Western civil society there have always been some conservatives. Over the next three decades Russell and I found that this fact was so distasteful to Marxists, liberals, and their allies among so-called "neo-conservatives," that they totally disregarded the evidence in the tradition of Burke's politics. Either out of invincible ignorance or moral perversity, they revealed a willful genius for self-deception. In order to denigrate the conservative tradition and deny it intellectual respectability, they claimed that American conservatism is of very recent origin, that it is centered in a mindless religious fundamentalism or jingoistic patriotism, and that it is devoted wholly to defending the *status quo*, especially the selfish interests of the business community. For more than three decades this has been the constant strategy of those at war with the conservative tradition, and it is a technique that will undoubtedly be used into the future.

In 1955 I wrote to Russell that I had been "elected by a whopping vote" to the Village Council of Trenton, Michigan, and that like Burke I was in the minority opposition party on the Council. For the next six years our correspondence was filled with discussions of local and state politics. On one occasion in 1956, a conflict over two opposite conceptions of American democracy surfaced when some "progressive" citizens proposed to change Trenton from a village to an incorporated city. Their project included annexing a large area of the adjacent township. For various reasons I opposed the city proposal. I looked up the laws of Michigan and learned that such an incorporation required not a simple numerical majority in the combined votes in the village and township, but separate concurrent corporate majorities. The law was consistent with the principle of the Founding Fathers that not simple majority will but minority, individual, and corporate rights were paramount in American democracy. Russell had defended this principle in the political philosophy of John C. Calhoun and in his praise of Brownson's "territorial democracy." The vote in the village was overwhelmingly in favor of the city proposal, but it lost in the township by four votes. The council members thought I was insane when I told them the proposal had failed. When the attorney general of Michigan confirmed my statement, my political enemies accused me of engaging in dirty Machiavellian politics.

I sent an account of my political victory to Russell: "Jacobin democracy has not prevailed. The principle of a concurrent corporate majority is still alive; Calhoun is vindicated by four votes in the muddy backwoods of Monguagon Township." Russell's response was ecstatic: "Humble felicitations, O Machiavelli of Downriver! Ferocious must be the tearing of hair and gnashing of teeth among the apostles of Progress, bound hand and foot and cast into the outer darkness. . . . I shall send the account of your victory at Actium to Jay Gordon Hall, who will be mightily tickled."

My political activities extended to the state level when in 1961 Governor G. Mennen Williams appointed me to a bi-partisan Constitutional Convention Planning Commission. Russell wrote to me that I was in a position to prevent much evil and possibly to do some good, since the purpose of the commission was to study the existing constitution of the State of Michigan, and to propose to the governor and legislature basic provisions for a new constitution. For the next two years Russell and I discussed the work of the commission, and I was able to incorporate some of Russell's ideas into the two chapters that I wrote — on the Elective Franchise and Education. The proposals advocated by the commission were ultimately incorporated into the new constitution.

Perhaps the most important recurring concern throughout our years of correspondence was the state of higher education in America. We agreed that religion and education together provided the main cultural basis of civil society. We both regarded the liberal arts and humanities as the soundest form of education, because such schooling developed human nature to its highest potential, and thus created a strong and healthy culture. We agreed that it was necessary to bring to the highest possible degree of perfection the intellectual, moral, social, and aesthetic virtues of our students, for their self-fulfillment and for their development into mature and responsible citizens.

Both of us began our professional lives as college teachers, but while I remained in the academy all my adult life, Russell created a crisis that compelled him to choose a different vocation. In the spring of 1953 Russell challenged "a progressive lowering of standards" at Michigan State College by the administration. Later that year he resigned from the faculty in protest. By admitting illiterate students, by expanding its curriculum to include such programs as "Outdoor Education," which offered graduate credits for courses in hunting, fishing, fly-casting, and canoeing, Michigan State College ("Cow College") grew swiftly into Michigan State University ("Moo U"), with over 30,000 students. Russell's colleague, Warren Fleischauer, also resigned in protest from Michigan State College, and went to John Carroll University in Cleveland. The following year, in May 1954, Russell wrote to me: "I don't think I shall ever seek any permanent university appointment again." He believed that rather than holding a full-time teaching position anywhere, he could do more good as an occasional lecturer at universities — and later, through journalism in his *National Review* column, "From the Academy."

For more than three decades Russell lectured throughout America, in over 200 colleges and universities, and his experiences provided him with ample subjects for his column and books. In such books as *Academic Freedom* (1955), in many essays in *Beyond the Dreams of Avarice* (1956), and in *The Intemperate Professor* (1965), he continued his war against administrators and faculty members who weakened or corrupted American higher education. In 1968 I sent him materials which helped him to write a powerful indictment of the administration at Michigan State University for its plan to buy national merit students, much as they recruited football players, by offering them a totally free program with a guaranteed degree for a minimum of work.

Russell also did all that he could to advance positive principles and programs in American education. In 1958 Warren Fleischauer and I founded Lambda Iota Tau, a national honors literary society, to raise the quality of literary studies in our colleges. In March 1959 we held a Midwestern conference of LIT at the University of Detroit, and I wrote to Russell on how the students had performed: "The intellectual quality of their comments, their skill in oral self-expression, the solid basis of their knowledge of dramatic literature and aesthetic theory, would have done credit to an advanced graduate seminar." Russell wrote a column on this conference, which prompted an editorial in *Life* magazine, and by December LIT had expanded to fifty-five chapters throughout the United States. At the national convention the following year in Cleveland, Russell's recent edition of Irving Babbitt's *Literature and the American College* (1956), provided the basis of the program.

Russell knew that town and gown audiences provided the best forum for presenting his philosophy of education, so that he wished to preserve a vital connection with American academia through temporary positions. He later held such posts at several schools, including Post College and Hillsdale College. Several times in the late 1950s I attempted to secure a temporary official connection for Russell at the University of Detroit, beyond his Daly Lectures, but without success. In November 1958 I learned that the administration of John Hannah at Michigan State University had poisoned the mind of the president of the University of Detroit against Russell, because he had criticized their prostitution of academic standards and courses. They painted Russell as a firebrand radical and revolutionary; their object was to destroy his reputation so that no university would accept him. They wanted quantitative growth in numbers, accepted mediocrity as their standard, and condemned anyone who had the courage to refuse to consent to the destruction of meaningful standards. Such administrators, and the faculty members who supported them, were to Russell the real radicals and revolutionaries.

The degradation of standards was by no means limited to higher education. The superintendent of education for the State of Michigan yielded to the pressure of the educationists and proposed a law to extend from twenty-one to thirty hours the number of credits required in courses in methodology for teacher certification, and to cut down the required courses for majors in subjects to be taught from forty to thirty hours. Russell exposed this proposal in his column, and provided a great resistance to the plan among liberal-arts faculty members in Michigan colleges and universities. Through Russell some faculty members and I organized the "Michigan Monitors of Education," which ultimately brought about the defeat of the proposal in the Michigan legislature, and resulted in the election of a new superintendent of education who opposed the plan.

The Michigan educationists also proposed to establish a Downriver community college in my home town, Trenton, an area which already had excellent available colleges. The faculty for their proposed college was to be drawn from the local high schools, thus weakening the high schools while not providing genuine college teachers. Even the heads of departments were to be trained in methodology courses rather than in their subjects. There were other anti-intellectual requirements built into their proposal. I believed that if the Trenton area really needed an additional college it should be a branch of the University of Michigan, so that meaningful standards and courses could be offered and maintained. My proposal to this effect was treated with contempt by the educationists, who obviously were more interested in extending their empire than in furthering sound education. I arranged a public debate on the issue. Russell came to Trenton, and together we convinced the Downriver community to reject the educationists' proposal. As a result of our efforts we were blacklisted by the educationists of Michigan for many years.

During the 1950s and 1960s we frequently met in Detroit, Trenton, or Mecosta, to discuss developments and plans for our various academic or political activities, or simply to enjoy good conversation on personal matters. For years my daughters particularly remembered our visit to Mecosta when they slept in Russell's "Old House," after he had told them ghost stories—for all night they had lain awake, expecting to see a ghost. In 1960 during a visit to Mecosta, Russell took me to Lost Lake, the perfect setting for one of his Gothic tales. On my return home I wrote to Russell: "I retain a lively impression of swirling firs and bounding woodchucks, the mists around Lost Lake . . . , Kirk's Landing and a faeryland blueberry patch, Van Tassels and blighted stumps, and rain." In *The Surly Sullen Bell* (1962), Russell gave his account of our day in an essay, "Lost Lake":

I own forty acres of woodland and pasture down toward this limbo. There I have endeavored to plant red pines and white pines and white spruces, but the field mice nibble the roots, and the droughts have taken their toll, and the premature spring thaws, with subsequent cold spells, freeze the hopeful sap in my little trees.

A few summers ago, I took to my forty parched acres a friend of mine, a professor of English from Detroit, to make a census of the surviving saplings. The weather seemed bent upon vindicating the Pathetic Fallacy; the weather forever does tricks, down Lost Lake way. A mighty wind arose while we walked across one of my desolate fields, making my old grove of sugar maples and elms creak dreadfully; enormous black clouds scudded across the sun; and out of nowhere popped a prodigious groundhog (which creature my friend Peter never had beheld before), running through the trees as if the fiend were coming up through his burrow.

Stopping stock-still, Peter looked cautiously about him, perhaps expecting any moment to catch a glimpse of the Weird Sisters on this blasted heath. "Don't you suppose," he said, precisely but with a certain awe, "we'd best go back to the car?" I understood; and we did.

Russell's account captured perfectly the style and temper of his Gothic imagination.

Over the years I was treated with fine specimens of that Gothic imagination. In 1954 I received a post card from the island of Canna in the Hebrides, where Russell was glorying in his visit to the monastic ruins and ancient graves of Canna. The next year he wrote me his euphoric account of his visit with the Duchess of Sermonetta at Ninfa, by the Pontine Marshes. She sounded like a witch out of a Gothic novel, and I warned Russell: "Your Duchess of Sermonetta sounds a little like Rappacini's daughter, so beware." Russell's Gothic taste manifested itself most clearly in the great house he built in Mecosta after he and Annette were married. In June 1969 he wrote: "We're in the midst of building Fortress Kirk, a brick structure of three stories (and cellars) adjacent to the Old House at Mecosta, and connected with it by passages." Since the Old House was ghost haunted, I was not too surprised, though terribly saddened, to hear that it had burned down in 1975. Russell promptly began an even more ambitious rebuilding project that took several years to complete. In 1977 he wrote: "You must come to see the Last Italianate house, with all its architectural curiosities." It took considerable originality to construct and live in a Gothic castle in Mecosta, but Russell did it.

During almost every visit to Mecosta, I met some unusual people staying as house guests with Russell and Annette. Russell's social benevolence led him to provide refuge and sustenance to persons in need, sometimes victims of Communist tyranny, and his home was frequently occupied by displaced persons lucky enough to have escaped to America. After the Hungarians revolted against Soviet occupation of their country, in December 1956 Russell wrote to me: "I have offered the use of my lake cottage, plus subsistence, to any refugee Hungarians the International Rescue Committee sends to me." Twenty-eight years later, in July 1984, Russell was still providing such help to a great number and variety of displaced persons: "We have with us at Mecosta four Croats, four Poles, one Italian, one Swiss, one Scot; we had two Ethiopians recently; also a congeries of Americans: A summer household of twenty-four, in all, ranging from eight years of age to ninety-three." Together with a steady stream of American visitors, teachers, students, and friends, and visitors from abroad, Mecosta was a gathering point for all sorts of persons who enjoyed Russell's hospitality or charity.

After Russell and Annette married, and I moved from Michigan to Rockford, Illinois, we necessarily saw less of each other, but continued to keep in close touch through letters. On the occasions when we met, we had much to discuss regarding our common interests, friends, and family matters. The spirit of our meetings was the same as at the very beginning of our friendship. In April 1982, I wrote after we had met at a conference: "After almost thirty-one years as friends I think it is wonderful that we have such perfect rapport that we can pick up our talk as though we had been together yesterday. That was the way it was with Robert Frost and me, so you are in good company."

In 1982, through the help of Russell and several other well-known conservatives, I was appointed by President Ronald Reagan to the National Council for the Humanities. For the next six years Russell and I frequently discussed the state of the humanities and higher education which revolved around the politics of what Russell called "Sodom-on-the-Potomac." Occasionally Russell came to Washington, as when we took part in a symposium on Irving Babbitt at Catholic University of America. Since he was chairman of the Academic Board for the National Humanities Institute, and I was on the Board, we met for the conference sponsored by the NHI, "Content and Character in Our Schools: The Renewal of American Education." The lectures we gave on that occasion were published in a small book, *Educating for Virtue* (1988).

In retrospect it appears that our interest in the renewal of American education, at all levels, was as enduring as our initial interest in Burke's political philosophy. In a brief memoir such as this much is necessarily omitted, but I can assert that as a true and tried friend Russell Kirk possesses all of the virtues of a Christian, gentleman, and scholar.

*   *   *

"Today the modern conservative movement is more than forty years old, and it is now possible to identify its origins, trace its development, and assess its impact. When one does so, Russell Kirk's name looms large at the very outset.

"It was in 1950 that Lionel Trilling made his famous observation that 'In the United States at this time liberalism is not only the dominant but even the sole intellectual tradition. For it is the plain fact that there are no conservative or reactionary ideas in general circulation.'

"Actually, Trilling was overlooking one aspect of the modern conservative worldview that had reasserted itself as early as 1944, in Friedrich Hayek's The Road to Serfdom: *the case for free-market economics. But economists of the Austrian school insisted upon calling themselves 'liberals,' in the original sense of that word, despite its application in the United States to the New Deal and its epigones. Incredible as it may seem, in 1950 the great intellectual tradition properly described as 'conservative' had no recognized interpreter or spokesman.*

"That omission was brilliantly rectified in 1953 by the publication of Russell Kirk's The Conservative Mind. *In this and subsequent books, Kirk revived the basic principles of conservatism, in particular as laid down by Edmund Burke, and applied them to modern America. Within five years, together with the principles of free-market economics, they had become the warp and woof of conservatism as we know it today.*

"And Russell Kirk performed one other important service as well: He gave this great movement its name."

— *William A. Rusher, 1992.*

An Exceptional Mind, An Exceptional Friend

by John Lukacs

I n the intellectual history of the United States in the twentieth century (historically speaking, the century from 1914 to 1989) Russell had a significant role. ("To have had a role" means more than to have "played a part.") Russell knows that, he has known it for a long time. But we seldom see ourselves as others see us — including our friends. So I think I should attempt to sum up my assessment of that role — or, more precisely, the significance of it. If my contribution has any value, this may be due to two things. One is my interest in the intellectual history of this country. The other is one of the things Russell and I have in common, different though as we are in our temperaments and in our provenance. Both of us are outsiders. I am not now referring to our ideas and principles but to our chosen station in life. I am foreign-born, a foreigner, who chose to remain outside the main centers of American intellectual life and commerce, in more than one way. Russell is a Midwestern American, with centuries of American ancestry behind him who, too, chose to live and work far from the madding (and maddening) crowd and from the fretful hubbub of those centers. Both of us are, and have remained, provincial, though not in the pejorative sense of that adjective. Often, it seems, we are content and perhaps even proud of that condition — sometimes at the expense of humility, I fear. Note that I wrote of Russell's "significance," rather than of "importance." The reason for this connects to the above. The conditions of intellectual commerce in the second half of the twentieth century were and are such that, had Russell become an Important Intellectual in the midst of that commerce, there would have been something wrong. He would have compromised his birthright, and many of his principles. He would have been celebrated rather than respected; and a Celebrity, as someone once wrote, is only someone who is famous for being well known. That kind of celebrity is almost always thoughtless, while respect earned is almost always thoughtful. Providence has spared Russell from occupying such a place in the center of American intellectual commerce where, with all of its ephemeral advantages and emoluments, the respect due to him would have gradually melted away.

I once referred to Victor Hugo's celebrated phrase of An Idea Whose Time Has Come, adding that in the twentieth century an idea whose time has come may not be any good. There are exceptions to this, and one is *The Conservative Mind*. Whether its publication in 1953 started, or coincided with the beginning of the American conservative movement is unimportant. What is significant is that *The Conservative Mind* was a catalyst, both as to its origins and in its effect. It was the work of an outsider. By this I do not mean Russell's personal situation at the time, nor the utter difference of his ideas from the then-accepted body of ideas in American intellectual life. What I mean is that, had it not been for Russell's years in St. Andrews during that work's creation, that book would not have been written — or it would not have been written in the way it was. This work by a then still young man was not only the result of his astonishing capacity of reading. There was the inspiration that an unusual atmosphere helped to crystallize in his independent mind. For the amazing thing in *The Conservative Mind* was not only the quantity of reading that its author had absorbed, but the quality of his account — dependent on a perspicacity that surges from something beyond intellectual experience. When I first read *The Conservative Mind* I was in the midst of studying much of the vast written heritage of Tocqueville, well beyond a reading of *Democracy in America*; and I was more than pleased, I was astonished to find how this, to me then-unknown or hardly known American author had been able to extract the most significant, the most telling elements from Tocqueville in a chapter of not too many pages. That was not merely the result of an economy of style; it was the proof of an exceptional mind.

Forty years have now gone by since the publication of that book. It is still Russell's prime and principal work. During those forty years something happened in the United States that has had no precedent in the intellectual and political history of the Republic. The majority of

Americans, including even intellectuals, have become "conservatives" now. Some intellectuals of this new-fangled majority refuse to admit that, of course. Others avow it all too easily, profiting therefrom. "Liberal" has become such a bad word that politicians now try to avoid it. Two years before the publication of *The Conservative Mind* even Senator Taft (one of Russell's heroes whom I sometimes respect but seldom admire) felt compelled to state that he was not a conservative but an "old-fashioned liberal." Seven years after the publication President Eisenhower (whom both Russell and I have considered, and still consider, to have been a supreme opportunist) announced that he was a "conservative." So a turning-point not only in the intellectual but also in the political history of the United States occurred during the 1950s. And the role of *The Conservative Mind* at that time is not to be gainsaid. Since that time Russell may have exaggerated the importance of politics, including his own political influences. Every person has his weaknesses — or, rather, vanities — good men included. There is Russell's tendency to see his larger political and philosophical principles absorbed and incarnated by temporarily important but, in reality, ephemeral political figures. In the long run this does not matter. The important matter is that Russell has been true to his original principles. Even now when he is the Old Sage (preferable to Elder Statesman) among the conservatives he is independent of most of them, and not at all by striking, or preserving, a pose. Forty years ago he knew, and said, that Economic Man is a myth; that the idea of Progress must not only be questioned but rethought; that Technology has nothing to do with culture and cultivation; that reason without faith may be as disastrous as is faith without reason. I will not and cannot sum up his principal beliefs except to say that he has remained true to them throughout, having rejected not only Karl Marx but also Adam Smith, because of their different, but perhaps essentially not unsimilar misreading of human nature, since the main motive (and purpose) of human beings is not that of "maximizing their profit." Samuel Johnson knew that well enough; so does Russell Kirk.

There are dualities in the character of every man. One interesting, and sometimes endearing, duality in Russell's resides in his origins and in his affections: Russell is both Tory and Puritan. He has propagated the restoration of medieval and bourgeois virtues sometimes within the same book or essay or article. His writings have reflected both the Royalist and the Puritan aspects of his *persona*, of the Cavalier and the Covenanter at the same time—though the former of these pairs may have gradually gained their ascendancy. He is more Cavalier than Covenanter in his aspirations, while perhaps both Tory and Puritan in his temperament.

*   *   *

Allow me now to conclude with a summary of our friendship. When I read *The Conservative Mind* in 1953 I was inspired enough to write Russell, who answered with his customary friendliness. Soon he visited us in our little apartment in Germantown, Pennsylvania, and then in my father-in-law's ancestral place in Chester County, and then often in our own dwelling, the Old Pickering School House. As Flannery O'Connor noted, Russell is a thinker and a writer rather than a conversationalist; but we had memorable evenings together, since I was aware that he knew what Goethe had meant when he wrote that the real mark of culture is knowing how to listen and not merely how to talk. (Not that I said much that was worth listening to, but still. . . .) During the last forty years we saw each other often, though perhaps not as often as we would have wished. He was the kind of guest that was an ornament of our house; I was his guest in Mecosta once. He had an abiding affection for my first wife and for my children; I was both happy and relieved to see his marriage and family with Annette, a pillar of his existence, domestic and otherwise. He was generous in assisting and recommending me when I was a young scholar struggling with the first draft of my *Historical Consciousness*. There may be a symbol in this. Our friendship has many roots, fibers, and threads, and the consciousness of history is not the least among them.

*   *   *

"I've just re-read your Academic Freedom*: and it comes out even stronger on a second reading. What a great gift it is to be able to convince and persuade, without antagonising (like I do)! It is, with* The Conservative Mind, *one of the most important books of this century."*

— *Roy Campbell, in an undated*
letter to Russell Kirk
written in the mid 1950s.

Russell Kirk: Past as Prologue

by Irving Louis Horowitz

My relationship to Russell Kirk exists in two distinct and discrete parts: as a young critic in the mid-1950s of *The Conservative Mind*; and as an aging publisher of Transaction Publishers issuing works in the tradition of that classic text. We bill ourselves as "publishers of record in international social science." As part of that "billing" we publish one series of books on conservative thought and another on liberal thought. I have never believed that denunciations of opponents, or dismissive approaches to those of different persuasions serve the common culture. Indeed, the spirit of fanaticism is, or at least ought to be, alien to honest social thought. And I believe the same is true for honest cultural analysis.

While I still believe my critiques of the new conservatism made nearly forty years ago remain essentially valid, I must also be frank and say that the liberal bastions from which those criticisms were launched seem far more vulnerable now than in the past. Indeed, both conservatism and liberalism are under assault from the forces of fanaticism. The neo-liberalism that would substitute assurances that we end up in the same place, however different people are in talent and interests, undermines precisely the classical ideal of every person counting as one. By the same token, the neo-conservatism that would demand allegiance to evangelical and/or fundamentalist persuasions deprives the conservative tradition precisely of the individual, anti-statist credo that has sustained it over time.

It is the infusion of "neo" that has done much to confound traditions of conservatism and liberalism alike. I suspect that both Russell and I now feel more comfortable in each other's company precisely because what is new, what is "neo," is what is so ersatz, transparent, and fanatic. In short these new credos do violence to the spirit of learning to which all people of the book are, in their nature, dedicated.

I would like to think that my relationship with Russell has not simply been one-sided. For while I readily confess to being profoundly influenced by his emphasis on the moral grounding of political life, I also suspect that he would modify his earlier assaults on the social sciences. He now appears to recognize that the great traditions which he represents are just as readily served by honest social science as by honest classical humanities. Russell knows better now than in the past that the key term in normative outlook is *honesty* of effort, not background discipline, or area of training.

Under the impact of Russell's thinking I have become more critical of established trends and tendencies in present-day social research as the title of my next book, *The Decomposition of Sociology*, should make quite clear. He, in turn, is now giving solid social and political science what I think fairer consideration. For example, some new titles for The Library of Conservative Thought, of which Russell is General Editor: *The Politics of the Center* by Vincent Starzinger, *The Italian Fascist Party in Power* by Dante Germino, *The Phantom Public* by Walter Lippmann, and *We The People: The Economic Origins of the Constitution* by Forrest McDonald. To be sure, these are hardly "mainline" works. But they do indicate ways in which social science studies and classical conservative traditions meet. It is to Russell's lasting credit that he can put aside old fears and incorporate the best of scholarship, whatever its professional sources.

Russell needs no further encomiums. He has received enough of these to last ten ordinary lifetimes. Certainly it is one of his great virtues that his head is not easily turned by praise. He has never rested on his oars, and continues to turn out work at a feverish pace, albeit with elegant results. And while he rarely forgets or ignores the long view, the long tradition as it were, he has a secret love affair with the present. He responds to the immediate with a far greater sense of urgency than might be imagined by casual readers.

In a world of assaults on American ties to Europe, under the rubric of Eurocentricism or Multiculturalism, he can fashion a book on *America's British Culture*. During the celebrations of the American Constitutional Tradition of 1989, he wrote major position papers on the character of that tradition, including the sort of acute analysis of the Bill of Rights that helps put in deep perspective the first ten amendments to the American Constitution. He has also spoken frankly in relation to presidential candidates and global matters such as the United States involvement in the Iraqi takeover of Kuwait. It would be less than candid to say that I share his positions on all practical or contingent matters. Clearly I do not. Just as clearly, I think that his views on practical issues do not necessarily issue from his general proposals on the nature of the political culture. Politics may have rich philosophical implications, but it is also a craft practiced on an everyday *ad hoc* basis. This double-edged nature of the polity is well understood by Russell.

But that said, we have in our midst a special sort of person — one who constantly fine-tunes the relationship of the general and the particular, the universal and the personal. His commitment is not now, and never was, to an economic system. Rather, Russell's faith is in a cultural order. Indeed, one suspects that capitalism may be as much anathema for Russell as it is for hard-bitten socialists. It is rather that Russell sees the present economic arrangement as far better than the utopian promises by the communists (and who could argue with that!). But it is the struggle for a culture, for a tradition of shared values, for a world in which religion is linked to practice at one level and morality at another, that characterizes Russell.

And I would say that at the very end of the rainbow, it is the cement of ethics rather than the grist of law that gives meaning to Russell's idea of justice. Without a morally centered world, Russell sees the contentions and conflicts engendered by the spirit of the laws as the last, but not the best, hope for survival. With a morally centered world, and one lodged especially in the Judaeo-Christian tradition (especially Anglo-Catholicism, if one places a fine point on this element) there is hope for the future because there is a prospect for social consensus.

Whether this sort of approach can actually resolve deep rifts and divisions within American or Western culture is a topic for a much fuller paper. It would require a re-analysis of my critique (in 1955) of the New Conservatism, and a re-evaluation in 1993 of what passed for old liberalism of the sort I represented in the past — and yes, still do. We may have shared values, but not necessarily shared heroes. I prefer to remain in a world of Leonard Schapiro, Morris Raphael Cohen and Jacob L. Talmon, to name a few. This is a world of unfulfilled prophesies to be sure, but one which raised the same warnings about totalitarian potentials in politics and culture that emanated from the writings of Russell's favorites: Irving Babbitt, Edmund Burke, and David Hume. But curiously, I think our decade-long relationship, close in every way, indicates that people of good will and good faith can live and work together in suspension of ultimate judgment, whatever the sources of cultural inspiration. Those lacking good will cannot so endure.

There is an area of common enterprise that has been possible because both Russell and I believe and practice the arts and crafts of publishing no less than professing. Over the years we have published not only our own works, but those of others. The idea of scholarship is not simply that of self-promotion or vanity. Collegial relations are feasible because a sense of the other is so real, so necessary. Russell and I have come to share what another colleague calls a conspiracy of excellence. This is not said in the spirit of snobbish righteousness, but simply in recognition that the act of publishing the works of others, no less than of ourselves, constitutes a statement of what is important, what is enduring. This has become a most powerful, if admittedly unstated, bond between us. This appeal to the majesty of the Word transcends differences in philosophies, ideologies, and even cultural backgrounds.

Perhaps we find a common bond at Michael Oakeshott's supper table: a place where dialogues replace daggers, and good wine does not have to be spiked with deadly potions. My faith in reason and Russell's faith in tradition, after all, derive from a common belief in persuasion not power, the authority of tradition and not the authoritarianism of raw force, and the evidence of the senses, not the fear of the truncheon. These, we hope, will ultimately determine the fate of people, nations, and civilizations.

In his farewell from American shores to the late Christopher Dawson, one of Russell's favorite figures, Richard Cardinal Cushing noted that he "is one of those rare human spirits who stands back from the world in which he lives and takes the true measure of time and man." Since I cannot advance a proposition which is more appropriate to a summary of the life and work of Russell Kirk, I dare appropriate the Cardinal's words and place him in the special pantheon of people who have taken the true measure of our age and of our spirit.

"The Box of Delights":
A Literary Patrimony

by Cecilia A. Kirk

"Bread" came alive one afternoon in our nursery. Having just read Maurice Maeterlinck's *The Blue Bird* together, my father, my sisters, and I created a dramatization of it in which the character "Bread" assumed a life of his own. In this play, two children wander through such magical scenes as the "palace of night" seeking happiness, symbolized by the Blue Bird. They eventually find contentment in their own home. I recall being rather perplexed by this conclusion. Of course, one implication is that perhaps happiness cannot be pursued, or that it comes from within. Naturally enough, I had not then articulated any analysis of the story, nor perhaps should I have, for the vivacious and perceptive story in itself was sufficiently appealing. *The Blue Bird* provokes our moral imaginations — possibly to a consideration of happiness, but more probably to an awareness of creatureliness and a solicitude for the two children.

Night after night my father read aloud to us, all of us delighted by the stories. Sometimes we listened for hours; this listening, unconsciously and inadvertently, brought a habit of attention. Occasionally, however, he was even more eager to read than we were inclined to listen: when we fell asleep, we were carried up the wooden hill — the stairs — to the land of nod. Always willing to read aloud, he introduced us to the marvels of good literature.

A cherisher of stories, Russell Kirk perceives their significance: they feed man's imagination, not that they intend to do so. While they are primarily to entertain, good stories simultaneously embody an understanding or a glimpse of truth. In conveying wisdom and providing insight, they reveal what it means to be human.

Of the many books that my father read to us, I cannot recall much of their plots or even many of their names, but I retain a vague sense of charmed awe and perhaps some benefit from their cumulative impact. In this respect, Lewis Carroll's *Alice's Adventures in Wonderland* naturally springs to mind. In that topsy-turvy, deliciously surprising wonderland, Alice maintains her common-sensical composure — despite the Queen's command, "Off with her head!" We all are astounded by the bizarre events, and admire Alice immensely. With Alice, we return to the real world, full of vivid memories, wiser after our strange adventure, and perhaps attentive to proportion, having witnessed the comical effects of disproportion. (Once, this book also was dramatized in our house — at a St. Valentine's Day costume party, with my father as the Cheshire Cat, my mother as the Queen of Hearts, my fortunate sister Monica as Alice, and me as the white rabbit, trained by my mother to repeat "I'm late, I'm late, for a very important date!" to our guests.)

Randomly selecting a few more books from our readings, I think of George MacDonald's *The Princess and Curdie*, *The Snow Queen* by Hans Christian Andersen, and E. Nesbit's *The Phoenix and the Carpet*. In all of these stories, likeable, courageous children are the protagonists, and sometimes must make unalterable decisions. Trusty Curdie confronts formidable dangers; the little girl withstands the evil Snow Queen. The six Bastable children — very English, very sensible, and very funny — discover that their carpet possesses magical powers, producing such extraordinary results as the appearance of a thousand Persian cats. Through these fantastic episodes, we experience an element of mystery, and discover the nature of character: Curdie's honesty and the princess's kind wisdom shine through, while the glistening Snow Queen is exposed for the deceiver she is. These adventures are not comfortable journeys; rather, at times the hero or heroine is nearly overwhelmed.

As my father observes regarding his own youthful readings, "I did learn much about the reality of human jealousy and ambition, ingenuity and fortitude, selfishness and charity, gloom and hope. I became aware that my own little physical environment was something local and not absolute. . . . I acquired some concept of abiding truths . . . . " In one of his favorite children's stories, John Ruskin's *The King of the Golden River*, the proud, cruel brothers Hans and Schwartz are transformed into stones in the river, while selfless little Gluck is rewarded abundantly. We are granted satisfaction with the justice of the conclusion. Although good literature is not necessarily morally instructive, by incorporating norms, standards of behavior, it provides measurement, familiarity with the diversity of human character and circumstance, and material for reflection.

Entering the realm of the fantastic, but often entirely real and detailed, J. R. R. Tolkien's *The Hobbit* and *The Lord of the Rings* provide the best examples of fiction that enlarges our vision. These tales fascinate us and appeal to our ethical consciousness. The affable and straightforward Bilbo, the greedy and loathsome Gollum, the talented, lithe, and mysterious Elves, all absorbed in a gripping adventure evoke powerful images, ones which certainly impressed me. My father also read to us from the five volumes of Mary Norton's *The Borrowers*, which narrates the adventures of a miniature family, its members only a few inches in height, as they endure the comical incidents and tribulations which accompany persons of that size. The Borrowers mimic in detailed microcosm the lives of bigger people. Inspired in part by these descriptions, I created my own little people. I built an entire town for them, which soon covered the floor of a small room at home, where I played for hours and years.

Continuing the element of the unusual, most vivid in my mind are the "unconventional" stories of our youth. *Struwwelpeter*, by Heinrich Hoffman, is the notorious example of this genre. My sister Monica was familiar with the terrors of *Struwwelpeter* (I do not necessarily recommend the book), whose cover depicts the unkempt Peter with exceedingly long fingernails, and wherein Johnny-Head-in-Air foolishly falls into a river. Then, there is the incident of the tablecloth where disobedient Fidgety Phil insists on tilting his chair back from the dinner table, resulting in its collapse upon him. There is most definitely a sense of responsibility for one's actions and of justice in the book! The milder *Goops*, by Gelett Burgess, depicts unmannerly behavior in a more playful and civilized mode.

The classic *Pinocchio* has won the devotion of generations with the mischief-making and easily misled, but good-hearted, Pinocchio, kind old Geppetto, and the talking Cricket. Yet it is no happy-go-lucky story, for the malevolent and deceptive Fox and Cat are thoroughly destructive, alerting us to the reality of harmful characters. Another traditional favorite, Robert Louis Stevenson's *Treasure Island*, similarly forewarns us of sinister circumstances, with its mysterious Black Spot.

Perceptive, normative literature, these tales serve as a preparation for life. Grimm's *Fairy Tales* are of this genre. Their unexpected endings delight us, for too many goody-goody stories are repellent and we justly reject them, while a diet of substantive stories is much more satisfying.

My father also read us fairy tales, including *Arabian Nights*, though these remained more to my sister Felicia's taste than my own. I liked *Dick Whittington and His Cat*, about a poor boy in London who eventually become Lord Mayor; while Monica treasured *Gertrude's Child*, about a doll that owns a child. *The Secret Garden* and *Charlie and the Chocolate Factory* especially pleased Monica. We all heard the same literature, but different stories sparked our individual imaginations. Although they may have possessed material of universal significance, these books appealed variously to our characters, moved by certain images. Andrea, my youngest sister, liked our father's own tales most of all, and she drew sketches of their characters. She was always fascinated by the pictures. After all, the illustrations first attracted us to the books and were often what we loved most about them.

Reviving the neglected art of storytelling, my father also invented his own tales. He related these stories as installments beside the fireplace, the traditional place for a community's stories, developing the characters and plots as he spoke. We followed "Hew and His Knife," "The Elusive Earl," and another tale set during the time of the Crusades (but whose name escapes me, as these oral narrations were never recorded). Often he would conclude an episode with the protagonists caught in a perilous predicament — surrounded by bandits or the like — which on one occasion so infuriated us that we demanded that he "get those children home to their momma." Laughing, he appeased us with a more satisfactory conclusion.

These stories acted reciprocally upon our household. Clinton, a genuine hobo whom we took in, appeared frequently in my father's tales, even assuming heroic roles — though Clinton himself denied being capable of any such self-endangering actions. My father was able, as he has written in another context, "to weave into the intricate tapestry of his romance certain little insignificant real happenings, making them important threads in his work." Unfortunately, my sister Monica soon learned to develop her own stories: one afternoon when we were supposed to be cleaning our room, Monica cleverly proposed that if I cleaned the room, she would tell me a story. In-

nocently agreeable, I listened to her tale of a horrible wolf (suspicious-
ly similar to that in "Red Riding Hood"), which culminated in the
malicious words, "And, Cecilia, the Wolf is Everywhere!"—causing
me to shriek with terror. My parents, who had been eavesdropping,
burst into laughter.

Those fireside tales were amazing and extraordinary; I have yet to
encounter their like elsewhere. During the telling of "The Elusive
Earl," I observed to my father that most of his characters were evil
(which also amused him); but I must admit that the hero or heroine,
despite any occasional suspicion or eclipse, invariably emerges as a
magnanimous person. What impressed me most about these tales was
simply that they existed at all, that he was able to create them, conjur-
ing them up out of nothing.

In my father's written, published fiction, very much for a more
mature audience, the characters evidence less felicitous qualities than
in his narrations for us. His fiction often considers the eerie, the
macabre, and even the diabolic. For the sheer pleasure of their
evocative titles, I specify: *A Creature of the Twilight, The Surly Sullen Bell,
The Princess of All Lands, Lord of the Hollow Dark, Old House of Fear,* and
"The Invasion of the Church of the Holy Ghost." A number of Kirk's
short stories, their anecdotes inexplicable, remain enigmas; some,
rooted in particular places and chance circumstances, portray harsh
spiritual battles beyond time and death. Such haunting works are far
removed from the children's tales, but they share a common element:
the appeal to the normative consciousness, touching upon struggles of
an ethical nature.

Encouraged by our father to take up our own reading, I began my
serious reading at the age of ten. That year, I fell ill and had to hobble
about on crutches for six months—which was providential, for I was,
for a time, thrown back on books. From the ages of three until seven,
my father had been similarly disabled, and so his mother constantly
read to him. While confined to sedentary activity physically, the
health of his mind thrived and became robust. During those early
years, he began to form an understanding—even a philosophical
habit of mind—and later suspected that he already had been aware of
certain truths at that young age, but only recognized them fully when
they were expressed years later. (This illative sense I have experienced
also, though in a much-muted form.) He was a precocious child, yet

he exhibited the customary love of play in that land of counterpane which has welcomed many of us, myself included.

The land of counterpane, a life of the mind, is intriguingly portrayed in *Tom's Midnight Garden*, by Philippa Pearce, in which the clock strikes thirteen and Tom enters his garden outside time. This heartwarming book possesses a rather eerie quality, expressing the experience of transcending time. It suggests the "eternal moments" during which time and the timeless coalesce, moments about which my father has spoken and which remind us that man was made for eternity. Those experiences inspire a curiosity that confirms that the world is more than physical matter.

Exploring the land of counterpane, I immersed myself in literature, absorbed by the stories. John Masefield's *Martin Hyde: The Duke's Messenger*, a historical romance, became my first serious book. After that, I read a number of Masefield sea novels, including two volumes my father had long promised me, though I was skeptical, with the curious titles *Dead Ned* and *Live and Kicking Ned*. Although he had attempted to read Hendrik Van Loon's *The Story of Mankind* and other historical works to us, his efforts were unsuccessful: we deserted him in favor of more conventional pursuits (namely, the neighbor's television; we did not have one of our own). Once attracted to historical novels, though, I read avidly: the medieval Polish *The Blacksmith of Vilno*, by Eric Kelly; *The Splendid Spur* by Sir Arthur Quiller-Couch; Willa Cather's *Death Comes for the Archbishop* and *Shadows on the Rock*; Joan Aiken's *Black Hearts in Battersea*, set in early nineteenth-century London; Scott O'Dell's *Island of the Blue Dolphins*, of an Indian girl alone on an island; and Lloyd Alexander's five-volume *Prydain Chronicles*, a romance based on Welsh legends. Also I read the strange H. Rider Haggard novel *She*, which is set deep in the African jungle where the inhabitants place pots on the heads of strangers and which concerns a mysterious and deathless Queen called by her subjects "She-who-must-be-obeyed"—a nickname my father and I adopted for my mother. My favorite was *The Boy with the Bronze Axe*, by Kathleen Fidler, set in a Stone-Age village in the Orkneys; today the remains of that actual village have been exposed by the winds.

By sparking my imagination through fairy tales, and by providing perspective and reason through historical novels, my father imparted a cultural legacy to me. For through the printed word, the wisdom of generations transcends the "provincialism of time" and speaks to us across the ages and the oceans. We acquire an understanding of tradition through the "eternal contract" of the generations, of the immediate and the timeless. Historical literature in particular provides a continuity and order; humane letters truly is conducive to a balanced habit of mind. The record of our collective and real stories, history reveals the enduring qualities of human nature.

The story is capable of expressing reality powerfully and precisely. Children's literature especially has a universal appeal and, we discovered, can transmit an imaginative, normative consciousness. As the aging Henry Ryecroft wrote, literature is "food for the soul of man."

*　　　*　　　*

"[Russell Kirk] is a compelling story-teller at a time when contemporary fiction sadly lacks a sense of story.

"I read all of the tales [in The Princess of All Lands*] with enormous pleasure and a most willing suspension of disbelief. It is also refreshing to find stories of heavenly and profane love which, also, are willing to deal with the grand theological themes."*

　　　　　　　　　　　— Madeleine L'Engle,
　　　　　　　　　　　1979.

*　　　*　　　*

"Building a personal creed for legislating is an absolute necessity. My own foundation has had many additions built upon the writings of Dr. Russell Kirk.

"I cherish most the personal conversations and the seminars given in conjunction with ISI at Piety Hill. Among the best was the 1978 visit of Malcolm Muggeridge as a guest lecturer. A fascinating interchange of ideas between two great writers reenforced my conservative foundation. Fun was not forgotten, especially at the New Year's Eve party, where Dr. Kirk's ancient parlor game of Snap-Dragon challenged players to see how many flaming brandy-soaked raisins could be snatched from the flames and eaten.

"During legislative discussion, I have found probably the most helpful of all Dr. Kirk's advice to be the admonition, "Politics is the art of the possible." In every debate a time comes when one must decide if what is possible is acceptable."

　　　　　　　　　　　— Michigan State Senator
　　　　　　　　　　　Joanne Emmons, 1992

The Importance of Russell Kirk

by Jeffrey Hart

Q uite often, when leading a college class studying a great poem, I begin by reading it aloud. When I finish reading it, instead of beginning comment and discussion, I read it again, perhaps even a third time. Among other effects, this concentrates the student's mind on the object, which is the subject. Commentary is ontologically subordinate to the poem, to its "quiddity," as the philosophers say.

I have somewhat the same impulse as regards Russell Kirk's *Prospects for Conservatives*. Though I will discuss it below, I would rather quote from it. The book has great quiddity, very definite existence. It is extraordinarily rich in thought and texture, and is timely in the 1990s precisely because of its timeless quality: It deals with permanent things.

This book exists in an important relationship to the author's famous work, *The Conservative Mind*, which appeared in 1953. The appearance of Kirk's book, seemingly from out of nowhere — no one had heard of Russell Kirk — was a tremendous event. And it was one because things were stirring. Lionel Trilling had been correct when he had written in 1950 that, "In the United States at this time liberalism is not only the dominant but even the sole intellectual tradition. For it is the plain fact that nowadays there are no conservative or reactionary ideas in general circulation." By liberalism, Trilling at that time meant the Progressive-New Deal-Fair Deal habit of mind, and he was largely right.

But, as I say, things were stirring. In 1944, Friedrich von Hayek, a leader of the Austrian school, published an improbable best-seller called *The Road to Serfdom*. Clearly written but not exactly a thriller, it sold thousands of copies and was even condensed in *The Reader's Digest*. Hayek challenged the liberal tendency toward centralization and government intervention and made a powerful case for the free market. Hayek, who considered himself an old-fashioned "liberal," that is, a believer in freedom, came as a breath of pure oxygen at a time when the entire intellectual establishment, the media and the federal government seemed headed down the road to ever-increasing government control. Hayek was walking around the liberal gas works with a lighted match.

In 1952 there appeared another key book, *Witness*, by Whittaker Chambers — a searing but also lyrical account of his transition from high-level Soviet spy to principled anti-communist. Like the Ancient Mariner in Coleridge's poem, Chambers had visited the abyss and returned to tell us about it. As Arthur Koestler remarked, Chambers had not returned from Hell empty-handed. Earlier, Chambers had identified Alger Hiss as a spy, and Hiss had been declared guilty after two famous trials. But the whole business went far beyond Hiss's individual guilt. Chambers's implicit point throughout was that there was a rotten connection between the liberalism of the Thirties and the Stalinist treason represented by Hiss. Liberalism was the soil in which the treason of Hiss had grown, and, even after Hiss was known to have been guilty, liberals defended him. They still do.

And then came *The Conservative Mind*, a fitting climax. So there was no tradition of conservative thought, eh? Kirk provided careful discussions of Edmund Burke, John Adams, Coleridge, Walter Scott, John Randolph and John C. Calhoun, Macaulay, Tocqueville, Disraeli, Newman, Maine, Lecky, Mallock, Irving Babbitt, and Santayana. In subsequent editions he extended the tradition to include T. S. Eliot.

Some objected that this was not an entirely American tradition, but it was Kirk's point that America is not an intellectual island but part of the Western tradition. The pilgrims brought with them to Plymouth Rock the spirits of Moses and Aeneas.

Whittaker Chambers, then an editor at *Time* magazine, told his editor Roy Alexander that "*The Conservtive Mind* is one of the most important books that is likely to appear in some time." *Time* agreed and devoted its entire book section to Kirk's book.

In this book, along with Hayek and Chambers, we have the three principal constituents of modern conservatism: Hayek's free market, Chambers's anti-communism, and Kirk's sense of tradition. It took about 30 years for these ideas to become dominant, but dominant they are, and bliss it was in that dawn to be alive.

One year after the initial edition of *The Conservative Mind* appeared, *Prospects for Conservatives* was first published under the title *A Program for Conservatives*. In it Kirk no longer spoke ventriloquially through Burke, Adams, Calhoun, Newman, or Santayana, but stepped forward in his own voice to become in effect part of the conservative intellectual tradition.

From the opening page onward what strikes the reader is Kirk's conversational ease among the greatest writers. He begins on a humorous note, which is also deadly serious: "In politics, the professor always plays the comic role,' says Nietzsche . . . Hilaire Belloc reminds us that the very eccentricities of professors, their peculiarities of gait, their squint, their oddities of gesture and speech, are a curse put upon them as punishment for their terrible sin of pride."

Those observations lead into the core of the book: the lethal power of abstractions in the hands of proud men who have little experience of, or love for, the actual world, the "sweet world" as Dante keeps calling it from the depths of Hell.

Kirk, and on this his voice should be heard with special clarity, understands that "conservatives always differ a good deal, among themselves." And unlike many conservatives today, he is concerned about the despoliation of the environment and about a "swelling" population.

But when he says that conservatives differ among themselves, he points to an important truth. That is, that there is no conservative ideology. The complex conservative quilt consists of free-marketeers, libertarians, monarchists, strict constitutional constructionists, Catholic traditionalists, anti-communists, Protestant fundamentalists, blue-collar ethnic traditionalists, and a vast number of people who merely want to be left alone by the busybodies.

Liberals, on the other hand, are on a specific continuum. They are, in varying degree, secular socialists.

Kirk can be devastating in his serene way: "One cannot re-educate a generation through a single book, or a thousand books, and therefore I do not really expect to be able to make my opponents into converts, as Burke converted [James] Mackintosh; for the modern liberal does not have the intellectual discipline of Mackintosh which made it possible to persuade him of his errors."

Timeless wisdom, drawing upon history, is also most timely: "Taxation, taken to the limit and beyond, has always been a sign of decadence and a prelude to disaster."

Kirk knows the great books. And he has contributed to them this masterpiece. As I said at the outset of this essay, I feel a constant tug here toward pure quotation: "Instead of endeavoring to make most men into gentlemen, we have been intent upon reducing any surviving gentlemen to the condition and manners of proletarians."

The word "wisdom" is not much in vogue these days, a fact that in itself is a cultural datum in the age of Madonna, Spike Lee, Phil Donahue and multicultural education. Wisdom implies a sense of the past, maturity, and humane learning.

Kirk not only is wise and not only knows tradition, he *is* tradition.

*　　　　*　　　　*

"My dear Kirk. First of all, let me thank you very much for your interesting article in Yale Review. *I was delighted (though what the hell you meant by saying what I lacked for perfection was . . . !); and secondly, let me say how much I enjoyed your three books, sent me by Regnery. You are the latest, and by no means the least, of that brilliant group of Americans advocating that of all unamerican things, the Traditional Spirit. Your praise of Edmund Burke is very much to my taste. Your witty prophecy of the immediate future should be enlarged."*

> *— Wyndham Lewis, in a letter*
> *to Russell Kirk dated*
> *August 29, 1955.*

*　　　　*　　　　*

"Monsignor Guardini has written that 'when a man accepts divine truth in the obedience of faith, he is forced to rethink human truth,' and it is such a rethinking in the obedience to divine truth which must be the mainspring of any enlightened social thought, whether it tends to be liberal or conservative. Since the Enlightenment, liberalism in its extreme forms has not accepted divine truth and the conservatism which has enjoyed any popularity has shown no tendency to rethink human truth or to reexamine human society. Mr. Kirk has managed in a succession of books which have proved both scholarly and popular to do both and to make the voice of an intelligent and vigorous conservative thought respected in this country."

> *— Flannery O'Connor, from a*
> *review of Kirk's* Beyond the
> Dreams of Avarice *in her*
> *diocesan paper,* The Bulle-
> tin, *July 21, 1956.*

A Proper Patrimony:
Russell Kirk and
America's Moral Genealogy

by M. E. Bradford

It is nowadays the fashion to think of these United States as a wholly "invented" polity, as the pure and miraculous handiwork of those gifted political craftsmen who were our honored forefathers and whose high achievements we celebrated during the Bicentennial year. It is also the conventional wisdom that our original revolution was *the* genuine revolution, the paradigm for all serious and progressive rebellions, early or late, and the fulcrum upon which the modern world has since been obliged to turn. It is obvious that the emphasis behind these assumptions is upon what was new about America, that break with the general Western prescription which should ostensibly account for our distinctive political habitude and origination. A corollary premise is that such a revolution is destined to continue on and on, perpetually unfinished, perpetually at war with whatever remains of the older world turned upside down when Lord Cornwallis marched out from his works.

What I have been describing is, to be sure, the basis for a variety of impious readings of the American past. In 1976 we heard or read about them all as part of the regular Bicentennial fare. And perhaps detected in the almost choral harmonies of the music they made together a fanfare sanctioning disorders yet to come. However, now as then, most of our countrymen are so thoroughly accustomed to the calculus which informs these interpretations that they notice its operation rarely, if at all. When told that the France of Robespierre, the Russia of Lenin, and the China of Mao are close relations to the America of 1776, that our "political religion" is a position defined by reaction against the structures, customs, and feelings which had informed the long record of Western man prior to the inception of our adventure with independence, they offer no objections. And even though the same solid citizens will, in all likelihood, act in their everyday affairs to belie such infamous analogies, the pressure of distortion gathers continuously in the absence of vigorous refutation. The results, in our contemporary social and political discourse, are something we experience with ever growing dismay.

Thus we face the paradox that what we are taught from authority concerning the American Revolution is the measure of our confusion on that subject. Here the influence of Louis Hartz and Bernard Bailyn comes quickly to mind. And I mention their names only to typify a more numerous breed—all of them relatives of the frenetic persona in Swift's *Tale of a Tub*, all, like that mad hack, gathering materials for "A Modest Defence of the Proceedings of the Rabble." *The Roots of American Order* presupposes, as a piece of rhetoric, no other state of affairs, no less formidable adversaries to confound. I use the word rhetoric advisedly. Praise of discontinuity, rupture, and drastic innovation is ever the song of the new ideological historians—of helpful, not baneful change: but change *identified as good by being identified as radical.* Kirk, however, writes no Tory apocalypse. He contends that our roots run deep and remain intact, that to know them is to recognize both their antiquity and their present hold upon us. His book is a calculated inquiry into the genesis of our national character which looks behind events and documents to remote antecedents and attempts to encourage a modest estimation of its originality, a thoughtful appreciation of how much and how far it was brought to these shores, and a quiet rejoicing that we remain, in our essential qualities as a people, so well and so anciently grounded in the funded wisdom of the ages. Kirk's amiable but unremitting determination is to require of our generation a grudging admission that America has a religious, a moral, and *therefore* a political genealogy: a patrimony that could be called *unrevolutionary* and not at all modern, whose order-giving strength owes, by accident or omission as much as by design, to continuities so axiomatic that we have rarely, until of late, felt any need to speak of them at all.

Thus came his book to be a special sort of anomaly: a study of America which devotes less than a third of its pages to life on this side of the Atlantic. Indeed, some of its larger components could be read with very little of a particular national theme in mind. One instance is the section on "Roman Virtue." Another appears in a few fine pages on Scotland's St. Andrew's University (the subject of a fine Kirk monograph—and his European alma mater). These excursions might puzzle the reader who likes to think of America in terms of disembodied ideals. But, given his purposes, Kirk had no other choice of procedures, no alternatives in emphasis. Most of the little that Kirk does write about colonial America or the formation of the Republic is included primarily to point his readers backward in time, to trends and authorities established among us long before we became our own kind of one and many.

Jerusalem, Athens, Rome, and London—the four great iconic cities for the Anglo-American and tropes for four distinctive structurings of social and political life, these plus an assortment of supporting figures who have made for our perception of these citadels as the sequence and a synthetic "given"—are the ingredients in Kirk's cultural dynamic. As a principle of order Jerusalem represents, of course, faith and pious submission. Athens signifies (apart from its force as a negative political example) reason and art: philosophy and the examined life. Rome is a simpler model. Rome is law and public order, a notion of the common good, of corporate liberty. After Rome comes Jerusalem again—the life, death, and resurrection of Christ. Medieval man sifted that first Jerusalem *and* Athens *and* Rome through the filter of the gospels, the fullness of God's revelation to His creation. And, most significantly for Americans, in and around the city on the Thames. Christianity taught of the integrity of the individual soul. In England that translated into liberty under law, in community. Kirk gathers up the threads as he goes. Mixed in with his discourse of cities and men is an account of certain habits and ideas, their slow and steady formation. And much church history. For the moral imagination has many of its roots there, as Kirk never allows us to forget, though the decorums which it nourishes take a prudential, secular form. These reverend patrimonies, religious and traditional, reach so far back into our composite past and have so nourished our identity that we are loath even to think of them unless they begin to lose their hold. And they *are* inseparable. Hear Kirk on the English absorption and combination of previous Western culture:

> From that time [of conversion] forward, despite conquest by the Danes and later by the Normans, despite the English Reformation of the sixteenth century and the Civil Wars of the seventeenth century, one may

72

trace the development of English law, English political institutions, and English civilization—a continuity that would spread to America in the seventeenth century and would provide fertile soil in which the American culture could take root. Knowledge of medieval England and Scotland is essential to a decent understanding of American order. During those nine hundred years between the coming of Saint Augustine of Canterbury and the triumph of Renaissance and Reformation at the beginning of the sixteenth century, there developed in Britain the general system of law that we inherit; the essentials of representative government; the very language that we speak and the early greatness of English literature; the social patterns that still affect American society; rudimentary industry and commerce that remain basic to our modern economy; the schools and universities which were emulated in America; the Norman and English Gothic architecture that are part of our material inheritance; and the idea of a gentleman that still may be discerned in the American democracy. This medieval patrimony was so much taken for granted by the men who founded the American Republic that they did not even trouble themselves to praise it so much as they should have done.[1]

A major purpose of this volume is to correct the distortion made possible by the silence of the "founders."

The centerpiece of *The Roots of American Order* may well be Kirk's discussion of Great Britain after the Renaissance and Reformation, from the sixteenth to the eighteenth century. It is a masterful synthesis of social, cultural, and political developments. That we are an extension of this record no one who reads these pages will hereafter be disposed to doubt. Yet this observation can mislead. And all the rest of his narrative of Western beginnings may charm us overmuch. We have had from Kirk's astonishing career proof of a profound interest in the acts and monuments of Europe. In truth, the demonstration of this concern is so considerable that hostile comment on the Wizard of Mecosta has sometimes argued from it that he is only a cultural expatriate, a connoisseur of archaic places, persons, and emotions. But, because of the fashion in which Kirk links this passion to his perspective on the formation of our nation, we can now insist that Russell Kirk was always occupied with the old world *chiefly because of his identification with the new.* He is an instinctive master in the reconstruction of a living social and political condition, the *Gestalt* of seemingly contradictory impulses and imperatives operating in configuration within or behind the thoughts and deeds of men and nations. His sketches of persons mighty in battle, in thought, or in the spiritual realm are illustrative of this gift. Yet in each of these portraits drawn for *The Roots of American Order* the teaching remains clear: they (or their kind) helped directly to make us what we are. Or what, at our best, *we should be.*

Never again will students of Kirk's career doubt that his absolute location in upstate Michigan and his identification with the "wise prejudice" of that ancestral place is consonant with his salutes to the classical, the medieval, the Scots, and (American) Southern regimes. In all of these explorations Kirk writes as a recognizable variety of American. And if that American speaks in the English idiom of an Old Whig or moderate Tory, the inheritance he applies to our situation has all the more authority in its application of the *mores majorum* formed and tested long ago by the intellectually most significant of our progenitors: a habit of mind built into the language it created and sanctioned by fruitful use.

This book is therefore not so much a dissertation on American history as a prolegomenon to the study of discrete components of that record and a context for such restricted inquiries: a Burkean preface to historical research *per se*, and a touchstone for understanding the specious eschatologies and mythologies which structure the narratives of our regnant historians. Since the filter through which the general Western prescription came into our system is a British one, the pivotal sections of Kirk's inquiry concern, *a fortiori*, the effect of that filter on the decisions which drove British America to pursue a destiny of its own. His great point is that the impetus was itself English, and after the Revolution continued to be English — at least until 1860. Kirk on the heritage of the English common law, the rule of *stare decisis*, as that mentality has shaped our common course adds, I believe, some valuable insights to the study of American politics: Kirk on Blackstone and his predecessors, whose authorities were not set aside with the rejection of George III. Hear again his words: "It was to the precedent of the Petition of Right [1628], among other constitutional precedents, that American Patriots would look in the 1760s and 1770s, and many of the grievances listed in the Petition would reappear in the American Declaration of Independence."[2] Kirk keeps us ever mindful that we were not "made" but, rather, thanks to new circumstances and "benign neglect," simply "grew." The institutions of representative government flourished from earliest times in almost every North American colony. Also a plurality of churches, some of them established; and the habit of religious toleration, at least outside of New England. Equally convincing are Kirk's observations on how we adapted the total British precedent without any sense of irreverence toward the model or much awareness that real modification was in process.

A body of transplanted English freeholders with a few town men thrown in, minus a nobility or powerful church establishment, could not, in a new land, have turned out any other way. At least, not after 1688 and the development of a legalist, xenophobic, and unphilosophical rationale for political justification of that most English and conservative of rebellions. The Declaration of Independence is a forensic, rhetorical document, the end of a series of such, designed to enlist recruits here and sympathy in England. It is intellectually an outgrowth of the Glorious Revolution. Understood historically and in its formal character, read as you would read a public poem, it tells us how to approach our departure from the royal protection. And as rhetoric, in what it specifies and what it neglects to mention, the Constitution is equally eloquent: in its ideological spareness, its derivation of authority from pre-existent states (resting on English charters, English history, and what legally had being); and also in its first ten amendments, drawn directly from England's own 1689 Declaration of Rights. The inference is unmistakable. *Separation came from the other side.* Americans remained within the inherited identity, keepers of that most basic and inviolate of compacts, between the living, dead, and yet unborn. From these materials has subsisted (in our author's terms) an "unwritten constitution" of our own. To this union we gave — on purpose, in the English spirit — only partial expression, chiefly in connection with new economic and political realities which were part of the American scene after the thirteen sovereign states achieved their respective autonomies. But a people with a real genealogy have no need of ingenious founders or the abstractions of contract. Kirk conceives of his work in these matters as a labor of restoration and recovery, not as a venture in intellectual innovation. However, as he well knows, to suggest such historically "self-evident" truths concerning 1776 and 1787 is, for this bemused generation, more shocking than mere originality could hope to be. To repeat, emphasis on the English filter is necessary to their demonstration.

In two other respects *The Roots of American Order* will scandalize those educated conventionally. I refer here to Kirk's insistence upon the authority of revealed religion among earlier Americans and his tributes to the ideal of the gentleman. The tenets of the Christian faith are the second prescription in his account of our roots. Right order depends upon the commitment of single persons to its ground, an acknowledgment of some outside authority. Excessive individualism is checked only by such extrinsic force, when it is freely admitted. Moral order within strong men binds the Commonweal to the Godsweal. Both rest finally on a sound ontology, without which no decalogue can operate with force. And gentlemen are the vessels of this sound ontology, those who are ever conscious that the gods alone assign our stations and exact a performance equivalent to their importance. In a nation where almost nothing was codified — where communities were very different, each jealous of its own character while still desiring a definite but restricted link to the rest — no more than a *de facto*, localistic religious/social structure made good sense; that is, if the balance of these conflicting imperatives was to survive.

Thus the customary reading of certain silences in our Constitution is clearly off the mark. Some of this learned distortion Kirk disarms with a few remarks on the merits of genuine "federalism." Other vulgar errors concerning "democracy," "competition," or "liberation" are negated by the aforementioned "characters": Jesus and Paul, Solon and St. Augustine, John Knox and Cicero, Marcus Aurelius and John of Brienne, to mention but a few. I value in particular his paired discussions of John Locke and David Hume. As regards their utility in the explication of an emerging national personality we have heard too much in praise of the former, far too little of the latter. Locke's notion of politics in a presocial vacuum had few advocates in the Philadelphia of 1787. Hume's skeptical prudence was more in evidence in the drafting of our Constitution than any theory of human rights as imperatives operating outside of a specific cultural continuum. For the same reasons, I admire the sketches of Sir Thomas Browne and John Bunyan. Again contrary to what we are told by the secularist authorities, their voices are still heard in this land, bespeaking an invisible communion all the stronger for being interior and beyond the prying eyes of such hostile examiners: audible in the hymnody in which most of us still join to celebrate our deepest loyalties in the time of worship. To reveal and display a bit of this submerged cultural iceberg is Kirk's enterprise. For, as he writes in conclusion, "Gratitude is one form of happiness; and anyone who appreciates the legacy of moral and social order which he has inherited in America will feel gratitude."[3] He ends his text proper with the most extensive of his sketches, an appreciative comment on a neglected predecessor in American thought — and, in many ways an analogue to Kirk himself.

Orestes Brownson, a New Englander by inheritance, after being exposed to all the "armed doctrines" of his day, settled in Michigan, and ended up a Roman Catholic and a traditionalist. Brownson wrote in his *The American Republic* (1865) the prototype of the book here under consideration. The old reformed radical praises "territorial democracy" and bemoans its decline. His is not a hopeful composition, nor were the years of its origination — not to a man like Brownson, or a man like Russell Kirk.

Which brings me to express uneasiness about one quality of *The Roots of American Order*, a quality made inevitable by the rhetorical objectives of the work but nonetheless deserving of mention in a full assessment. As I observed above, Kirk more or less concludes his account with the War Between the States. This emphasis is a tacit admission that the objections I have in mind are very much in order. For it is necessary to recognize that almost coeval with our oldest roots are components of the national temper which have perpetually threatened to poison the healthy springs on which they feed. The locus of these obnoxious elements is the New England of the worldly but still "holy" covenant, of antinomian, chiliastic politics; and their principal distributor into the American intellectual bloodstream is our chief of men, the Illinois Cromwell, Abraham Lincoln. The City upon a Hill, once renamed "Union" and refounded by "fire and sword," is not really the Republic of Kirk's reverence. And to join the two is to nourish both. True enough, our native gnosticism is a "sometimes thing," even in its principal champions. For instance, the regimenting Federalists deserve credit for arresting the spread of French "isms" and for preserving the common law. And Lincoln often contradicts the heresies boldly trumpeted in the House-Divided, Gettysburg, and Second Inaugural Addresses. In one situation the Great Emancipator may arrogate to himself, by argument *and* language, an especial intimacy with the Divine Will. He is prepared, when seized by the afflatus, to declare that the multi-faceted union ordained by the Fathers has brought upon their sons (and especially upon moderate men in the North, long comfortable in this "divided house") a judgment from on High. On another occasion he will offer to the "sore thumb" of our internal variety, the long accepted fact of black slavery, a constitutional guarantee more rigid than what was needful to secure a confederation in the first place. Sorting out this network of conflicting opinions is a thankless task, a labor requiring the skill and the example of a Russell Kirk. Yet, for reasons he has taught us, it must be done. And with the instruments he (among others) has put into our hands. It is enough to say that if Kirk's Federalists and his Lincoln were as plausible as the ambiguous villains of my own syncretic typology, we could endure them well enough. Then might we occupy ourselves more with cultivating than with protecting the old stock tree that we both love well.

But for the moment we must take advantage of the impetus given to us by *The Roots of American Order* and perform some of the labors which it (like earlier Kirk studies) challenges us to undertake. The futurists who construe the past according to the measure of a tomorrow they can only imagine—a dream, usually bad, which hopefully will never come true—must be confronted in connection with the discrete segments of the American record. And with reference to the history of American *disorder*, of which Kirk speaks only by comparison. Spurred by his achievement, let us have narratives, mixed with generous portions of biography and analogue, and a quiet emphasis on commitments shaping the actions of those involved long before they have found theoretical expression. Let us demonstrate how the bonds of faith, friendship, family, and common experience have ordinarily obtained in our national affairs, whatever abstract explanations are imposed upon them after the fact. However, as we follow this example, let us pay tribute to its source, recall who has been and continues to be such an anchor of our political sanity and for so long the special keeper of this prescription for Americans who call themselves conservative. Where the study of these roots is concerned, we all begin with Russell Kirk.

NOTES

1. Russell Kirk, *The Roots of American Order* (La Salle, IL, Open Court Publishing Co., 1974), p. 178.
2. *Ibid.*, p. 261.
3. *Ibid.*, p. 475.

Natural Law or Nihilism?

by M. D. Aeschliman

"The Scripture tells us," writes Swift in a brilliant passage, "that 'Oppression maketh a wise man mad.' Therefore, consequently speaking, if some men are not mad, it is because they are not wise." Stung by the continuing, oppressive folly and evil of our nightmarish century, Russell Kirk has nevertheless not been maddened by it. Though he knows how hard the tempest of our time really rages, he has not fled or been driven to the heath like Lear or Lear's fool. Instead, he cultivates a "cell of good living," for himself and others, amidst the chaotic follies, vices, perversions of value, and subversions of norm that prevail in much of the high and middle culture—and in most of the low culture—in our time. His insight, piety, and equanimity—his wisdom, Godliness, and virtue—are especially apparent in *The Wise Men Know What Wicked Things Are Written on the Sky* (1987), a volume of lectures which takes its title fittingly from the greatest long poem of our century, G. K. Chesterton's *Ballad of the White Horse* (1911).

Dr. Kirk is a figure in that noblest of all our heritages, Christian humanism. To go no further back, one should start listing his models and forebears with Shakespeare's Ulysses, with Richard Hooker, and then mention John Milton, the great Augustans Swift, Pope, and Johnson, Edmund Burke, the great ethical Victorians Arnold and Newman, and more recently Chesterton, Irving Babbitt, P. E. More, C. S. Lewis, and T. S. Eliot. It is altogether fitting that Eliot and Kirk should have been good friends, and that Russell Kirk should be the author of the single finest study of Eliot that we possess, *Eliot and His Age: T. S. Eliot's Moral Imagination in the Twentieth Century* (1971), which is now available in a handsome paperback edition from Sherwood Sugden & Co. It is also altogether fitting and right that Russell Kirk should be the editor of *The Portable Conservative Reader* (1982) and that a new edition of his *Edmund Burke: A Genius Reconsidered*, originally published in 1967, again should be made available in the momentous bicentennial year of the grisly French Revolution, the ghastly commencement of modernity.

Dr. Kirk's profound equanimity comes, I think, from the rare feat of having drunk so deeply at this well of humane and Godly wisdom that he can thoroughly understand the nihilistic revolution of our time but not be tainted, contaminated, or possessed by it. It is outside and around but not *inside* him. The nihilistic revolution (whose guiding lights—avowed or unavowed—are Sade and Nietzsche) provides, as Flannery O'Connor said, the very air or gas we breathe, culturally and socially. But this gas is neither breathed nor marketed on Kirk's street in Mecosta or in his books. Within our country this revolution is not mainly Marxist (which menaced here to a larger degree 50 years ago, when Kirk was coming to maturity), but liberal-libertarian-libertine. Its corrosive consensus has managed to propagate widely and deeply the view that there is nothing authoritative or obligatory that is "anterior, exterior, or superior" to the individual self. The self is deified. In the lapidary formulation that the late Sergei Levitzky used to paraphrase Dostoevsky, "The relativization of the Absolute leads to the absolutization of the relative." Yet at the same time—"insane conjunction," as Kirk says—"collectivistic prejudices and libertarian prejudices frequently coexist within the same person." (As if one could say, "There is no basis to ethics, but there are many things you *ought* to do.")

The fact that the liberal-libertarian-libertine revolution is morally nihilistic, that it is lethal to ethics and thus to *any* sane *res publica*, does not seem to worry too many of our artists, comfortably tenured humanists and scientists, newspaper and magazine editors, or other ornaments of the intelligentsia. The logical outcome of this nihilistic revolution—the *real* revolution of modern times—is a world of criminals, devils, and lunatics, on the one hand, and the decent remnants of the race, deprived of moral common sense and thus rendered powerless against weaknesses, follies, and transgressions, on the other. In light of this, Dr. Kirk has never enlisted in the army of the "knowledge class," made up of glibly feckless and endlessly talkative intellectuals devoted to their esoteric specialisms or urgently fashionable crusades. He is no degenerate son or "man of the hour."

He is, instead, a man for all seasons, one who has come to understand, internalize, live by, and eloquently transmit what C. S. Lewis called "the ancient orthodox tradition of European ethics." This is to say that he is a Natural-Law thinker, one in whom the leaven of Aristotle and Cicero has been married to the Judaeo-Christian revelation. (Its Eastern form, as Joseph Needham, John Wu, and Lewis have pointed out, is called "the Tao." Kirk's chief lesson is an old one, but one that is "yet ever new" to each individual and each generation if they would be sane and decent; it is "the pearl of great price": "In the Christian teaching," he writes, "freedom is the submission to the will of God."

> This is no paradox. As he who would save his life must lose it, so the person who desires true freedom must recognize an order that gives all freedoms their sanction.[1]

He knows from a long and varied life and from wide and deep reading of history that "much of the time, in ages past as today, men have used their moral freedom to choose slavery or anarchy instead of ordered liberty".[2] Dr. Kirk has thought long and hard about liberty, its real and its counterfeit, its healthy and its toxic forms. In the tradition of Matthew Arnold and T. S. Eliot, he sees the superiority of Cicero to John Stuart Mill (and of course to Sade and Nietzsche, even greater heresiarchs):

> Mill was unaware of any difficulty in closely defining "liberty" — unlike Cicero, who saw the necessity for distinguishing between *libido* and *voluntas*. To Mill, "liberty" might mean "doing as one likes" or "pursuing one's own good in one's own way" or acting "according to one's own inclination and judgment."[3]

Of "right reason" — that most precious of all intellectual commodities — there was little in Bentham or Mill, and none at all in Sade or Nietzsche. The liberal-libertarian-libertine revolution is a "liberation" from wisdom and virtue, from Natural Law or Tao and from its author, God. This romantic-Faustian-Promethean-existentialist "liberation" is radical voluntarism, the assertion of freedom not *within* the moral universe (as in Cicero and all Godly humanism), but of freedom *from* the moral universe. "I have killed everything in my heart," says one of Sade's characters, "that would have gotten in the way of my pleasures." Man's ultimate metaphysical destiny, Nietzsche wrote, is "beyond good and evil"; life is "an aesthetic phenomenon."

This is the creed of all aesthetes, but also of all tyrants and gangsters — whether Caligula, Heliogabalus, or Nero; whether Mussolini or Hitler — or the rapacious libertarian wastrels of our own time. "Viva la libertà!" sings Don Giovanni, but he is a libertine, a cynical seducer, not a free man in the moral sense.

Yet "right reason" tells us, in the words of an old adage, that "be you ever so high, the law is above you." Of course the decent naturalist — the Hume, the Mill, the T. H. Huxley — never goes as far as Sade; no, if he lives decently he lives like a parasite off the momentum and residue of beliefs that he neither avows nor nourishes. What conceivable reason, Alfred North Whitehead asked, could men like Hume, Mill, or Huxley have given for *any* moral views they held, "apart from their own psychological inheritance from the Platonic religious tradition"? They were "decent Godless people," their ethics a guttering flame, a dying fire.

Dr. Kirk has seen this and much else, and he knows that it is not being seen or said for the first time. He knows that this truth was seen by the men and women of the New Testament, by Cicero, by St. Thomas Aquinas and Shakespeare, by Milton and Burke, and by Dostoevsky and Solzhenitsyn (who in *The Gulag Archipelago* quotes Goethe's *Faust* to mock the liberal fantasy of collective progress and the liberation from ethics that it encourages: "the whole world changes and everything moves forward;/And why should I be afraid to break my word?"

These are the central matters and regulative truths of a real civilization, of a sane *res publica* and decent Godly order. Without them it cannot exist *as a civilization*, no matter how many laboratories, nuclear reactors, computers, automobiles, condoms, abortion clinics, television sets, and satellites it has. "The less civilized a society," Kirk wrote in a previous book, "the more generally will and appetite prevail unchecked," The nihilistic revolution worships and exalts change, speed, power, force, will, and appetite, "rejoicing," as Kirk puts it, "in a devil's sabbath of whirling machinery." In a striking, ominous, resonant piece of rhetoric and insight he writes of our age, "when the flood-waters of the world are out . . . it will not suffice to be borne along by the current, singing hallelujah to the river god."

The distinction between true and false freedom, like the distinction between authority and power, is indispensable to a civilization, as opposed to a tyranny (such as prevails in various forms across most of the globe today) or to a mere squalid aggregation of competitive selves (such as seems to prevail in our own land). The fluorescent and seductive temptation of "liberation" is a hereditary and perennial enemy of real, proximate liberty, ordered liberty, liberty both conditioned and conditional but ultimately real and of infinite value. Russell Kirk repeats this lesson in season and out, and doing so puts himself in the noblest of company. Milton's Abdiel challenged the glozing liberal-libertarian-libertine rhetoric of all the ages when he defied a haughty apostate indulging his "style of radical will." Ordered liberty within the moral universe is not servitude, the faithful angel tells Satan:

> This is servitude,
> To serve th'unwise, or him who hath rebell'd
> Against his worthier, as thine now serve thee,
> Thy self not free, but to thy self enthrall'd. . . .
>
> (*Paradise Lost*, VI: 178–181)

"Radical" freedom is the freedom of the savage, the fool, the lunatic, the criminal, or the devil, "beyond good and evil" and "beyond" decency, humanity, and sanity too.

I have chosen to concentrate so far mainly on one point, a crucial one, in Dr. Kirk's thinking, partly in order to show his luminous and obstinate orthodoxy: he sings no "hallelujah to the river god." In each of his essays the act and the art of prudence are evident, as befits so careful and faithful a reader of Burke. The proper relation between principle and practice can only be regulated in our sublunary world by the cultivation and application of prudence, of a deep, intimate, and extensive knowledge of the relations and tensions between ends and means, as between souls, minds, and bodies. Utopianism and cynicism are extremes to avoid, not in the interest of the human muddle but of the humane middle. "Reason rightly used" safely guides our steps, as rationalism, empiricism, and subjectivism never can and never have.

Dr. Kirk frequently uses the phrase "humane letters" to remind us of the nature, nobility, and tasks of true humanistic culture. He is at once a moralist, a historian, a social or "public" philosopher, and a man of letters, a confluence and conjunction of talents that reminds us of the high Victorians, especially of Arnold and Newman. As social philosopher he follows in the line of Eliot, a line developed nobly in our time in a large body of more technical social science created by kindred spirits such as Daniel Bell, Peter Berger, David Martin, and

Robert Nisbet. As a moralist, religious thinker, and writer he also reminds one of Eliot, Lewis, and Malcolm Muggeridge, with their profound but pugnacious orthodoxy and satire that aims to lash the vices and mitigate the follies of the age. But as an historian, religious thinker, and writer Kirk has something of the statesman in him too, in this regard perhaps making one think of Reinhold Niebuhr, who also came, late in life, to acknowledge the greatness and relevance of Burke.

This legacy and ballast are very important, for the responsibility of the intellectual and the writer in our time is very great. The momentum of the past, the cake of custom, the nurture of sane tradition, have all been broken or severely reduced in effect and authority: the automobile and the television are, as Kirk somewhere says, "mechanical Jacobins." An undissociated sensibility, Russell Kirk eschews the tempting excesses always so palpably present to the intellectual: histrionic subjectivism and self-indulgence (e.g., Susan Sontag's "styles of radical will" and the toxic literature of Ginsberg, Mailer, Miller, and company); moralistic, collectivistic liberalism (ethically relativistic and individualistic in personal affairs, morally absolutist, simplistic, and collectivistic in public affairs); feckless, esoteric intellectual specialism (largely caused by what Jacques Barzun called "the Ph.D. octopus"). Quite rightly did Forrest McDonald (quoting M. E. Bradford) call Kirk "the American Cicero,"[4] as his interests are in the lasting rather than the ephemeral; the normative rather than the unique, idiosyncratic or exotic; the true rather than the new.

This balanced, eloquent, humane learning is everywhere evident in *The Wise Men Know What Wicked Things Are Written on the Sky*, essays originally given as lectures at the Heritage Foundation in Washington. Each one brings water from the well of the ages, but brings it to that part of the garden that needs it most, in the amount the terrain requires. Vast learning is lightly worn and judiciously applied; and chaste hope is given. "America's Augustan Age?" is full of the virtue and *Romanitas* that it commends, succumbing neither to boosterism nor pessimism. "The American Mission" chastens arrogance, expansionism, and cynicism all at once by drawing on the unjustly neglected insights of Orestes Brownson (1805–1876) to remind us of the grandeur and the limits of "ordered liberty." "The Illusion of 'Human Rights' " criticizes the disastrous simplicities of Wilsonian liberalism in the light and in the interest of true Natural Law, described by Sir Ernest Barker as the "justice . . . conceived as being the higher or ultimate law, proceeding from the nature of the universe — from the Being of God and the reason of man."5 "Prospects for the American Family" commends and defends the family against its witting or unwitting enemies and against the extremes of anarchic, atomistic individualism ("the freedom of the wolf") and compulsory collectivism (where "children become wards of the state"). A brilliant documentary essay in, of all places, the *Washington Post* (25 September 1988), "Is Day Care Ruining Our Kids?" makes Dr. Kirk's essay look even more apposite.

And so it goes in each of the remaining essays, where insights of great accuracy and power are found on every page, often with clear implications for personal practice or public policy. "Prospects for American Education" returns to the civic subject for which Dr. Kirk is perhaps best known — the possible improvement of our public-education system, whose quality is deplored from all sides. His insistence on pointing to the importance of and using the *word* "norms," as opposed to "values" (inherently or inevitably a relativizing word, thus fatal to clear argument and sane consensus), is characteristic and salutary. How much more light would be available if educators came to recognize and use ideas of the "normative" and the "normal" as representing "right reason" and "ordinate response"! ("Nothing," C. S. Lewis wrote, "is abnormal until we have grasped the norm.") This is a battle that Dr. Kirk has fought not only in the contents but in the very titles of his books, one of them being *Enemies of the Permanent Things: Observations of Abnormity in Literature and Politics* (second ed., 1984). "Can Virtue Be Taught?" and "The Conservative Purpose of a Liberal Education" are essays in the great tradition of Christian humanism, refining, applying, and extending its truths and tenets, articulating its aims and hopes, such as the desirability and possibility of a "remnant": a "number of people in many walks of life who would possess some share of right reason and moral imagination; who would not shout the price of everything, but would know the value of something; who would be schooled in wisdom and virtue."6 Here, as so often, one hears the voice of Burke, unique in its very generality, championing the Natural Law. "But what is liberty," Burke wrote prophetically two hundred years ago, "without wisdom and without virtue? It is the greatest of all possible evils."

These are Dr. Kirk's characteristic concerns and insights, their value and truth being, in St. Augustine's words, "ever ancient, yet ever new." Their appropriateness to our present circumstances is shown, and thus we have in hand no work of mere inkhorn abstraction or esoteric speculation, but one of active and particular prudence. Nor is it the prudence of "Mr. Worldly-Wiseman," but of citizens, sages, saints, and statesman, of men and women who have seen and said, with Dr. Kirk, that true "freedom cannot endure unless we are willing to nurture that religious understanding which is its sanction."[7] The "body of transcendent norms" which Dr. Kirk articulates and transmits "gives purpose to existence and motive to conduct."[8] In a crazy age whose processes and products, from high culture to low commerce, oscillate from the toxic to the trivial and are redolent of "the bondage of purposeless freedom," Dr. Kirk's writings serve and bear witness to sanity and humanity, with grace, eloquence, and precision.

NOTES

1. Russell Kirk, *The Wise Men Know What Wicked Things Are Written on the Sky* (Washington, D.C.: Regnery Gateway, 1987), p. 108.
2. *Ibid.*, p. 102.
3. *Ibid.*, p. 106.
4. Bradford, quoted in Forrest McDonald, "Russell Kirk: The American Cicero," *National Review*, 31 December 1985, p. 92.
5. Barker, quoted in Kirk, p. 36.
6. Kirk, *op. cit.*, p. 83.
7. *Ibid.*, p. 103.
8. *Ibid.*, p. 104.

*　　*　　*

"I am rereading The Conservative Mind, *which, like all really good books, gives something more at each reading."*

— *Whittaker Chambers, in a letter to Russell Kirk dated January 19, 1954.*

The Terrors of the Soul

by Andrew Lytle

The subject of most ghost stories is profane. The supernatural is usually spurious. At its best it is magic, the effort to force nature to act beyond its properties. The illusion so evoked is often sentimental. It depends upon the victim's acceptance of fantasy instead of the profound meaning of symbol, such as a fragment of the concupiscent sheet inserted beneath the bark of a tree to force the lover's return. This reduces the erotic to lust. The profane ghost belongs to this category. The shock of meaning does not finally convince. The mystery with which the tale begins remains unacceptable at the end. Not so Mr. Kirk's ghost stories.

Their terror is often the concrete showing of damnation. They restore in a secular time the very terror of that threat. The effect goes beyond punishment for the violation of moral laws. This is to say that the action renders up the insoluble mystery, particularly in the title story, behind moral law. The souls in *Watchers at the Strait Gate* have left behind even the deadly sins, but the border they cross is no interregnum before judgment. The abyss through which the petitioners must pass threatens even the spirit. There the sinister watchers at the gate can smell the intangible filament of flesh not yet dissipated. In this Mr. Kirk goes beyond any known theology with such a threat.

The theology of the stories is Christian, belief in which has been supplanted by Progress with its heresy of the perfectibility of man. This presumed Progress frees sinners and particularly criminals — they think — from the restraint of the Four Last Things. There are occasions where physical strength is invincible, in prison for example. Its exercise is brutal, unrestrained, and unpunished. In "Lex Talionis" it takes the ghost of one of the criminal's victims, who had challenged his power and lost, to bring the criminal to judgment.

Mr. Kirk's ghosts often appear as retributive agents. Evil in these tales is more than absence of good. The priest in "The Invasion of the Church of the Holy Ghost" accepts the presence of Satan as actual. His machinations become, then, an objective force. Like the dragon that lies beside the road, Satan and his minions remain a continuous threat. But it is nothing, no thing, unless the unwary, tempted, accept it for the truth. The intended victim is almost always seized through the sensibility. This precipitates the drama of the soul — salvation or damnation.

The effort to possess the soul of another is the action of the first three stories: "The Invasion of the Church of the Holy Ghost," "The Surly Sullen Bell," "The Peculiar Demesne of Archvicar Gerontion." What wonderful titles! The physical decay of part of a city is the terrain for the action. There are no citizens. A few desolate souls lurk in and about the abandoned buildings — winos, the sinister, most of the detritus of society. At night they seem to flicker, or they are dark presences, ghastly as shades. The derelict buildings themselves are ghosts of structures in which life once thrived. As in "Lex Talionis" there is something uncanny about a restaurant operating deep into the night. Everywhere there is silence, even when there is speech. The dark outside presses against, as it isolates, the restaurant. Within, the patrons give the sense of unseeing witnesses. A ghost is not distinguishable from human kind, if human they are. The criminal and the spirit who is to bring the malefactor to his doom sit at table, but the reader does not recognize one as a shade any more than does the criminal. Yet the author has given us a clue. The avenging agent does not allow himself to be touched. To reveal, at this stage of the story, what he is would be to warn the murderer and so lose the story.

These abandoned segments of cities are more than spooky atmosphere. They are the symbols of the dire results of what happens when the Puritan mind tries to set down the Heavenly City upon earth: that is, to replace God by man. In the "Archvicar's Demesne," it is a ruined and sacked city of desolation where the hero, Manfred, finds hmself trapped by necromancy, there to dwell forever alone. As such it is the archetypal place which the slums of the other cities vaguely reflect. The corpse candle as will-o-the-wisp, a flame the height of a man, has one cry, "I must have your body!" The Archvicar fails, as Manfred clutches the ikon of Christ over the ruined altar and falls back into life, at which moment the *ignis fatuus* flares and dies.

This is almost allegory, but there is too much of life's concrete detail for such an abstraction. The struggle, perhaps, could be the basic allegory underlying all great actions, in literature and out. The soul occupies perilously the body. It is by the flesh that it is saved or lost. This is made clear in "The Surly Sullen Bell."

I like this story almost best of all. The action takes place by and in the edge of the Old Town of St. Louis, which represents the early French and American past. Its neglect and decay is the judgment upon the inheritors. Nothing is sound but the cathedral. The dwellings are awaiting the bulldozer and that flinging ball, to put up a memorial park, which will benefit no living people but the politicians and the progressive town, in which the air stinks from the breweries and from other fermentations.

The action proper concerns the old complications: the woman, the husband, the rejected lover—Nancy, Godfrey Schumacher the husband, and Frank Loring. They meet after ten years at the Schumachers', a Victorian house a few blocks from the decayed and doomed Old Town. We learn that Loring lost the girl because he would not fight for her. The vigorous, the lover of power, the fraternity president, fought and got her. But something is wrong. His power fails him with Nancy. She has a disease the doctors cannot diagnose. She is so frail that to the rejected lover she seems the flower maiden he loved and courted and lost. This is appearance. The reality is disease and approaching death. Both men have betrayed her, in different ways.

The husband's love of power failed him in worldly matters. He taught languages, but failed even to become a dean. Every office needs the power to execute it, but Godfrey's appetite was insatiable. His need to possess served no specific knowledge. An ego without commitment is forever hungry, as it must turn cannibal. Easily a malign force entered and possessed him. Godfrey, failing elsewhere, vampire-like fixed upon his wife's spirit. But this he could not break. The evil images he fed her became no more than bad dreams which she abhorred. Gradually he fed her poison in black coffee to weaken her resistance. But he failed in this too. Not her will or spirit but her life-force gave way at the end. Six months before, the rejected lover, Loring, was brought in. Godfrey sensed that he represented in his wife that part of her which resisted him. He would poison both and so triumph. The end did not gratify his expectations.

89

Loring foundered in the Old Town, with Godfrey's face at an empty window staring down at his victim. The face finally disappeared before Loring's will to resist and live. To such a test was Loring brought, that of life or death, for refusing to enter the stresses of life. He crawls to a police station to say he has been poisoned. When the police arrive at the Schumacher house, Godfrey retires and shoots himself. Nancy is already dead. Loring has failed her twice: in fighting for her; in February, not understanding what she was trying to tell him. He could have saved her then and saved himself. The reader wants to say, "Can't you see he is poisoning you both?"

Loring's obsession with innocence, then, the opposite of the husband's abuse of power, was as obstructive to life. Loring was given a third and last chance, with his life to pay if he failed. And this was because he was capable of love. He did pay for his delay which led to Nancy's death. Her small son, her very image, he was asked to take and rear. The rival's son would always be there to remind him of what he had lost and had caused his beloved to lose — the fullness of life. That would be his punishment, for he never can forget what his sin of omission has done.

Forever deprived, he is a warning that the looking back, the refusal to accept what growth demands, is a pillar of salt. Appetite is governed by the will and the sensibility. Its explicit temptation is to be as the gods, knowing both good and evil: that is, the temptation is power beyond man's capacity to control it. And Godfrey was not a god. He was equal to only one part of knowledge. His will, being human, was unequal to his appetite. The implicit refusal of mastering appetite, not engaging it, Loring was guilty of. You cannot fall from innocence. You quicken into what we know as Life, the Wilderness of Time which offers all the opposites we encounter as we grow. As the story demonstrates, what with will and appetite, to hunger after what is lost, after the state of innocence, becomes as destructive as the selfish exercise of power. That leads to death. Innocence become substantial is death-in-life as well.

Not all the stories have such grim or profound subjects. There are humor, venial sins, the smaller ironies; but always somehow the malefactors of whatever degree of turpitude find themselves judged and punished in the light of virtue. There is not a story which does not carry the reader along to the end, for the skills are the skills of a good craftsman who understands his subject and its perils.

II.

REDEEMING THE TIME:
ESSAYS BY DIVERS HANDS

"The state of Michigan is fortunate to count Russell Kirk among its citizens. And I am fortunate to count Russell Kirk among my friends. I met Russell and Annette early in my career as a state legislator. As Piety Hill was in my district, I called on them over the years for advice, insight, and good conversation.

"What a wonderful anachronism, Piety Hill. What a welcome refuge for the Remnant who have pledged fealty to time-tested ideas. Russell has encouraged civil discourse in an uncivil age. He has defended traditional values in a culture that restlessly seeks the shock of the new. Through numerous writings and lectures, conversations, and seminars, he has taught Americans about America—about its deeply conservative habits, about the roots of its constitutional order, about the Burkean influence on our Founders.

"Anyone who has made the pilgrimage to Piety Hill understands the quiet strength of this man of ideas. But there is another side of Russell that I have witnessed, and that is his strength as a man of action. When called upon, both Russell and Annette are willing not just to write about, but to take part in, the sometimes messy business of politics. As Senate Majority Leader and as Governor of Michigan, I have witnessed and appreciated their mediating role in the state's Republican Party. They played an especially crucial role in the 1988 primaries, when Jack Kemp, Pat Robertson, and George Bush were struggling for control of the soul of the state GOP. Their commitment to the 'politics of prudence' has leavened political discourse in Michigan, and I shall always be grateful for their contribution.

"Nor do their activities stop with politics. (They understand the limits of politics and government in the American Republic.) Deeply religious and committed to serving their fellow man, Russell and Annette have given generously of their time and abilities to improve the lives of those less fortunate. They have provided a home to the homeless, to political refugees, and to outcasts who had nowhere else to turn.

"Michigan is blessed to be home to Russell and Annette Kirk. America is blessed by their contribution, in letter and in deed, to our way of life. On behalf of the people of our state, I salute the Kirks with gratitude and appreciation."

— The Hon. John Engler,
Governor of Michigan,
1992

Poetry and Prophecy

by Cleanth Brooks

Studies in the humanities — history, philosophy, literature, the languages, and other arts — have a peculiar value for any culture but especially for a culture like our own. Indeed, they have it precisely because of the triumphs of science. A little reflection will show why this has to be true. What do the sciences like physics and chemistry deal with? They deal finally with cause and effect, with process, with the means through which physical things happen and by which society lives and gets its work done.

Yet a society that knows only means and is vague or confused as to the ends for which the means are to be used is indeed a confused society. For though it might have the most superior science at its disposal, it could use it to accomplish the most foolish enterprises or wicked purposes. Witness Adolph Hitler. His use of German scientific resources is a prime example.

The layman, impressed as he has to be with what science has accomplished, wonders why, if we can put a man on the moon, we can't abolish poverty, or why we cannot find out what makes human beings behave as they do. But the problems involved are not of the same order. Science has achieved its accuracy and its objectivity by eliminating the subjective factor, what used to be called the "human equation." But when questions of why? for what purpose? to what end? arise, the variable human element cannot be eliminated.

I am not conscious of saying anything new here. The greatest scientists have said this again and again. Nor am I speaking in disparagement of science. The true scientist knows what his job is and in our time has been doing it magnificently. But he also knows and respects the limitations of his specialized knowledge.

Yet in a world in which applied science is so powerful, it is perfectly natural that many of us are confused on these issues or, fascinated by our increasing ability to control nature, give no thought as to what the ultimate values are or dismiss the problem as unimportant with the cheerful assumption that the proper goals will take care of themselves — we just don't need to think about them. Some may respond to this line of reasoning with a question of their own: "Well, from what source should we get our values? You don't really believe that a study of literature, say, will provide objective values for mankind, do you?" To which I should answer, "I certainly do not."

I know of no source that can reply to our questions with the objectivity of science; not established tradition, nor history, nor philosophy. And even religion ultimately bases itself on faith: "Faith is the substance of things hoped for, the evidence of things not seen."

My contention, however, is this: Since it is idle to hope for truly scientific answers when we face the question of ultimate choices, we would be foolish not to see what the humanities may be able to tell us. Even literature, the least objective of all the humane disciplines, may have something to tell us about our inner selves and about how human beings behave with relation to each other.

How does literature do this? Principally in two ways. First, by articulating with sensitivity and discrimination the states of mind that we find difficulty in expressing and, by fitting them to proper language, helping us to experience them in all their subtle shadings so that we can make them a part of ourselves. In short, the articulate members of the culture may help us to become more articulate ourselves with the consequence that the blurred and confused world of the emotions becomes clear and well defined.

Second, by entering, vicariously at least, into all kinds of human situations, we can as readers widen our knowledge of other human beings, and again, of ourselves. Though our personal lives limit the number of crucial or even significant experiences we may experience directly, literature displays for us an almost infinite number of experiences in which the protagonist makes choices and faces the consequences of those choices. Thus, if literature cannot of itself dictate our choices for us, it can broaden and deepen the full meaning of many choices.

A technological society most of all needs such sustenance, for as I have indicated its members tend to be very knowledgeable about means but often poorly educated as to ends. The member of a technological society should not have to make his life choices basically on gut feelings. I would prefer to team his intelligent brain up with — not his alimentary canal — but his heart. That is where we used to look for the deepest truth.

We need, however, some concrete instances of what the humanities — which I insist appeal to the whole man — his heart as well as his brain — can do. Consider the following little poem by Wordsworth:

A slumber did my spirit seal;
  I had no human fears:
She seemed a thing that could not feel
  The touch of earthly years.

No motion has she now, no force;
  She neither hears nor sees;
Rolled round in earth's diurnal course,
  With rocks, and stones, and trees.

These eight short lines are packed with enormous force, and how complicated rhetorically is this little poem. That fact is worth pondering. The lover who has lost his loved one confesses that he was caught up in a strange sleep, a slumber that sealed his "spirit" so thoroughly against any human fears — that is, fears that the girl might not be immortal — that he couldn't believe that she could die. Now, however, her unlooked-for slumber in the arms of death has waked him out of his own strange slumber. Whereas he had thought that she was so ethereal that earthly things could not touch her — that she was impervious to the motions of time and force — now she has no force of her own and, no longer instinct with life, is as inert as any rock or stone. Her only motion is not willed by her spirit but imposed upon her body by the very whirl of the earth. She is now caught up in the turning of the earth that measures out earthly days and years.

I have said that the poem is complicated rhetorically, but far from hampering it and making it clumsy, the complication adds to its force. The poem communicates the shock in which the lover, so bemused that he once thought his loved one was not made of dust, like all the rest of us, knows that she is now simply part of the dusty earth.

There are other ways, however, to think of the body of a loved one that the earth has closed over. Here is a poem by A. E. Housman. It is short enough to be quoted in full.

The night is freezing fast,
  To-morrow comes December;
    And winterfalls of old
Are with me from the past;
  And chiefly I remember
    How Dick would hate the cold.

Fall, winter, fall; for he,
  Prompt hand and headpiece clever,
    Has woven a winter robe,
And made of earth and sea
  His overcoat for ever,
    And wears the turning globe.

Here the mourned-for person is not a young woman but a man. However, as in the Wordsworth poem, mourning itself is not put forward directly; it is only implied. Yet, how different is the tone of this poem.

Notice how circumstantial the poem is. We can date it exactly: the poem begins on November 30. The speaker writes as if winter began on December 1. That was what I was taught in my youth. In the later decades, we have become much more exact. We now regard the first day of winter as the day of the winter solstice, and that occurs on December 21 or December 22. Yet this point is unimportant. What is important is that it is the onset of winter that brings Dick to his living friend's mind. His memory of Dick's hatred of the cold initiates the poem. Dick's dislike of the cold may not be a very important element in his character, but it is the kind of thing that sticks in a person's memory and so provides a plausible reason for his friend's almost playful praise of Dick

The poem, thus, begins realistically and even casually. The stress is on Dick's admirable capacity to deal with any kind of situation. It is implied that Dick even know how to handle the problem of the grave itself. There is no hint of the lugubriousness of "Bury me not on the lone prairie" or "Massa's in the cold, cold ground."

Even in death, Dick, with his "prompt hand" and his clever "headpiece," dominates the situation. He has made of the earth a comfortable garment to keep him snugly warm. The poem has reversed the situation of Wordsworth's young woman. Instead of being helplessly whirled about in earth's daily course, Dick triumphantly *wears* the "turning globe."

Is the idea absurd? Of course it is, but no one knows this better than Dick's friend who speaks the poem; one of the ways in which we face up to death is to be able to joke about it. In this instance joking is particularly appropriate, for such a ploy is one that praises the dead friend in an affectionate manner that the dead friend would himself have appreciated. There are many ways to pay tribute to the dead and thereby express one's sense of loss.

Which of these two poems is the better? The question is absurd. Each is excellently fitted to its occasion. We would not give up either, and they are so different in tone that competition is out of the question.

It is interesting and broadening to our imaginations to note how many attitudes and states of mind can be elicited from what seems at first glance the same scene or the same object or topic or state of circumstances. Take, for example, the theme of nature. Let us begin with a section from William Wordsworth's famous poem on Tintern Abbey. The passage I shall quote tells us what nature came to mean to Wordsworth.

> . . . and this prayer I make,
> Knowing that Nature never did betray
> The heart that loved her; 'tis her privilege,
> Through all the years of this our life, to lead
> From joy to joy; for she can so inform
> The mind that is within us, so impress
> With quietness and beauty, and so feed
> With lofty thoughts, that neither evil tongues,
> Rash judgments, nor the sneers of selfish men,
> Nor greetings where no kindness is, nor all
> The dreary intercourse of daily life,
> Shall e'er prevail against us, or disturb
> Our cheerful faith, that all which we behold
> Is full of blessings.

This is one of Wordsworth's most eloquent statements of his faith in the power of nature to quiet, console, stimulate and exalt the spirit of man. When we are betrayed by other men or sneered at by them, or cuffed about, or simply have our lives dulled by the everyday intercourse with them, nature is always there to revive us, to bring us back to pure and lofty thoughts. I am, of course, being unjust to this great passage in detaching it from the rest of the poem, the imagery of which does so much to load, charge, and qualify the passage when we come to it. At the moment, I'm concerned primarily with the attitude that Wordsworth takes towards nature as compared with, let's say, the attitude that Keats takes in his famous ode to autumn. Keats seems primarily interested in building up in our minds the quality and atmosphere of the "season of mists and mellow fruitfulness." The poem is loaded with sensuous detail, just as the season of autumn is loaded with a sense of the ripened harvest. For example,

> With fruit the vines that round the thatch-eves run;
> To bend with apples the moss'd cottage-trees,
>   And fill all fruit with ripeness to the core;
>   To swell the gourd, and plump the hazel shells
>   With a sweet kernel; to set budding more,
> And still more, later flowers for the bees,
> Until they think warm days will never cease,
>   For Summer has o'er-brimm'd their clammy cells.

Obviously, autumn meant a great deal to Keats, but he does not spell out for us any particular solace of the spirit that the autumn gives. He is content simply to evoke it in all of its fullness and drowsy majesty. In this he is so successful that he manages, imperceptibly, to turn the abstract season into a goddess

>   . . . sitting careless on a granary floor,
> Thy hair soft-lifted by the winnowing wind. . . .

Comparisons are indeed invidious. I am not trying to make one poem better than the other, but simply to compare and contrast the two attitudes to show the vast variety of attitudes possible. Suppose we take up one further contrast, this time with a poem by Housman, a poem I think we shall have to quote in full if we are to see the total attitude and how it is developed.

> Tell me not here, it needs not saying,
>   What tune the enchantress plays
> In aftermaths of soft September
>   Or under blanching mays,
> For she and I were long acquainted
>   And I knew all her ways.
>
> On russett floors, by waters idle,
>   The pine lets fall its cone;
> The cuckoo shouts all day at nothing
>   In leafy dells alone;
> And traveller's joy beguiles in autumn
>   Hearts that have lost their own.

On acres of the seeded grasses
   The changing burnish heaves;
Or marshalled under moons of harvest
   Stand still all night the sheaves;
Or beeches strip in storms for winter
   And stain the wind with leaves.

Possess, as I possessed a season,
   The countries I resign,
Where over elmy plains the highway
   Would mount the hills and shine,
And full of shade the pillared forest
   Would murmur and be mine.

For nature, heartless, witless nature,
   Will neither care nor know
What stranger's feet may find the meadow
   And trespass there and go,
Nor ask amid the dews of morning
   If they are mine or no.

In each of these three poems, nature is regarded as beautiful and the poet shows that he has fully taken her beauty into account by the rich detail in which he has described it. This fact is more apparent in the last two poems than in Wordsworth's, but if one read all of "Tintern Abbey" with its brilliant description of the panorama of the Wye valley and its charming details of woodland and meadow, one would see that Wordsworth too knew nature intimately and could describe it in as careful and specific detail as either Housman or Keats.

In fact, the layman, reading these poems with any care, must exclaim to himself how very observant these poets are, how much they see that he didn't see and that most of us don't usually see; how well the poets can describe it in every detail and every nuance.

Yet, what different views of nature the three poets take. For Wordsworth, nature is something of a spiritual presence. One can return to nature for sympathy, consolation, refreshment: for all the things that fortify the spirit and make like meaningful again.

There is no question but that Keats also loved nature, but in his wonderful poem to autumn he is content with simply describing its mellow fullness and richness, its lulling quiet, a kind of sleepy satiety, an outpouring of the whole cornucopia of the harvest. He, too, turns autumn into a kind of goddess, drugged with her own ripeness; but

Keats doesn't expect that she will take any notice of him; he makes no prayer to her. In fact, if there is a kind of worship in the poem, it could be best described as a quietly contemplative sense of awe.

Keats treats his goddess almost tenderly. To many people autumn means an ending—it is the season of farewell. Springtime is the season that prompts joy and promise. But as if to console autumn, Keats points out that autumn has her music too and describes that music in beautiful detail. The tone is not that of melancholy, rather a kind of wistfulness.

When we come to Housman, we are in the modern world with a vengeance. Housman also loves nature. He enjoys it in all its seasons: winter, summer, spring, and harvest time. It is no idle boast when he says that he knows the enchantress in all her ways. But he has no illusions about this beautiful witch who has for so long held him in thrall.

As for nature's never having betrayed the heart that loved her, Housman knows that nature is completely faithless. She doesn't care who her next lover will be. Nature is indeed, as he says in his last stanza, "heartless" and "witless." She

> Will neither care nor know
> What stranger's feet may find the meadow
> And trespass there and go. . . .

Why does Housman use the word *trespass* here? Because he had thought in his folly that these were his special meadows, a domain that he had won for himself by his walks there in communion with nature. Someone else coming there would be breaking in, trespassing on his own property. But he admits at the end his delusion. He'd never owned those meadows; nobody can own nature. Nature will indeed never

> . . . ask amid the dews of morning
> If [those footsteps] are mine or no.

Nature is unconscious of man. She doesn't know or care whose eyes gaze with wonder on her beauty.

Someone will want to ask "but which of these is the 'best poem?' " Again, I'm not sure that there is any answer here. All of them seem to me perfect expressions of a possible view of nature and they also impress me as full, authentic expressions of what a person of a certain sort, and of a special temperament, and in certain circumstances might feel about nature. They are all "good" poems. Does that mean then that poetry is irrelevant as far as human preferences are concerned? No, not at all. We have many moods, and, to tell the truth, there are many natures, for we ourselves are a part of nature and when we look at any natural scene, we put part of ourselves into it.

A botanical analysis of a landscape would be rather too abstract for most of us. At an even deeper level, a landscape described in terms of its chemical elements would be so abstract as to be unrecognizable. If we broke it down further to its atomic and subatomic components, we would have reduced it, I believe, essentially to a mathematical description. I point this out not to disparage such analysis. It has its own truth, and it is a very important truth. It would reveal a world that we could use, but not one that human beings could "live" in.

An illustration here may prevent misunderstanding. A scale map and an oil painting of the same landscape are both "true," but their truths are different and they serve different functions. It is desirable to have them both.

Lest I seem to value too little the scientific and technical power of the American universities, let me report on a documentary which I saw recently on television. The principal person interviewed was, I believe, a Japanese, but he taught mathematics at one of our midwestern universities. He was stressing the scientific prestige that is attached to American universities and offered as proof the great number of foreign-born scientists who had been attracted to them and, as an even more impressive fact, the number of graduate students attracted to our universities from abroad.

Yet, another faculty member saw in the same figures not a high praise for our institutions but something more sinister. He said the situation reminded him of the latter days of the Roman Empire when the philosophers at Rome were imported from Greece and the Roman armies were composed largely of non-Roman people — barbarians he called them.

I do not know how seriously this doom-sayer meant to be understood, and I doubt that his analogy of the U.S.A. to the imperial Roman Empire is fully applicable. Nevertheless, superpowers do have their problems and we are getting some twinges from some of ours. At least people are beginning to ask about them. Some of our economists, many of our politicians, and nearly all of our radio evangelists have something to say about our future.

101

What have the poets had to say? A good deal, though the three poems I shall cite are scarcely hot from the press. Most of them were written some 50 or 60 years ago; but then poets take long views.

The British poet, Robert Graves, who died a few years ago, wrote a brilliant poem called "The Cuirassiers of the Frontier." The person speaking the poem is one of the heavy armed cavalrymen who were the mainstay of the Eastern Roman Empire that held back the barbaric forces for centuries until 1456 when the Turks finally overthrew it and took Constantinople. This poem then is not about the fall of the old Rome, but of the new Rome which the Emperor Constantine founded on the shores of the Bosporus. The man speaking is one of the barbarians who, by this time, filled the armies of the new Rome as well as they had filled those of the old Rome. He is quite contemptuous of the capital city of Byzantium. He scoffs at the Christian establishment with its great churches like Santa Sophia. He has no patience with the pederastic senators and the wealthy citizens of the metropolis, or the mobs betting on the races at the Hippodrome. What he proudly claims is that those barbarians who have taken the Roman oath and are now serving in the Roman armies on the frontier represent all that is left of the real Roman spirit.

What they manifest is an *esprit de corps*, a sense of comradeship, a sense of professionals who do the job they are paid to do and do it well with no nonsense about the usual rhetoric of fighting for God and country. It is a bitter speech, but when we take into account the man who speaks it out of his special situation, it makes a kind of sense: At all events, he ends his tirade with a very brilliant simile. He says,

> We, not the City, are the Empire's soul:
> A rotten tree lives only in its rind.

The simile is scientifically accurate. The living part of the tree is that layer just under the bark. Go further down and you strike dead wood, simply a lifeless beam on which the rind grows and climbs. The simile makes the soldier's point: the capital city is morally rotten.

Here is another poem on the subject, written by the late W. H. Auden. He frankly entitles his poem "The Fall of Rome."

> The piers are pummelled by the waves;
> In a lonely field the rain
> Lashes an abandoned train;
> Outlaws fill the mountain caves. . . .

> Cerebrontonic Cato may
> Extol the Ancient Disciplines,
> But the muscle-bound Marines
> Mutiny for food and pay.

Cato, the Censor, was a famous Roman statesman noted for his bitter criticisms of the loss of the old Roman virtues, but "cerebrontonic" is a fancy, psychological term right out of our own century. So it goes.

Auden's point is very close to that made by Robert Graves. The Roman Empire, this time of the West, is seen as tired, bored, disorganized. It has lost its soul. It is decadent in all the senses, from top to bottom. No wonder it will eventually collapse.

But the poet gives the poem a very special turn with the last two stanzas, which I shall quote here:

> Unendowed with wealth or pity,
> Little birds with scarlet legs,
> Sitting on their speckled eggs,
> Eye each flu-infected city.

> Altogether elsewhere, vast
> Herds of reindeer move across
> Miles and miles of golden moss,
> Silently and very fast.

What is the poet saying in these last stanzas? What does he mean by bringing in the little birds sitting on their nests and the reindeer making their annual migration across the tundras of the north? Simply this, I think. Such matters as the rise and fall of empires and all else connected with civilization are peculiarly human problems. Such problems do not affect nature at all. The birds and the beasts cannot choose a course of action. They simply do what comes naturally to them, and nature does not make any mistakes. To the birds it matters little whether Rome rises or falls, and it matters not at all to the reindeer as they pursue their immemorial migrations whether some superpower rises or another superpower goes to pot. It is a sobering thought and well worth our remembering.

These may seem to be rather dismal poems to end with, but I don't mean to end on a lugubrious note. I should say that these are thought-provoking poems. They suggest, among other things, that we might give a closer look at ourselves and what we are doing. It is all very well to sing "America the Beautiful," and certainly America has many things that are beautiful. But her "alabaster cities" *are* stained with human tears. America has plenty of problems which thoughtful citizens need to think about and to try to solve.

Nevertheless, I do not want to end with a fixation on our *American* problems. I am thinking of civilization generally, and this is the matter to which our great literary artists, including the poets of the twentieth century, have been thinking about from time immemorial. W. B. Yeats, the Irish poet, who is probably the greatest poet of the twentieth century, wrote a wonderful poem called "The Second Coming." He obviously took his title from the Christian prediction of the second coming of Christ, but what he describes is the second coming of a kind of anti-Christ, a force that will represent the antithesis of the gentle child born in a manger. He too, therefore, is describing a crisis in the history of civilization in which all that we have known and valued for the last 2,000 years is being challenged and overthrown by something hostile to it all.

The poem begins with a brilliant image, that of the falconer and the falcon. The bird has been loosed and is now swinging in wider and wider circles above the falconer's head. But the falcon has now got so high that he can no longer hear the voice or the whistle of the falconer. We have a symbol of power broken loose from command: power simply on the loose. The poem goes on to say:

> Things fall apart; the centre cannot hold;
> Mere anarchy is loosed upon the world,
> The blood-dimmed tide is loosed, and everywhere
> The ceremony of innocence is drowned. . . .

The poem thus goes on to describe what happens when power and wisdom fall apart. The civilization breaks up, "the blood-dimmed tide," as the poet calls it, is loosed and "the ceremony of innocence is drowned." One has to read a good deal more of Yeats to know what he means here by "the ceremony of innocence." I have time only to suggest what I think he meant: that innocence, true innocence, is not something that comes automatically at birth, but from ritual, from discipline; in short not from nature but from nurture. At all events, from wherever it comes, the poet's foreboding vision sees it drowned in blood. There then follow the wonderful lines:

> The best lack all conviction, while the worst
> Are full of passionate intensity.

104

I came first to appreciate these two lines back in 1938 as Europe was preparing to go to war. The parliamentary democracies which we thought of as surely the best, England, France, seemed listless and unable to act, while the totalitarian powers were indeed full of "passionate intensity." The poem proved to be an extremely accurate prophecy of things to come, for this poem was first printed in 1920, nearly twenty years before the Second World War began. Yet it is not the predictive power of poetry that I want to claim for it. I prefer the old-fashioned term "prophecy." Indeed, "prophecy" originally did not mean prediction at all. It originally meant the statement of a truth, a statement of some important truth as revealed from on high. Only later did the word "prophecy" take on the meaning of prediction.

The great poems are prophetic in this first sense. They do tell us the truth about ourselves and about the state of our culture. Writers of the quality of Eliot, Yeats, Faulkner, and Warren, at their best, do write with prophetic power, not in the sense that they can tell us in which year there will next be a stock market crash or a war or a revolution. They give us something better than that. They remind us of the eternal truths, of the basically unchanging character of human beings and of the perils and yet the triumphs possible in carrying out the human enterprise. They keep measuring us against the eternal verities and the universal values. That is why in a technological age like our own, in which we tend to become absorbed with means and machinery, we need most of all the wisdom of poetry and of literature and history. It is at our own peril that we disregard the funded wisdom of mankind.

*   *   *

"Russell Kirk is a writer who comes as a great relief to anyone looking desperately around for some element of sanity in an increasingly lunatic world. In the misleading categories of our time, he is a conservative—which simply means someone who refuses to accept the notion of change necessarily as progress, or to see in an evidently declining and dissolving civilization intimations of a bright new future. He has the almost unique distinction of being able to write about education without either lapsing into incomprehensible gibberish, or finding it necessary to detect in the largely infantile protests of students the promise of moral and spiritual regeneration to come."

— *Malcolm Muggeridge, from a*
review of Eliot and His Age
in Esquire, *November 1972.*

An Ohio Masterpiece: Prospects for Renewal

by Louis Filler

There have been several books in our time which reflected national unfoldings and larger feelings of community, rather than merely personal attitudes and experiences. They have reflected modern psychology and concerns while retaining lifelines to earlier times. They have even attained a curious fame or notoriety, and may yet be heard of again. I think for example of Ross Lockridge, Jr.'s *Raintree County* (1948), which included in its large-scale drama, revolving about the Civil War and its enigmatic aftermath, young John W. Shawnessy and Professor Jerusalem Webster Stiles—the one an idealist who sought reality, the other a cynic who hoped there was substance in his friend's dreams—who carried on an intermittent dialogue of sorts amid metaphors of national and mundane events. *Raintree County* seemed to ask whether, considering the character of our people, the American experiment was a failure or success—and, indeed, whether life is worth living at all.

The country gave Lockridge all it had to give at the time: a bestseller and Elizabeth Taylor to play a lead part in the motion-picture version of it. It may have been Lockridge's conclusion that the case for America was shaky. For with a good Indiana family and large prospects, he elected to commit suicide.

Such authors—there are others—appear to have lost energy and drive at least in part because they encountered among their countrymen and their critics a lack of spiritual direction, of shared dialogue and discrimination in the success they were handed along with that also given common bestselling entertainers and yarn-spinners. But a deeper, more tenacious purpose made a premier novelist of Helen Hooven Santmyer of the little town of Xenia, Ohio, some 60 miles north of Cincinnati. Born in 1895, she found herself struck in the 1920s by the concerted attack on all she held dear in life by a new, brilliant array of post-World-War-I authors who found family and traditions suffocating and false.

A world with the Black Bottom, the Shimmy, the Charleston was no world in which Santmyer could happily join. Dorothy Parker, working — as she said — to keep body and soul apart; Ernest Hemingway, responding to feeling and nature, not at home but in Spain; H. L. Mencken, with his steely hatred of the American booboisie did not appeal to her spirit. Even John Dos Passos, a decent artist reporting chaos and hypocrisy wherever Americans congregated: his were not the scenes Santmyer had known and loved. Her treasured memories jarred awkwardly with the changing fashions, the rising businesses and pursuits — and, with the advent of the 1930s, what she bluntly called socialism. But it was Sinclair Lewis who wounded her sensibilities most; for he, too, had come from a small town, which he reported as dried and soul-killing. Reading his books in the 1920s, notably *Main Street*, roused in Santmyer an ambition to report to readers her world, which she felt passionately deserved the regard of other true Americans.

Meanwhile, she had a life to lead, a career to make. Out of the smallest and most inconsequential of towns, Santmyer had graduated from Wellesley in 1918. She served as secretary to a *Scribner's Magazine* editor the next year. Her almost life-long goal to be a writer proceeded slowly, but resulted in a manuscript of what became *Herbs and Apples*, published in 1925. That same year she entered Oxford, graduating with a degree in literature two years later. In 1929 appeared her one early effort to create characters, *Fierce Dispute*. Neither this nor the earlier book suggested a living or career.

In 1927 she became a librarian in the Dayton and Montgomery County (Ohio) Public Library, but left after several years to teach English at Cedarville College, a small Presbyterian school outside of Xenia. There, in 1953, she was made head of the English Department and Dean of Women. A change of administration and new connection with the Baptist Church caused her to leave and return to the Dayton library as a reference librarian. There she stayed, commuting to her family home in Xenia until her retirement in 1960.

Santmyer then took up the manuscript of what became ". . . *And Ladies of the Club*", probing her vivid and minute memories for characters and events. A by-product of her interests was *Ohio Town* (1962), in which she set down personal reminiscences and historical details about Xenia's churches, library, courthouse, and other features of the town and its activities. It was paradoxical that, in *Ohio Town*, she made of Xenia's cemetery, where she had often wandered among the tombstones, a living place — the touchstone of vital dialogue among those soon to be laid in its aisles and others who carried out their last rites.

In the next decades Santmyer labored faithfully at her great task, unmoved by every anti-family, anti-small-town tendency bruited in homes and public places, tendencies which were somewhat less so in such a town as Xenia: itself no more prepossessing in turbulent times than it had been in the years following the Civil War, from which her novel took off.

Nevertheless the town had maintained features which gave it a natural distinction. As an Ohio town it had been part of a vast basin of land and water for the travelers and settlers who had populated the Old Northwest. Here, from the Ohio River to the Great Lakes, had been fought a major war with the Indians. This had made famous such places as Zanesville and such personalities as Mad Anthony Wayne, who had cleared the area of Indians. After this conflict ended, families and entrepreneurs had come to settle and exploit the region's natural resources and terrain.

From Cincinnati, farther south, had radiated facets of trade and the products carried by river boats. Blacks had crossed the Ohio River from Kentucky and headed north, settling significantly in Wilberforce, just outside of Xenia. Catholics loomed large in Cincinnati, and had made inroads into Xenia life and business. In addition, utopian-minded seekers had come to the Glen, ten miles north of Xenia, to set up colonies for others like themselves in jagged tracts near which the Ice Age had ended. Seminaries favored particular sects, but also suffered pressures from abolitionists and those favoring women's education; and all labored for the philanthropist's dollar. Xenia itself gained a ladies institute for its better-to-do daughters. A

newspaper, *The Torch Light*, transmitted news from its citizens and exchange papers.

None of this added up to drama in the gaudy sense, but it contained the more significant drama of life and death, the founding of
homes and rearing of children: a living world which reached out to
other Ohio communities and beyond. Santmyer's guiding principle,
as she probed her half-a-century's worth of memories and knowledge,
was that it *was* a living world which, with all the rough justice and injustice of life, brought to its inhabitants pain but also purpose and
fulfillment.

Xenia had sent her youth into the Civil War. Some had died;
others emerged with wounds and honors. The town had sent some of
its women abroad, to study at Oberlin, at Wellesley (as we have
seen), and even to England and the Continent. Xenia had known
distinguished men. General William T. Sherman was an Ohioan,
and Xenians had served under him. Political leaders—U. S. Grant,
the Tafts of Cincinnati, Marcus A. Hanna of Cleveland—respected
the Republican vote in Xenia and met with its outstanding citizens in
the state capital, in Washington, and even at home. Xenia was far
from isolated or ignored.

But that was why one read history, not a novel. A novel carries the
heartbeat of humanity, the record of individual men and women who
made choices of work and life partners, and were made and molded
by the large world. What had Xenia to say that merited the world's attention?

By 1960, one would have guessed, not much. Even in post-Civil-
War times great movements and cultural changes had passed lightly
over Xenia. In early years, monopoly in land deals sponsored by the
government had made George Washington and Benjamin Franklin
rich. Monopoly had eventually passed on to rangy entrepreneurs,
who had sought control of oil, sugar, beef, corn, wool—whatever
might be necessary to people. Populist movements had risen to resist
them. The telephone had helped communication, and the automobile
had challenged the horse.

It was not history as such which dominated Santmyer's manuscript
as it unfolded during her years of writing, though history marched
tandem with her main theme. It was the Xenians themselves, with
their changing but overlapping patterns of carefully described dress,

interests, and relationships which absorbed her. At the front Santmyer placed the women she had known or known about who formed,
as she underscored, not a "female circle," to respond to life as auxilliar-
ies, but a *woman's club*, to explore literary and cultural themes and
to implement each other's private concerns. Here was a "feminism"
of whose power and direction later sophisticates would know less and
less as history and imaginative understanding blurred.

Santmyer's central perception was little recognized by those who
later acknowledged her sensational emergence as a national bestseller;
it was that culture, though apparently "trivial" on the face of it, is
critical to any direction women might take. Papers on Wordsworth,
Compte, and the German Romantics might look like little or nothing
to those who see culture as a side-dish to important matters. There
would in time be a hundred other matters for women to explore in the
Progressive era and beyond, in avenues which affected the psychology
of the nation, as women voted, helped create unions, opened clinics,
and judged government according to their insights. But the heart of
their enterprises was their cultural awareness of human needs. When
that dried up, when agencies became money-getting outlets and
public women merely more functionaries or stipendiaries, their services would become expendable, interchangeable, even harmful to
those who hungered for completion. As Nietzsche said: Not freedom
from what; freedom *to* what.

Santmyer's canvas begins with the young ladies' graduation from
Waynesboro Female College in 1868 and the forming of the Ladies'
Club. (Waynesboro is Xenia, the substitution made to keep the tale at
arm's length, away from the actual scene.) With the principals introduced, sketched, and set in motion, their story catches up the
aware reader into the natural dynamics of marriage, business activity,
children, and the aging town's people. Many figures enter the skein of
the narrative, often first as names only, later to emerge as more fully
sketched figures. The interchanges of family, homes, and circumstances move as steadily and deterministically as weather.

The novel moves through the late nineteenth century with the
growth of families and the accession or loss of individuals. Amid this,
the Ladies' Club makes steady progress through hectic and affluent
times like a well-balanced skiff in changing waters. Each year the club
produces its annual events, with papers ranging in topic from the
Greek historians to the more respectable cultural leaders of the recent

past and even the present. George Sand presents delicate problems for discussion, as does the French exotic Pierre Loti. But the ladies meet these and other problems as best they can. They offer the most acceptable townspeople entertainments, including firmly edited scenes from Shakespeare. Their entertainments also include wedding receptions and housewarmings, as well as the more shadowed funeral services for family and club members. They take in new members as others leave spaces, all while effecting social influence reflecting their religious conservatism and their husbands' firm Republicanism.

Their influence goes further than family; it takes in community. This is demonstrated in their 'reform' efforts against beer and spirits, with the conducting of street prayer and hymn singing at demeaned resorts. Less controversial is the ladies' role in opening a town library, made up of locally donated books and requiring the voluntary services of the ladies themselves. The library campaign reaches to town officials and helpful men, and takes on the aura of a heroic drive. It leads also to a more democratic concern for the poor in local schools. The ladies are not levellers; they see limited potential in the poorer East-End Irish and blacks. But their very concern for their own progeny brings them to broader vistas which serve the larger Waynesboro.

The novel ends as Santmyer's town, having seen the economic crashes of 1883 and 1893 — and the good times following — moves into the twentieth century and faces the great shifts in values and issues of the time.

To one not wholly lost in the novel, it will be evident that blacks, so considerable in our own world, appear only as servants and workers in Santmyer's novel. They are whole-heartedly members of the white families that employ them, but their presence fades in the novel when they return to their own homes in the East End. More notable, considering Santmyer's sense of the crucial value of education, is the total absence of a fictional treatment of Wilberforce University, just outside of town, though it had been in its heroic stage under the great black educator, Bishop Daniel A. Payne.

A word must here be said, one that was better known in his time than now; Payne had been born of free Charleston, South Carolina Negroes, and had shown scholarly aptitude almost before his teens. His teaching of other blacks to read and write was so effective that the state legislature passed an ordinance directed at him to end his teaching. Payne went north, where he earned ministerial credentials and continued his own education, learning ancient and foreign languages and developing a passion for history. He disturbed his black congregations by not welcoming their "farmhand ditties"—spirituals—but spent years gathering fast-disappearing materials for an imperial history of the African Methodist Episcopal Church. Payne took up bankrupt Wilberforce, originally founded for the education of Kentucky slaveholders' illegitimate black children, and by sheer will paid off its debt and turned it into an academic institution which graduated sternly educated ministers to carry their disciplines to black congregations and communities.

None of this receives notice of any kind in Santmyer. Nor does she so much as notice Horace Mann's then-vital Yellow Springs community ten miles to the north, alive with enterprise—alarmingly so to anxious competitors in Xenia. Yet, in imaginative reconstruction, Santmyer's narrative loses nothing by its close-knit tale. Parochialism has been given a bad name in recent decades, but often without dynamic insight. Parishes have produced masterpieces, as witness the Brontë sisters and Jane Austen. Because their authors focussed on individuals, such great literary works reveal high values and fulfilled lives which needed no larger stage. In Austen, the Brontës, and Santmyer we learn that parochialism can mean love, as well as other things.

We noted that it was the scorn poured on the small town, notably by Sinclair Lewis, which inspired Santmyer to her great task and kept her patiently at work on it amidst an adverse world. Yet it may be noted that she misconstrued her foe. Lewis, a complex and turbulent man and artist, was not the enemy of her people she thought he was. Lewis was certainly a critic of the small town, but an upbuilder, rather than a demolisher. And while Lewis was certainly influenced by Twenties scorn of the old fashioned and outmoded, he wanted to see a better small town.

The small town *had* eroded, since its expansive years in the post-Civil War years. The builders, the givers, the doers of whom Santmyer wrote *had* given ground to lesser ladies and businessmen, who followed routines rather than creativity, and were increasingly bemused with things at the expense of culture. World War I had encouraged a shoddy bragging and propaganda at the expense of thoughtful pursuit of goals, certainly of traditional goals. There had been a falling away from days of strong disciplines and Carnegie libraries. Santmyer herself had in her own Twenties book, *Fierce Dispute*, noted Xenia's vulgarity and dullness.

Santmyer's true foes were the cynics of journalism who wanted not so much to improve the small town and the families which supported it, but to demean it as a burden on individual self-expression. They were helped in their cause by the ethnic and immigration complexities of the time, and the inadvertent help given them by civic-minded Progressives. In 1905, for example, one of the most thoughtful of them, Frederic Howe, published *The City: The Hope of Democracy*, which emphasized the city's receptivity to new immigration from the South and abroad, unwanted in the small town. Howe dreamed of the city as leading the nation toward a happier joining of disparate WASPs and ethnics in a union of tolerance and creativity. Unfortunately, the Howes of that time could not foresee that the city could also encourage anonymity and attacks on the family as an institution.

Santmyer did not directly or indirectly cope with such a calculated opponent as Dreiser, whose books were in his time seen fuzzily as compassionate and telling the truth about life in America, unfulfilled in its sexual depths and false to the facts of people's carnal needs. The truth about Dreiser's "crusade" has only recently been spelled out by academics for academics, whose editions of his letters and diaries reveal his bare. all-but-empty world of selfishness and hypocrisy. (Dreiser's *American Diaries: 1902–1926* offers particularly strong evidence of this.)

From hindsight we can now see the process which led from permissiveness and indulgence to the darker shades of our present social dilemmas. In cultural terms—the terms so momentous to Santmyer—one can clearly see the decline of perspective from such as Dreiser through the shallows of Henry Miller and other obsessed characters to James Jones and Norman Mailer. Such authors, and those who welcomed them, made comprehension of the values in family and continuity all but impossible to grasp.

By the time of the youth "revolt" of the Sixties and Seventies it was generally recognized that relativism had rooted itself strongly in popular culture so that genuine students of the larger society could hardly be separated from mere egotists who traced their petty dissatisfactions in prose. For example John Steinbeck, author of the imperial *Grapes of Wrath*, though erratic in production, felt inclined to apologize for having received the Nobel Prize. Similarly, James Gould Cozzens, as a recipient of the Pulitzer Prize, was feverishly attacked by influential academic and popular critics.

In such a climate of opinion Santmyer's *". . . And Ladies of the Club"* was fortunate to so much as see print in 1982, when it received almost no regard by first readers: a novel out of time and irrelevant to the world of pop music and narcissistic tales. Its unexpected explosion in popular esteem—its week-after-week appearance at the top of bestseller lists—was a phenonemon of 1984 and dragged its critics reluctantly to the fore. Who read it? What did it derive from?

Several seasons later it can be reported that though it is not examined in literary discussions, where tendentious novels and tales seeking novelty continue to be written and reviewed, Santmyer's novel seems secure in the homes of perhaps a million purchasers and the minds of millions more who have found relief in its recognizable people and family concerns. The book is not easily found at second-hand book stalls or on library shelves; those who have it keep it, and would doubtless buy other works which honor life.

But a Santmyer is not readily found. Publishers can order more books of the same sort, but they can't order the creation of genius. Family is not easily reconstructed, for the benefit of the market. And so, though successors to *" . . . And Ladies of the Club"* cannot be predicted, the need for stable relations, not to say family is now fairly recognized, even in the most permissive cities. The small towns and suburbs have no comparable problem.

They are aware of what constitute bases in society, and they struggle with the perplexities that adult and young delinquents pose. The role of culture in these concerns is still less tangible in handling, still difficult to grasp, and may take time to reestablish. It is still subject to aggressive attack. But the plaque which the town of Xenia has placed on the family house in which Santmyer spent most of her years is only the first such plaque which may be anticipated for others of her quality. Because of her life and art the future of the small town and its leading inhabitants looks more promising than it has in many years.

Virtue: Real and Imagined

by Claes G. Ryn

I t is widely agreed that Western society needs to be morally in-
vigorated. Many intellectuals express themselves in favor of "justice," "human rights," "virtue," "universal values," and the like. Unfortunately, the moralistic fervor of such discourse is sometimes in in-
verse proportion to its intellectual stringency. A lack of philosophical
and historical discipline is common both in the universities and in the
churches, journalism, and politics. It cannot be assumed that the
surge of moralistic sentiment stems from a yearning for ethical universality. Talk of "moral values" is sometimes mere adornment for the
idiosyncratic ideological preferences of groups that want to impose
their will on others. Key terms of moral discourse cover a wide range
of meanings. For example, Christian "love" and "compassion" are
cited in support of conduct or social arrangements that would have
dismayed Christians of earlier centuries. Terminological appearances
are often deceiving, as when traditionalist-sounding calls for virtue
and justice that invoke the authority of Plato and Aristotle turn out to
hide egalitarian and democratist beliefs that the Greeks would have
dismissed. Some conceptions of individual and social responsibility
that are treated as closely related are actually incompatible. A failure
to make appropriate distinctions is closely connected to a disinclina-
tion to explore ideas with regard to their concrete and practical meaning, to examine them in a manner simultaneously historical and
philosophical.

One urgent but largely neglected need is to distinguish between
conceptions of morality that emphasize personal character and conceptions that discount it. Notions of the second type can be quite different. They may stress incisive ratiocination or tender emotion, or a
combination of the two, as the source and hallmark of virtue. But

whether morality is associated primarily with abstract principle or with sentiment, the need traditionally seen for improving self by protracted and often difficult exertion of the will is deemphasized or ignored. According to the older view, by contrast, virtue is, broadly speaking, sound character in action. Humane social relations are seen as possible in proportion as individual human beings are able to tame the lower inclinations of their own souls. Social tensions and injustices have their origin in those inclinations. While rationality and sentiment are integral to man's moral life, they are conducive to good only if ethically informed and structured.

Equating social responsibility with individual moral character has deep roots in the classical heritage, although there the emphasis on sound willing sometimes blends with more intellectualistic elements. The identification of morality with character has been powerfully influenced by Christianity but is not necessarily bound up with a particular theology. Rationalistic or sentimental notions of virtue, or tendencies in that direction, are found throughout human history, but they have acquired particular strength in the modern, "post-Christian" era.

Although these philosophies often employ the same or similar terms to indicate what they consider virtuous, they can be shown to be fundamentally different. The nature and extent of the contrast between them can be demonstrated by analyzing their ideas, not in the abstract merely, but with attention to the concrete conduct, social relationships, and institutions that they entail. Some of the substantive entailments of the old Western stress on moral character may be brought out in an examination of some key features of traditional American society. Certain ethical predilections have produced particular personality traits and social and political structures. A juxtaposition of the traditional American moral ethos and the moral ethos of Jean-Jacques Rousseau is illuminating, as is a comparison with the ideas of John Locke. Although Locke is often regarded as having expressed the spirit of the founding of the United States, his ideas turn out to be in important respects dissonant with American theory and practice. Both in the case of Rousseau and that of Locke, attention to the specific socio-political entailments of ideas reveals the tension between their thought and American tradition. Taking account of the concrete substance of ethical ideas will clarify the meaning of genuine ethical universality.

Central to the old Western understanding of morality is the idea that human nature is divided between higher and lower potentialities. Man is capable of nobility and civilization but also of great viciousness and baseness. Besides a potential for community with God and other human beings, Christianity finds in man a perverse attraction to what is destructive of his higher humanity. Christianity refers to the chronic nature of this dark propensity as original sin. Whether specifically religious and theological or more humanistic and nondogmatic, the traditional Western ethic sees the key problems of personal and social life as stemming from the duality of human nature. For man's higher potentialities to be realized, he needs to discipline his lower self. Social wrongs have their ultimate origin in the weaknesses of human nature. The purpose of society and government is to protect against the worst manifestations of human nature and to assist man's moral, intellectual, and aesthetical education and self-education. Because man finds his deepest satisfaction in the ethical ordering of character, society must take special care to encourage his moral development. Upbringing in the family, education, social conventions, and laws are needed both to restrain man's lower tendencies and to buttress his higher. According to the ancient Greeks, whose view was incorporated into Roman and Christian thought with various modifications, man's nature is social and political. Only in cooperation with others can he hope to grow as a human being. Man's essential nature is discovered not in some primitive, presocial, or extrasocial condition but in the civilized community where his higher self is nourished. Life in groups and associations of various kinds manifests his higher potential.

The traditional Western view of man is nowhere more radically challenged than in the writings of Jean-Jacques Rousseau. To him and similar thinkers can be traced a redefinition of morality that is transforming Western society. For Rousseau, man is not a mixture of higher and lower inclinations. His essential nature is good. Injustice and unhappiness are not due to some primordial flaw or perversity within the human soul that necessitates a strengthening of character but are caused by distorting and oppressive social institutions and conventions. Man's original, spontaneous goodness has been denied expression by historical society. On every side natural man is hemmed in by artificial rules, expectations, and obligations. In Rousseau's famous words, "Man was born free, and he is everywhere in chains."[1] In order to liberate human nature, Western civilization with its dualistic view of man must be overturned. Like his descendants today, Rousseau uses much of the vocabulary of the older Western traditions in ethics and social thought. His language sometimes gives the impression that he wants to restore ancient ways of life—for example, those of Sparta. But occasional and superficial similarities between him and the Greeks cannot conceal that he is giving an entirely new meaning to terms like "virtue" and "citizenship."[2]

Rousseau contends that humanity once existed in a primitive, presocial state of nature. Human beings were good, equal, and self-sufficient. They lived independently in peaceful anarchy. Free to follow the impulse of the moment, they were also happy. Rousseau insists that a primitive autonomous life is natural to man. Humans are not social beings. From his belief in man's original and spontaneous goodness Rousseau derives the theory for a new society and government. Having once entered society, men cannot "return to the woods." But it is possible to recover the original purity and simplicity of nature in a new form while remaining in society. This will require that the oppressive constraints of existing civilization are removed. A people who overthrow those traditions will form a new community of equality and brotherhood. They will have a sense of common purpose, a general will (*volonté générale*). This will of the people, the spontaneous voice of nature translated into politics, is by definition virtuous and must have unrestricted power. Rousseau wants not only complete political equality but the removal of every constitutional check on the majority. In the new society the unrestricted freedom that used to belong to the individual in the state of nature is transferred to the citizen as a member of the general will.

It is important to note that Rousseau associates groups and associations with the civilization that has enslaved man. They introduced partisan and therefore illegitimate interests into the body politic. Groups threaten the virtuous unity of the people by dividing their loyalties. To guarantee the moral rectitude of the majority, such influences external to the individual should be eliminated. For citizens to participate fully in the common identity of the general will, they must belong solely to the undifferentiated whole of the people.

This short comparison of two contrasting notions of moral virtue is merely suggestive. To show the full extent and significance of the difference between them it is necessary to examine further the concrete personal and socio-political manifestations of each. The meaning of the old Western stress on moral character can be elaborated by analyzing it in relation to important elements of traditional American life and by indicating how the society fostered by traditional morality differs not only from the egalitarian collectivism of Rousseau but from the social atomism of John Locke.

Long-standing intellectual convention has it that the United States is a liberal society. It is widely believed that John Locke provides the intellectual paradigm for understanding the "founding" of the United States. Louis Hartz speaks of America's "Lockian settlement."[3] That the United States has marked liberal traits and that its political and intellectual debates give prominence to the rights and freedoms of individuals can hardly be denied, but it needs to be emphasized that terms like "liberalism" and "individualism" can have sharply different meanings. If there is a sense in which American tradition is individualistic, it can be argued that this individualism is of a special type that must be carefully distinguished from other possible types. It is a mistake to regard individualism and private initiative in American tradition as centering upon an autonomous, self-enclosed individual, the kind assumed in Locke's social-contract theory.

A salient feature of American life that is poorly accounted for by a Lockean understanding of individual and society is one that Alexis de Tocqueville found striking and recorded at length in *Democracy in America* (1835–40). Tocqueville observed in the United States an extraordinary proliferation of groups and associations, churches prominent among them, writing, "In no country in the world has the principle of association been more successfully used, or more unsparingly applied to a multitude of different objects, than in America." Tocqueville describes a strong inclination among the citizens to join together privately and locally to meet their needs. The way of Americans in the 1830s was not to turn to some distant authority for remedies to problems but for the citizen, in private cooperation with others, "to rely upon his own exertions." Through an elaborate network of partly overlapping and more or less formal groupings a large number of tasks were performed which, in a people of more passive individuals, might remain unaccomplished or be entrusted to government. Tocqueville illustrates the pervasiveness of local and private initiative: "If a stoppage occurs in a thoroughfare, and the circulation of the public is hindered, the neighbors immediately constitute a deliberative body;

and this extemporaneous assembly gives rise to an executive power, which remedies the inconvenience, before anybody has thought of recurring to an authority superior to that of the persons immediately concerned." Americans would turn to a higher authority only if quite unable to meet their own needs. They tended to view government with a measure of mistrust and even anxiety.[4]

A willingness on the part of citizens to assume social responsibility in their families, neighborhoods, and local groups powerfully counteracts the growth and centralization of government. In America it has been traditionally assumed that, if a public authority should become involved, it ought to be one that is as close as possible to the problem or need. Citizens have turned first to semi-public local associations, then to the township, county, or city, then to the state government, and only in exceptional instances to the federal government. Decentralized responsibility and corresponding structures of government have made it possible for small political entities close to the people to exercise real power and independence. In general, the social and political ways of old America offer a concrete illustration of the ancient principle of subsidiarity, according to which social tasks should be entrusted to organizations at a distance from the people directly concerned only if those tasks cannot be satisfactorily performed by an authority closer to the citizens.

Consciously or unconsciously a certain view of human nature and moral responsibility was enacted in the socio-political relationships and institutions just described. These patterns were closely related to the religious and ethical beliefs of those who set the tone in society. In a similar way, the enormous expansion and centralization of government in this century reflect the rise of different beliefs. It is crucial to recognize that much is revealed about ethical ideas in the socio-political habits that they imply and engender.

The nature of traditional American individualism cannot be fully understood apart from the social context in which it took shape. Even today, the old propensity for associating with others and taking private and local initiative survives. In the United States, perhaps more so than in any other Western country, the energy of the individual is channeled, from childhood on, through a sometimes intensive group life — first in a person's own family, then in the families of friends, in the scout troop, the sports team, the Sunday-school class, the school orchestra, and so on. A habit of entering into cooperation with and adjusting to others is formed early. It eventually gives to the aspirations of the individual a social dimension; personal wishes become increasingly difficult to distinguish from the wishes of the person's most cherished groups. If individual moral responsibility is first of all responsibility for self, so that a person's less admirable traits are not inflicted upon others, that self-restraint also tends to buttress communal relations.

The ethical significance of these observations is easier to see if individualism that is affected by life in intimate groups is contrasted with another possible kind of individualism. One can imagine a society so dedicated to the autonomy and independence of the individual that its citizens receive little or no habituation or encouragement in showing consideration for others. The interests of the individual are allowed to center upon the desires of the self in isolation. Human beings of strongly egocentrical disposition are everywhere common, but a society can be more or less solicitous of the partisan ego. Within the traditional American pattern of association and cooperation the individual must repeatedly take the wishes of others into account. The person is called upon again and again to perform little acts of self-denial. The individual is able to improve his standing in his social circle only by sacrificing some of his time, energy, and property for others. Initially there is perhaps little but enlightened self-interest to motivate a person to act as he is expected to act and, for example, do his part in local affairs, attend church, or help with charitable work. But his way of life becomes a habit and with time perhaps even a source of meaning and satisfaction. One's personality is shaped by how one acts and relates to others. Group memberships constantly encourage the individual to make the views of others his own. In the end, the individual is unable to separate his own interests from what family members, relatives, colleagues, and others find important. The effect of his memberships is to temper the egotistical impulse and make him apply personal initiative at least partly in behalf of goals beyond the solitary self.

American tradition has fostered a kind of individualism that is poorly explained by theories of human nature and society that view individuals as discrete and autonomous beings not dependent on association for their essential humanity. It is an individualism that integrates concern for the freedoms of individuals with the human need for community. The self-assertion of the individual has been molded within an ethos begetting communal structures. Man, American tradition proclaims, is a social being needing others to develop his humanity. Americans have shown themselves to be in this respect more the descendants of Aristotle and mediaeval Christianity than of John Locke, the social atomist.

The structures of traditional American government correspond to and support the old preference for decentralization and life in groups. This is not the case with the form of popular government proposed by Jean-Jacques Rousseau. His majoritarian, plebiscitary notion of democracy assumes the desirability of equality and unity. The people should not be made up of a multiplicity of groups and have many levels and centers of authority. For the virtuous General Will to manifest itself the people must form an undifferentiated whole, all individuals counting the same. There should be, in the current phrase, "one man, one vote," but not simply in the sense that each citizen should be able to vote. To guarantee the ascendancy of the General Will society must rid itself of what differentiates the citizens and gives them unequal influence. Rousseau has a profound mistrust of groups within the state. Political and social subdivisions are for him partisan, conspiratorial interests that divide the loyalties of the citizens and divert them from the good of the whole. If the General Will is to assert itself, Rousseau writes, "it is imperative that there should be no sectional associations in the state." The popular will must be purged of the prejudices and partialities of a traditional decentralized and subdivided society. The common good has for Rousseau nothing to do with accommodating the needs and interests of human associations other than the all-encompassing political collective. To become a part of the General Will the individual must be truly autonomous, "make up his own mind for himself" (*n'opine que d'après lui*), which means ridding his consciousness of the influence of groups.[5] The virtuous union of the General Will is between individuals who consult only their very own ego and who discover in that ego a common purpose. Rousseau is at the same time an uncompromising individualist, one who insists on separating the individual from groupings, and an uncompromising collectivist, one who regards the state as a whole as the sole framework for virtuous human striving.

Rousseau's idea of popular government is a frontal assault on socio-political institutions and habits that American tradition deems central to human well-being. Classical and Christian thinkers had assumed that man develops his higher potential through life in more or less intimate groups. For Rousseau, it is social entanglements of this sort that have perverted man's nature. They have imprisoned his natural goodness, partly by destroying his independence. Rousseau would therefore abolish associations intermediate between the individual and the state, the kind of independent organizations that Robert Nisbet calls "autonomous groups."[6] Man should think and act not as a member of regional, local, or private entities but as a part of the undifferentiated whole. The individual is to become the state, the state the individual. The citizen, writes Rousseau, should receive from the collective "his life and his being."[7]

Rousseau's attack on sectional associations is integral to his moral philosophy. Without the careful consideration of these concrete social and political entailments of his thought his notion of virtue cannot be fully grasped. Rousseau understands well that groups like the traditional family both generate and transmit habits and preferences that are inimical to his own idea of individual and collective life, and that these groups are a natural outgrowth of the ethical and cultural assumptions of traditional Western civilization. The freedom and virtue envisioned by Rousseau requires the eradication of the social patterns and institutions from which that older ethos is indistinguishable. Those who want the new society must be ready, Rousseau writes, "to change human nature, to transform each individual."[8] During the French Revolution the Committee of Public Safety expressed the same need: "You must entirely refashion a people whom you wish to make free, to destroy its prejudices, alter its habits, limit its necessities, root up its vices, purify its desires."[9] To that end social structures have to be transformed.

Far from undermining or destroying man's sectional associations, the traditional American system of government encourages, protects, and empowers them. American popular government shows no interest in the people as an undifferentiated mass and, specifically, gives it no political authority. The people in that sense are not recognized by the U.S. Constitution. Under it Americans have political standing only as members of sectional associations. Similar preferences pervade traditional American government in general. Citizens share in power as residents of a particular state, congressional district, state legislative district, county, city, or other political subdivision. If by "one man, one vote" is meant that each person should carry the same weight at the ballot box, that principle is flagrantly violated by the Constitution. In spite of huge differences in population, Delaware and New York, Wyoming and California send the same number of senators to Washington. Residents of Delaware and Wyoming thus have many times the voting power of residents of New York and California. Voting is weighted also in elections to the House of Representatives, for even states with tiny populations are entitled by the Constitution to at least one representative. Not even modern presidential elections provide an outlet for the people as a national and undifferentiated mass. The citizens actually vote for presidential electors in the several states, and electors are apportioned to each state in the same number as it has senators and representatives in the U.S. Congress, which means, again, that the votes of people in small states are, as it were, counted more than once. Both by design and spontaneous evolution, America's decentralized and decentralizing political structures extend privileges to countless subdivisions, making it possible for them to exercise real authority and assert their interests. These institutions of government interact with and protect a plethora of diverse private groups and organizations. It is assumed that vital sectional associations and elaborate decentralization are conducive to a humane society. In this regard, American society clashes not only with Rousseau but with Locke, whose chief concern is not the needs of groups or persons as members of groups but the rights of discrete individuals.

Just as the undifferentiated mass is a concrete manifestation of Rousseauistic virtue, so is a decentralized and group-oriented society like traditional America the enactment of a very different view of virtue. The former can be said to be an ethic of the collective, the latter an ethic of community. Before going to the heart of the ethical issue, more needs to be said about the individual as a member of groups.

To live in community is not to be a part of humanity in the abstract or in general. Community means first of all to be associated with particular individuals. The social nature of man is most clearly evident in autonomous groups marked by close and repeated personal contact—for example, families, workplaces, local churches, clubs, union chapters, schools, and neighborhood organizations. As Nisbet has so incisively argued, people find their deepest sense of belonging and security in their more intimate associations, the family preeminent among them.[10] Here the individual is recognized and treated as a person. Whether as child or adult the individual knows that the other family members care about him. His needs and wishes matter, and he in turn is prepared to consider and accommodate the others. The individual is somebody. He is missed when absent. Others depend on him. In the small group particularly, the individual is acutely aware of being responsible not just for himself. It matters greatly what the person does and does not do. The individual is powerful in the sense that his actions affect the group and others beyond it in a direct and tangible manner. He also senses that he is liked and respected in spite of mistakes and weaknesses. Should he behave badly, censure is to be expected, but so is tolerance, understanding, and forgiveness. Yet he is expected to measure up to the highest possible standards. The family plays a central role in transmitting the moral and other expectations of the civilized society to the individual and habituating him to those expectations. In the small social unit it is not possible for the individual, at least not for long, to convince others that he is better than he actually is. Moralistic posturing is mercilessly exposed when a person's actions do not measure up to his words.

Any group can fail in its higher purpose. Particular individuals in the association or the influence of the surrounding society may have a detrimental effect. Neither should the possible drawbacks of social intimacy go unmentioned. If a society stresses the values and interests of groups to the exclusion of freedom for the individual, the result is likely to be normative rigidity, intolerance, and narrowness of mind. Particular groups as well as society at large need some deviation from and challenge to established ways. Social life needs to be continually renewed and refreshed by the originality of individuals.

Edmund Burke has remarked that the main source of warm feelings for state or nation is the affections that we form for "the little platoons" to which we belong. It needs to be added and underlined that serious problems in these same groups are very likely to undermine man's broader attachments. In a people of disharmonious, disintegrating, and neurotic families a general disaffection with the larger society is to be expected. When the family and other social organisms are at their best and interact vitally with a larger and creative civilization they contribute immeasurably to the individual's moral and cultural development and to his sense that life is worth living. In an environment of relative harmony and safety the individual learns the concrete meaning of personal responsibility, of work, initiative, sacrifice, and compromise — all characteristics that are basic to the wider duties of citizenship. The individual moves beyond a narrow concern for self. Tocqueville says about this formative power as it exists in America's intermediate associations that it disciplines citizens in "habits of regularity, temperance, moderation, foresight, self-command," leading them in the direction of virtue.[11]

To relate these points to an earlier theme, individualism and freedom can be practiced by rootless and self-centered persons who have grown up in a society of weak or disintegrating autonomous groups or by rooted, considerate persons formed by life in healthy associations. Individualism here has entirely different meanings representative of entirely different societies. "Democracy" and "market economy" are examples of abstract terms whose content must vary drastically depending on the presence or absence in society of the kind of individual responsibility and corresponding decentralized and group-oriented structures that have been discussed. Both the form and substance of democracy or the market economy are shaped by the moral predilections of the individuals who act within either system. The purposes of society vary accordingly.

The ethical import of the contrast between traditional American social and political patterns and those of collectivism must be analyzed further. Two fundamentally different notions of virtue correspond to two fundamentally different societies. Perhaps the main source of ethical confusion in our time is the failure to distinguish clearly between them.

People today who speak the most about social justice, including those who stress the need to assist the weak and the poor, typically voice a generalized caring for nobody in particular. Their concern is not for this or that person, which presumably would be too confining. Their compassion might seem more generous: it encompasses all suffering humanity. On this generalized benevolence many modern people base their claim to having moral sensibility. These lovers of mankind seem to take much pride in their own moral sentiments and to expect the praise of others for being the conscience of the world.

People who do not share their view of social responsibility can be looked down upon as morally inferior.

Modern humanitarian sympathy is often expressed in the language of the old ethical and religious traditions of the West. Has there then finally appeared a morally superior breed of human beings who are actually carrying out such old Christian admonitions as love and charity? The new moral type seems to exude compassion. To discern the substance of the new moralism it is necessary to consider its concrete manifestations in personal behavior and socio-political arrangements. In that perspective, the terminological resemblance to the older traditions can be seen to conceal a drastic change in the meaning of morality.

It should be noted, first of all, that the humanitarianism at the heart of the new morality does not have moral character in the traditional sense as a prerequisite. It is possible for a person to be ruthless and intolerant toward people at close range, such as colleagues or family members, and yet feel love for humanity in general. In the classical and Judaeo-Christian traditions man is viewed as flawed and often selfish. Love and charity are fruits of a protracted and sometimes difficult improvement of self that makes the person more capable of considerate action. An enticing feature of modern humanitarianism is that it does not presuppose any painful moral self-scrutiny and laborious strengthening of character. In that sense it is virtue made easy. In comparison with the improvement of character that makes a person easier to live with, it takes little effort to care for the oppressed, the starving Third World, or the exploited proletariat. These are not individuals with names and faces. They are abstract categories, people in distant places where the caring individual does not risk encountering them. In fact, the object of compassion usually exists only in the imagination, on the television screen, or in the newspapers. Another advantage of this benevolence of the emotions is that it somehow always transfers the obligation to act elsewhere, to government perhaps or to an international organization. The caring individual may be charged some money in taxes, which is a low price for feeling morally admirable. The new virtue makes it possible to bask in self-approbation without having to show any strength of character. The lover of humanity can be as odious as before in dealings with people up close.

The profound difference between generalized sympathy and traditional virtue is coming into view. Christianity did not admonish people to adopt a self-congratulatory and sentimental benevolence towards nobody in particular. It taught instead—let it be carefully noted—love of neighbor. Though crucially important, the significance of this commandment is all too easily missed by people of flesh and blood with whom the individual may come into personal contact in daily life. It is indicative of the change that has been wrought in the moral life of Western man that today little attention is paid to why love of neighbor should once have been regarded as central and distinctive to morality. Here lies a key to distinguishing between different ideas of virtue.

To the friends of mankind, loving one's neighbor may appear confining and niggardly. Does not real virtue have greater scope and liberality? But such feelings of moral generosity may signify an escape from responsibilities that place concrete demands on the individual. To love people in the immediate environment requires the kind of strength of will that used to be known as character. It means the ability to act for the welfare of one's spouse, child, parent, colleague, student, teacher, employer, employee, etc. While caring for humanity in the abstract imposes no particular burden, acting responsibly toward living, breathing people here and now can be difficult, partly because these "neighbors" may be disagreeable and have interests at odds with one's own. They may make uncomfortable demands on one's time and energy. For these reasons love of neighbor can be said to form the core of authentic traditional social morality. It is in concrete personal relationships and not in the arena of rhetorical moralizing that real moral worth is displayed and tested. Little or nothing can be said about an individual's moral character on the basis of professions of caring for abstract categories of people at a comfortable distance. Better evidence of virtue, or its opposite, is found in a person's more intimate relationships.

The belief, increasingly dominant in the Western world, that a virtuous disposition is a state of emotion—specifically, a feeling of sympathy—owes greatly to the influence of Rousseau. In his view, morality is not an *effort*, for man's real nature is spontaneously inclined to good. But Edmund Burke, who knew Rousseau both as a person and thinker, comments that Rousseau's professions of universal sympathy came from one whose "heart was incapable of harboring one spark of common parental affection." (Burke has in mind Rousseau's insistence, over the tearful protests of his mistress, that each of the children born to them be abandoned to an orphanage—which, given the nature of such institutions at the time, meant the likely death of the children.) In general, Rousseau had great difficulty getting along with other human beings, a problem that only intensified with age. For Burke, the essential nature of the "new-invented virtue" of Rousseau and the French revolutionists was "benevolence to the whole species, and want of feeling for every individual."[12]

The old Western ethic clearly did not want social obligations to be restricted to people within the individual's personal circle. But it assumed that real morality gets its start and is practiced chiefly in close-up relationships. In that setting morality involves concrete responsibilities and action. Genuine virtue both requires and builds strength of character. Having been nurtured and tested in the family and other intimate groups, morality can be expected to spread outward into society and politics. Citizens molded by a society of this kind are bound to define social goals and problems in other ways than citizens who grow up in a more centralized and undifferentiated society and for whom the essence of virtue is the love of humanity. It makes a great difference whether social responsibility is rooted in character or in moralistic sentiment, whether it is the natural extension to the larger society of virtue already achieved in personal life or the application of a merely abstract "justice."

Classical and Judaeo-Christian ideas of virtue were enacted in a group-oriented, decentralized society that followed the principle of subsidiarity. By multiplying opportunities for personal initiative and contact, society gave expression to and encouraged individual responsibility. It also made possible the adjustment of measures of social amelioration to the special needs and circumstances of persons and groups.

Christianity did not expect universal love of mankind from the ordinary person. Behaving charitably towards "neighbor" was hard enough for most people. Christianity associated a wider love of man with the truly exceptional person of character. In the saintly individual, the overcoming of the selfish ego through protracted effort of will leads beyond love of neighbor to loving identification with humanity at large—love, however, not in the form of sweet, teary-eyed, and self-congratulatory emotion but in the form of readiness to act selflessly. Modern love of mankind presupposes no such difficult transformation of individual character. The type of moralism that parades under banners of "justice," "equality," and "brotherhood" affords Western man an opportunity to bypass the demanding effort of moral self-improvement, including its more elementary stages. Anybody can put forth the imaginary beneficence of sentiment. Behind the assumptions of moral purity in the benevolent soul one detects a Rousseauistic belief in the goodness of man. Lovers of humanity who wish to remake society need show no evidence of having already improved themselves. They can go directly to the improvement of society and — why not? — reform of the entire world. Are not their abundant warm feelings for the world's unfortunate sufficient proof of their moral qualifications? The more ambitious the plans for a just new order, the stronger the evidence of an exalted morality.

People resisting the humanitarian plan could only be morally perverse, and their opposition must be broken. If the reformer is viewed with suspicion even by those he claims to be helping, he is no less to be thanked for his benevolence. Consciously identifying himself with his greater mentor, Rousseau, Robespierre wrote: "The consciousness of having willed the welfare of his fellow men is the reward of the virtuous man. The gratitude of the multitude, who surrounds his memory with honours, bestows on him the due which his contemporaries denied him."[13]

The scope and significance of the change in the understanding of morality can hardly be exaggerated. If the test of virtue is the warmth and intensity of feeling, old-fashioned training of moral character is no longer needed. The social and political consequences are potentially profound and far-reaching. It becomes possible to be a passionate friend of humanity and to be simultaneously ruthless in the treatment of actual human beings: to be, as Burke said with special reference to Rousseau, "a lover of his kind, but a hater of his kindred."[14] Rousseau, Robespierre, Marx, and Lenin had hearts full of brotherly feeling. They wanted a better world for mankind. But when such visions are implemented the streets run red with blood. "Freedom, equality, and brotherhood," the French Revolution proclaimed. In practice it employed the guillotine. Egalitarian revolutionaries care deeply for the downtrodden, but, as Irving Babbitt pointed out, their invitation "be my brother" has a corollary: "or else I must kill you."[15] And with the rule of virtue there arises some version of the Gulag archipelago.

The translation of the abstract and sentimental brotherhood of man into social and political practice follows a logic suggestive of its substantive meaning. Its claim to being the essence of morality has a curious ring. Does it not in fact sanction and mask a will to unlimited power? Should anything be allowed to stand in the way of such goodness? The demand for equality and brotherhood somehow exempts the one making the demand from mere membership in the egalitarian mass to be created. Does not the friend of humanity belong to the political or intellectual elite that will construct the new society and there benevolently rule a grateful people? Behind the humanitarian mask lurks the potential for pitiless inhumanity. Anatole France warned that when one starts with the assumption that men are naturally good, one ends by wishing to kill them all.

By contrast, virtue as understood within the older Western tradition is embodied in concrete good actions conducive to community. It builds social relations of some intimacy that tolerate personal diversity. Whereas the lover of humanity may be unable to live harmoniously with particular people, the person of moral character tends to thrive as a member of groups.

In the modern world the most obvious and blatant threat to the old morality and to the decentralized, group-oriented society from which it is indistinguishable has come from totalitarianism. The latter correctly views the autonomous groups and the initiatives that emanate from them as standing in the way of the centralization of power. The totalitarians know that groups like the family keep alive and give rise to values and behavior that clash with the intended new order. They consequently try to destroy or weaken private and freely formed associations, for example, by undermining traditional loyalties, as when youth organized by the Movement are told to inform on parents or siblings. The assault on the intermediate associations divests the citizens of old social identities and places them unprotected before the increasingly powerful state. Before, the citizens were organized in freely formed groups for mutual support, self-help, and private initiative. Now is created a people of isolated and insecure individuals, able to turn for a sense of belonging only to the all-encompassing collective. There appears the undifferentiated and passive mass, the lonely crowd. The Movement wants this people to march in step for the final victory of justice in the world. Perhaps the ultimate stage in the transformation of traditional morality and com-

131

munity is the "brotherhood" of the rootless crowd that shouts its predictable assent to moralistic totalitarian slogans.

What totalitarians try to accomplish through direct and open assault on traditional society, other intellectual and political movements are achieving in more indirect, gradual, and subtle ways. In the United States a form of abstract individualism has acquired great power that is increasingly difficult to distinguish from collectivism. Elements of Locke and Rousseau are blended in a pursuit of "equal rights." The objective is not a limited one, like removing racial discrimination, but to push the principle of equality before the law in a radically individualistic and egalitarian direction. Citizens should no longer be treated as social beings, according to traditional group memberships and responsibilities, as fathers or mothers, males or females, members of families, residents of states or localities, but only as individuals having equal rights. Before the law the citizens should stand socially naked, stripped of the roles that heretofore defined their personhood. Government and society in general have long given preferential treatment to social arrangements that from time immemorial have been regarded as indispensable to civilized life. By making the abstract, socially undefined individual the reference point for policy and legislation and by cancelling supports extended to man as a member of groups and subdivisions, the ideology of equal individual rights promotes the atomization of society. The American people are moved in the direction of the undifferentiated mass, the condition regarded by Rousseau as requisite for virtuous popular rule. The analysis here offered shows this atomization to be the political, social, and cultural dismantling of the classical and Judaeo-Christian moral ethos. As Rousseau recognized in his own way, the undifferentiated mass represents the obliteration of the values of traditional civilization.

Some who call themselves libertarians and have much in common with Lockean individualism want the removal of supports for particular socio-political arrangements so that individuals can have greater freedom to pursue their own preferences. Others, calling themselves socialists or liberals and drawn more to Rousseauistic collectivism, want a new egalitarian order established by the state. The difference between these groups is far smaller than might appear from their language. They both want to abolish privileges that define and bolster the decentralized society. As these advantages are withdrawn through the application of political power, that power can only grow, because it undermines the many competing centers of influence engendered by traditional moral preferences. Also, it falls to central government to handle needs previously met by groups and associations that are losing their efficacy.[16]

According to Rousseau legitimate laws must spring equally from all and apply equally to all. Rousseau deeply influenced Immanuel Kant, whose notion that we should act so that the principle of our own action could be raised to universal law has strong egalitarian implications. Kant's idea makes light of the element of uniqueness in all individuals and all historical situations. Because of that element, human actions cannot be replicated. Only if individuals and circumstances could somehow be made the same would the conditions be present for universalizing our own action. Only then could any principle apply equally to all.

The logic of the doctrine of abstract equal rights can be illustrated with reference to the idea that all people in a democracy should have the same voting power. If taken literally, "one man, one vote" would disenfranchise citizens as members of traditional political subdivisions. In the United States power has been given to citizens as members of regional and local political entities to ensure the effectiveness and independence of those entities. The principle of equal voting power is most blatantly violated by elections to the U.S. Senate, which give preferential treatment to citizens as residents of the several states and give particular privileges to residents of the smallest states. Favoring persons as members of political subdivisions by empowering those subdivisions is pervasive in America. For each citizen to be treated merely as one and for numerical majority rule to be possible these intricate decentralized political structures would have to be dissolved. With them would disappear the moral and cultural ethos from which they are indistinguishable.

"One man, one vote" purports to give the people more power. Does it then strengthen the individual's ability to shape his own life? Abstract individualism separates the political rights of the person from political and social subdivisions and prepares the way for the huge, all-encompassing collective. Rule by the undifferentiated mass of individuals, according to the wishes of the numerical majority, is difficult to distinguish from a totalitarian form of government in which the individual is nothing and the state and its elites are everything.

When does the citizen feel most influential? Is it as an active member of regional and local groups through which he can directly affect his own life and that of his community, or is it when those groups have faded away and he can go to the polls as one of millions of equal voters to elect rulers in the nation's capital? The present analysis shows centralized mass democracy to deprive the individual of concrete power. But this loss of influence is merely symptomatic of a larger transformation of society. As the citizens lose opportunities for personal initiative in local groups and associations their social nature is starved, which is another way of saying that the morality of character is receding. If genuine virtue is enacted most fundamentally, if not exclusively, in strong and vital intermediate associations, then continual centralization and expansion of government indicates a growing moral vacuum in the people. Official government professions of "justice" and "compassion" cannot hide the loss of the substance of morality.

The modern welfare state is due in large part to the disappearance of an older Western understanding of the nature of individual and social responsibility. Love of neighbor has been more and more replaced by love of mankind. With the redefinition of virtue has come a destruction or transformation of traditional groups and associations which has made it necessary for people to look to government for some semblance of security, charity, and belonging.[17] It is nevertheless misleading to view the welfare state, as it has actually emerged in a country like Sweden, as wholly the creation of modern humanitarian morality. True, that inspiration accounts for the general direction of the evolution of the welfare state, away from local control and diversity to central administration and standardization. But the historically existing welfare state has not been built and operated solely according to the collectivist ethic that has been its main inspiration. In practice it has drawn upon the moral resources of the traditional society it is trying to replace. For example, the various institutions of the welfare state — government social agencies, hospitals, retirement homes, etc. — have been manned by people whose way of dealing with others still, to some extent, reflects the personal and social habits of love of neighbor. The welfare state has been able to put in its employ a character type that it has not itself created and whose disappearance is actually implied in its own ideology. To that extent, the welfare state has been parasitic on an older society and been able to take credit for forms of responsibility that it has no plans for keeping alive. If the welfare state no longer has quite the reputation it did among its advocates, one reason may be that the old moral capital is running out and that the system must operate more and more on its own abstract humanitarianism and in the environment of centralization and bureaucratization that the latter tends to produce.

This analysis of the substantive entailments of ethical ideas has shown that the social atomism of individual rights is only in appearance the opposite of collectivism. If by individualism is meant the liberation of the individual from traditional social ties and responsibilities, it is but another version of the moral and social dynamic that creates the centralized mass society. Social atomism and collectivism are somewhat different forms of the abandonment of the morality of character. John Locke and Jean-Jacques Rousseau are generally representative of these two related tendencies, although in Locke some elements of thought could be cited that mitigate his atomism. Only the concrete social and political entailments of their ethical ideas disclose the full import of those ideas. Similarly, the meaning of the morality of character cannot be understood without considering its embodiment in concrete action and a group-oriented, decentralized society. It should be clear that a modern ethic of either humanitarian sentiment or abstract rationality differs fundamentally from an ethic of character. Obviously, many other particularities than those examined above are relevant to the meaning of moral virtue, but the ones stressed in this analysis appear essential to any satisfactory definition.

The argument presented here has offered support for the ethic of character that is deeply rooted in the classical and Judaeo-Christian heritage. It is not assumed, however, that a particular philosophy of the past adequately addresses all pertinent issues. It has already been suggested that the moral community needs a balancing of the needs of groups and individuals. True ethical universality requires individuality and creativity, qualities that in important respects are better understood by modernity than by earlier periods. There is no necessary connection between the modern discovery of the centrality of personal uniqueness and freedom, on the one hand, and social atomism, on the other. Individuality that recognizes a transcendent moral obligation is a necessary source of the enrichment and deepening of community. To manifest ethical universality, social habits and

135

structures must be continually refreshed and reinvigorated by the creativity of individuals. It is ultimately in this sense that ethical universality is a synthesis of the universal and the particular, the transcendent and the immanent.

NOTES

1. Jean-Jacques Rousseau, *The Social Contract* (Harmondsworth, England: Penguin Books, 1975), bk. I, ch. I, p. 49.

2. For an extensive analysis of Rousseau's ethical and political ideas that substantiates the interpretation here offered, see Claes G. Ryn, *Democracy and the Ethical Life*, second expanded edition (Washington, DC: The Catholic University of America Press, 1990), esp. pp. 92–151.

3. Louis Hartz, *The Liberal Tradition in America* (New York: Harcourt Brace Jovanovich, 1983; first published in 1953), p. 10. So strong does Hartz consider Locke's influence on America that he describes it as a virtual "tyranny."

4. Alexis de Tocqueville, *Democracy in America* (New Rochelle, NY: Arlington House, n.d.), vol. I, p. 177.

5. Rousseau, *Social Contract*, bk. II, ch. 3, p. 73.

6. Robert Nisbet, *The Quest for Community* (New York: Oxford University Press, 1953).

7. Rousseau, *Social Contract*, bk. II, ch. 7, p. 84.

8. Rousseau, *Ibid.*

9. Quoted in Robert Nisbet, *Conservatism* (Minneapolis, MN: University of Minnesota Press, 1986), p. 10.

10. See, in particular, Nisbet, *Quest for Community*.

11. Tocqueville, *Democracy in America*, vol. II, p. 131.

12. Edmund Burke, *Letter to a Member of the National Assembly* in *Selected Writings and Speeches*, Peter Stanlis, ed. (Chicago: Regnery Gateway, 1984), pp. 513–14. In recent years, the appalling nature of Rousseau's personal life has attracted growing attention. A popular treatment of this subject is the chapter on Rousseau in Paul Johnson, *Intellectuals* (New York: Harper and Row, 1988). Johnson's account only hints at the relationship between Rousseau's life and his ideas. The most perceptive study of Rousseau's writing is still Irving Babbitt's pioneering and long-controversial *Rouseau and Romanticism* (Austin, TX: University of Texas Press, 1977; first published in 1919), which has yet to be as widely read as it deserves. In spite of a certain one-sidedness on the subject of romanticism, the book brilliantly and penetratingly analyzes and explicates the ethical and aesthetical ideas of Rousseau and their vast influence. it also explains how Rousseau's life and ideas belong together.

13. Quoted in Bruce Mazlish, *The Revolutionary Ascetic* (New York: Basic Books, 1976), p. 86.

14. Burke, *Selected Writings*, p. 514.

15. See Irving Babbitt, *Democracy and Leadership* (Indianapolis, IN: Liberty Press, 1979), esp. ch. II.

16. The affinity between the individualism of Lockean social contract theory and social democracy is apparent in the work of John Rawls. See his *A Theory of Justice* (Cambridge: Harvard University Press, 1971).

17. The relationship between the emergence of the modern welfare state and the weakening of traditional groups is perceptively analyzed in Nisbet, *Quest for Community*.

Paternalism, Patronage, and Potlatch: The Dynamics of Giving and Being Given To

by Grace E. Goodell

Rooted in M. G. Smith's analysis of corporate categories and groups,[1] this essay explores how being given to affects corporate integrity. The discussion focuses on paternalism, examined from many angles primarily to throw light upon its dynamics and especially the effects of state paternalism on groups within the state's domain. This question is of theoretical interest to anthropologists, first, in deepening our comprehension of the nature and formation of corporate and "loosely structured" groups, especially as constituent units of state-level society; secondly, in raising new issues about the emergence of the state and "economic development"; thirdly, in deepening our understanding of how bureaucratic ministrations and their effects on "beneficiaries" vary cross-culturally; and fourthly, in exploring further the nature of the "gift." It should also be of interest to studies of ethnicity and boundaries. Paternalism is increasingly central to our field research because fewer and fewer of our subjects can any longer be studied apart from the paternalistic "development" thrust of the Third World states that engulf them. Anthropologists frequently play an active role in or at least study ostensibly benevolent "development" projects launched by the state for its people. Yet we bring but a rudimentary theoretical and empirical grasp of the dynamics of giving and "helping" and of their effects on a society's sociopolitical foundations.

A slight modification of Dworkin's definition of paternalism will introduce us to the discussion: Paternalism is interference with others' autonomy justified by reasons referring exclusively to their welfare, good, happiness, needs, interests, or values.[2] One advantage of opening the discussion with this definition is that it focusses attention on the theoretical issue of autonomy. Salient in any discussion of paternalism must be its ideological claim to benevolence. The persuasiveness of this ideology may partly explain why many who study the causes of poverty pay little attention to paternalism. In this essay I frequently refer to the paternalist as "benefactor" (rather than donor), the recipients as "beneficiaries," and what is given them as "benefits." In doing so I do not imply a normative judgment about paternalistic transactions but, rather, attempt to keep in the forefront the crucial ideological claim that is integral to paternalism.[3]

Examples *par excellence* of comprehensive state paternalism affecting anthropologists' subjects are the vast World Bank irrigation systems placed upon the populations of fertile agricultural basins in the Third World, the massive relocation schemes of Iran, Tanzania, Indonesia, and elsewhere for peasants' material benefit (which sometimes in fact results), and the various health and education programs, government cooperatives, and land reform efforts so often imposed by edict from on high. While these programs — as do many acts of paternalism — offer economic benefits in an often dire economic context, they also have political and social consequences.

Research on Paternalism

Studies of the effects of paternalism in various related disciplines and in anthropology have on the whole found the negative consequences of *being helped* as pervasive and profound as those of being "exploited." Philosophers, in the footsteps of John Stuart Mill, continue a lively discussion about the moral implications of paternalism.[4] Many of them are legal scholars whose considerations provoke interesting sociocultural questions and, in turn, might be enriched by anthropological research.[5] In medicine, too, paternalism has become an intensely debated issue, perhaps best known to academics from the controversial works of Szasz.[6] In social welfare and urban studies "a new generation of reformers, drawn to an unprecedented degree from the ranks of lawyers and the dependent groups themselves, are challenging the wisdom and propriety of an ideal of the state as parent."[7] In labor relations and geriatrics the importance of the topic is widely recognized. In social psychology, such provocative research on paternalism is being carried out that I will return to its findings below.

Enlarging our understanding of the political dynamics of being given to, scholars and professionals in the field of human rights (for instance, the New York Civil Liberties Union) have called for radical reconsideration of government programs that impose "benevolent" protections and controls on large classes of people.[8] For some decades now sociologists and political scientists have examined paternalism in the state's social policies.[9] Selznick's early study of the Tennessee Valley Authority remains a classic.[10] Brilliant analyses of paternalism in race relations pervade ven den Berghe's works, among others.[11] Polanyi, Thompson, and many of the younger British social historians have documented the oppressive effects of state paternalism on deviants and the poor.[12] In a fascinating historical study of colonial domination, Crozier contrasts the bureaucratic and paternalistic French rule with the more laissez-faire and locally determined British policies.[13]

Many of these studies cite the recurrent combination of bureaucratic rationality, efficiency, and planning with the ideology of benevolence. They raise challenging questions for anthropologists studying the state and its relationship to its constituent social units. Much of this work would be enriched by anthropologists' interest in placing dyadic relationships within the context of *the whole* society and in cultural variation in the ideology and behavior of bureaucracies and those they act upon. Applied anthropologists could contribute significantly to this literature by using cultural, socio-structural, psychological, and political analyses to discover patterns among the many cases already in wide discussion.

Interestingly, the basic issues these studies of paternalism — especially the more analytical ones — raise over and over again cluster around the same core of concepts and questions with which the existentialists began to wrestle a generation ago.[14]

Anthropologists are in a much better position than other social scientists to appraise the sociopolitical and even economic benefits of paternalism because, by placing ourselves within the recipients' social system, we observe outsiders' initiatives from the inside. We often locate ourselves towards the bottom of the social hierarchy, by definition the most likely target for help. Having no doubt about the maturity of people there, we are less likely than others to underrate their ability to help themselves, to decide for themselves after listening to alternative proposals, and even to gain in the long run from making their own mistakes. Living with them rather than surveying them, we see the pragmatic, enduring value of their initiative and spontaneity and their organizational forms, which must be weighed as seriously as crop yields and bank loans.

Nevertheless, although anthropologists have often placed themselves in the midst of paternalism, their research has been notable for *not* seeing the dynamics identified by other disciplines.[15] For instance, in the extensive anthropological research on plantation systems and company towns one rarely finds paternalism analyzed in any depth.[16] Indeed, not infrequently anthropologists—whether writing as applied anthropologists or not—advocate more paternalistic intervention and bureaucratic guidance at the very time they are lamenting the erosion of local structures or lack of local control.[17] If espousing self-realization on the one hand and demanding more bureaucratic assistance on the other are not incompatible, recommending both simultaneously at least calls for explicit analysis.[18] Anthropologists working on Africa seem to come closest to the issue of paternalism, but few explore its implications. For instance, some endorse Nyerere's ujama program for its ideological claims while documenting its quite opposite effects.[19] Surely it is the task of the anthropologist to see the ideology of benevolence and benefits for what it is and to confront the tradeoffs of paternalism scientifically.[20]

Paternalism's Effects on Corporate Categories and Groups

Despite anthropology's neglect of the issue, the dynamics of paternalism touch upon a central concern of our discipline: corporate groups. If extensive anthropological research and theory attribute social *cohesion* to collective challenge, can we infer that by preempting challenge, paternalism may prevent incorporation? In the work of Darwin, from which anthropology inherits many conceptual models, competition elicits a species's clear-cut identity, fixes its "corporate" boundaries, defines its "exclusive common affairs," and sustains its structural integrity. Marx and of course Simmel find conflict decisive in forming and maintaining structure; Marx was quite aware of the fragmenting effects of security. In Weber, God's unrelenting test concentrates the Protestant's self-discipline.

Beginning with Radcliffe-Brown, British social anthroplogy again and again demonstrates that only higher-order challenge will unite segments in confederation. For Sahlins, "complementary opposition *creates* structure."[21] Severe external pressure evokes corporateness in the Bohannans' work, in Fortune's Dobu, in Chan Kom, in threatened Tikopia, in Geertz's oppressed Java, and among Bateson's alcoholics. For Goffman, the self preserves its identity when it must confront others; for Mary Douglas, danger intensifies the search for corporate purity. Even the anthropological literature on economic development offers examples of challenge eliciting collective initiative and corporate cohesion among peasants — Hill's cocoa farmers, for instance.[22] Applied social scientists have achieved some success in "catalyzing" the organizational transformation of corporate categories into corporate groups by prompting concerted action, specifically through conflict.[23] These examples only suggest, and by no means constitute an exhaustive review of, anthropologists' enduring interest in the effects of challenge on social cohesion.

Does this diverse evidence imply that benign circumstances cause structure to disintegrate? That security may make corporate groups revert to categories? That prolonged abundance may preempt political life, hence corporate organization? To be sure, I am lumping together here in the concept of "challenge" two distinct dynamics — the call to *defensive* conflict and the need (perceived or created) to *fill a vacuum* through initiative. Most — although by no means all — anthropological research about the effects of challenge on structure pertains to the former, while the question at hand, state paternalism, refers more directly to the latter. However, the two may be closely related.

Finally, while we see that social groups can realize a new organizational level by rising to meet a challenge, we must also explain two other observed responses: that some feel no impetus at all to meet it and that it may cause some groups to disintegrate. These differences may often be due to the different types of bureaucracy ministering to them or, more fundamentally, to cultural differences.

This paper does not attempt to answer these questions; rather, it seeks to bring M. G. Smith's analysis of corporate categories and groups to bear upon them in order to shed light on the workings of paternalism. After all, it is often *the way* paternalists "help" and the sociopolitical *effects* of this process on their would-be "beneficiaries" that call for question, rather than anything concrete that they provide.[24] I will base my discussion of the relationship between the paternalist and his "beneficiary" primarily on material presented in Paine's *The White Arctic,* in Selznick's research on the Tennessee Valley Authority, and in van den Berghe's study of Caneville, a South African company town.[25] (Although Caneville does not deal with *state* paternalism, for our purposes here — and for the residents of Caneville as well — the Company virtually substitutes for the state.) Finally, I will draw on my own field research on paternalism in state "development" projects in Iran and the Philippines.

Smith describes a corporate group as an "enduring, presumably perpetual group with determinate boundaries and membership, having an internal organization and a unitary set of external relations, an exclusive body of common affairs, and autonomy and procedures adequate to regulate them."[26] These distinguishing characteristics reflect his emphasis on self-directed, dependable, and possibly long-term transactions with similarly accountable — though possibly quite variegated — entities in a large field. Corporate groups often overlap. Individuals can play one off against another or create new ones. Because of these groups' clearly bounded identities, established procedures, and self-direction, their members as well as outsiders and even strangers can deal with them as reliable, compact units. Such groups are by no means limited to tribal or Western societies.

In contrast to corporate groups, corporate categories lack "exclusive common affairs, autonomy, procedures adequate for their regulation, and the internal organization which constitutes a group" even though they are clearly bounded, identifiable, and permanent as aggregates. Slave groups, serfs, and many minorities are corporate categories,[27] calling to mind Embree's "loosely structured societies"[28] and network theory.

This essay hypothesizes a causal relationship between initiative (that is, behavioral expression of autonomy), which is of central concern to Dworkin, and corporate integrity, of concern to M. G. Smith — a relationship frequently implied in anthropological research but rarely elaborated. The opposite of group initiative, *reactive* common endeavor, generates little integrating power, especially when it is called forth by an external or superior authority.[29] Initiative fosters integrity because it embodies behavioral commitment to the group's *own* definition of itself, whereas action elicited by a superior affirms his control.

Two of the most penetrating studies of state paternalism's erosion of corporate groups, one conducted in rural Senegal and one among blacks in New York City, both attribute corporate cohesion to group initiative, "the difference . . . between 'developing' and 'being developed'."[30] In Smith's terms, this lies partly in the distinction between *determining* policy and carrying it out (or being its object). The former is a political activity, competitive, and hence conducive to incorporation because it requires self-generated internal organization for initiating action; the latter — administration/implementation — is inherently hierarchic, hence neither competitive nor political[31] and certainly not conducive to initiative. The element of competition in the segmentary relationship comprises more than just challenge: it defines one in contrast to similar others, hence tests one's boundaries and autonomy.

That peasants or tribal peoples no longer live in isolated closed corporate communities and instead must become part of Popkin's economically rational world does not mean that they must give up corporate organization[32] (nor does their ability to retain or develop corporate integrity have anything intrinsically to do with the capitalist versus the socialist "mode of production"). Indeed, through the dialectic of "segmentation" the cohesiveness of autonomous groups may structure other groups with which they interact, as well as the overall political order; this is described for Africa, for instance, in Richards and Kuper and especially Jones.[33] An important challenge for applied anthropology is facilitating the conversion (as part of larger social entities) of corporate categories into autonomous corporate groups.[34]

If paternalism's central thrust is to block or destroy the corporate autonomy of its would-be beneficiaries, how does it accomplish this? Turning to the empirical evidence provided by our several ethnographies, we can see how paternalism undermines each of the requisites of the corporate group as Smith has defined it.

First, *determinate boundaries and membership*: In each of our case studies, clearly identifiable and permanent aggregates struggle to find or maintain their distinct identities in the face of paternalism's efforts to erase the boundaries that distinguish them from others. In the

Northwest Territory the Canadian "tutelage" of the Inuit determined to "dismantle" their ethnicity. In Caneville the Company's insistence upon the overarching Caneville "Family" levelled all distinctions between groups. Selznick watched the TVA simply "absorb" the well-articulated state and county extension services into Washington's domain, again by generalizing their functions.[35] This is the essence of colonialism.

Secondly, *exclusive common affairs*: While an aggregate may have determinate boundaries through which society makes it a category, its members have to form themselves into a corporate group by taking into their own hands a project of their own. In Caneville it was impossible for residents to identify any exclusive common purpose because the circulation of information was closely controlled and public opinion was made irrelevant to the shaping of their lives. Both there and in the eastern Arctic, the paternalist provided all the important services that anyone needed, while forbidding controversy. All three ethnographies show the paternalist leaving people only the most trivial exclusive common affairs, making aggregates which crystallized around them trivial themselves. The enervation of organized initiative which results from being subjected to almost any type of *professional* overhaul — professional welfare, medical care, technological "development," etc. — has been extensively documented.[36]

Having but a trivial or fleeting purpose denies a group's *permanence*. Chalmers shows that, under state paternalism in Latin America, organized groups without any opportunity to engage in important policy making are left with only defensive and opportunistic roles and therefore tend to degenerate into factions.[37] Indeed, Hamilton argues in his study of paternalism in New York City that benefits are distributed strictly on an individual basis to prevent the poor from discovering any perduring common interests.[38]

Even when paternalism cannot prevent groups from forming to carry out their own projects, it can destroy their healthy *internal organization and procedure*. Caneville's administrators were quite conscious that by maintaining a constant downward flow of (apparently benevolent) initiatives of high frequency and intensity, they could simply block all channels for lower levels' interaction among themselves.[39] This points out that in understanding paternalism's effects on corporate categories and groups we must examine the latter's horizontal relations, not just the vertical dynamic.

One of paternalism's classic strategies for destroying internal organization is divide-and-rule, again a matter of horizontal interaction between aggregates. All the ethnographies describe this debilitation of middle-range associations between the top and the bottom of society, which leaves the top the only potential source of all benefits.[40] A second paternalistic strategy for destroying a group's internal structure is to coopt its leaders by keeping their leadership intact but shifting their role from that of organizing group initiatives to that of funnelling downward benefits and directives. In colonial Africa chiefs were simply made civil servants. Keenly aware of this device, a delegation of village headmen told one British administrative officer that "they would sooner be allowed to collect one shilling a year from each peasant as personal tribute than be paid a salary equivalent to twice that amount." One village headman explained, "If you pay me to wash my table it will then become your table."[41] These headmen had a clear grasp of the Smithian distinction between administration and policy making.[42]

Finally, *unitary external relations* are of course impossible to maintain if a group's internal organization is eroded. In Caneville, in the New York poverty programs Hamilton studies, and among the Inuit, as in paternalistic World Bank development projects, the paternalistic state cordons its "beneficiaries" off from the rest of society. By thus isolating them it would force them to define themselves vertically as indistinguishable from itself (having no boundary of their own, no separate affairs, etc.); at the same time, by obstructing their horizontal relations it deprives them of the potentially favorable effects of segmentation and competition on corporate cohesion. In Selznick's study,[43] the federal government established itself as the *only* agency through which outsiders could deal with citizens' groups or local organizations and these could interact with one another.[44]

Relevant Studies in Social Psychology

Recent research in social psychology has greatly advanced our understanding of paternalism's effects on the key dimensions of corporate integrity within individuals; reviewing these findings will allow me to summarize the principal concepts and variables of my analysis. I do not, of course, propose any direct correspondence between social and individual (psychological) phenomena, nor do I argue that a social group or category is merely the sum of its constituent individuals' psychological states. Rather, I am suggesting that anthropologists interested in homologous structures and relationships in *systemic* terms will find questions raised by the study of the individual suggestive of hypotheses for the study of larger systems. We share with psychology many theoretical concerns about hierarchy, the nature of interaction, the emergence of structure, boundaries, and autonomy, and the connection between initiative and meaning, though we recognize that, just as psychological attitudes are distinct from social behavior, so psychological structures are distinct from social structures.

Social psychologists have found that "self-induced dependence" results from allowing someone to help one do something one could have done oneself. This leads a person to question his own competence, perform less proficiently the tasks in which he has accepted assistance, and find them more difficult than do subjects who are not helped in doing them.[45] The loss of a sense of one's own boundaries through such dependence can cause severe psychological disturbance.[46]

In her wide-ranging investigation of learned helplessness, Langer has explored conditions which cause one to feel a lack of control and thus lower self-esteem.[47] Salient among these conditions are the deprivation of responsibilities (not being expected to make decisions and never being held accountable) and the absence of choices about what to do, how to do it, or its consequences. The illusion of incompetence or dependence results in poor learning and lack of persistence; one who has learned to feel helpless experiences much greater pain in a stress situation than one subjected to the same stress but thinking he has control over it.[48]

Seligman and others suggest an interesting paraphrase for paternalism in their studies of the effects of "uncontrollable reward" on both humans and animals.[49] In these experiments the subject keeps receiving rewards whatever he does; they just "drop from the sky." Such largesse appears to impair the "beneficiary's" learning skills, dull his competitiveness and sense of self, and undermine his overall ability to respond.

From such research many psychologists conclude that the need for a sense of "mastery" is innate in human nature. Indicatively, this sense of mastery derives (at least among American subjects) from *choice* and *competition*, which draw one into involvement.[50] A sense of mastery is seriously jeopardized when one is treated condescendingly by bureaucratic personnel and experts, when one is helped in something one can do for oneself, and when one receives from others rewards for a performance originally undertaken for its intrinsic meaning.[51] That a sense of mastery develops through testing oneself against others partly explains the disintegrating effects of isolation.

Finally, from research on stress psychologists have found that it serves as an "organizing signal" when it is moderate (in Simmel, it heightens "concentration") but may destroy organization when extreme.[52]

These findings, far too briefly summarized here, echo Smith's analysis of the effects on corporate integrity of challenge and competition, self-asserting action (policy making and not just administration), choice (boundaries), independence (autonomy), and responsibility (affairs exclusively one's own).

The Role of Ideology

Most studies of paternalism credit the paternalist with benevolent rather than Machiavellian intentions.[53] Though many anthropologists would set this question aside, it cannot be denied that the paternalistic state and, certainly, many of its bureaucrats appear genuine to many observers — in paternalism's more limited forms, even to many of its "beneficiaries." Its proclaimed benevolence is all the more plausible when backed up by what many (if not always the "beneficiaries" themselves) consider to be the *real benefits* that it extends.

The more convincing the ideology of concern and help, the more enmeshing the relationship with which it embraces those given to. This is intensified by the ideological ambivalence of some paternalists, who, although it is *they* who usually insist upon helping — and often quite lavishly — all the while claim it is the *beneficiaries' condition* that demands their gifts and constantly warn that their largesse is contingent upon both the beneficiaries' need and their success in helping themselves. Laing attributes the schizophrenia of some of his patients to such "Catch-22" paternalism.[54] Furthermore, as these paternalists may periodically require their "beneficiaries" to prove (or at least advertise) their weakness publicly, over time the "beneficiaries" are likely to internalize their most successful begging acts.[55]

Peasants and many ethnic poor who still live within the moral economy Scott describes are particularly vulnerable to the sense of obligation from receiving help heavily laden with ideology.[56] Thus it is no wonder that the state rarely actually requires them to finance the government services they receive or repay government loans, while now and again severely punishing token delinquents among them. Keeping fresh the tension of unrequited debt—the entire peasantry's unrequited debt—is far more useful to the state than what the poor might in fact repay, especially if in doing so the latter might feel independent. Meanwhile, by publicly dramatizing its largesse the state normalizes its duty to continue providing.[57]

If I may be permitted further reference to psychologists' findings, according to Szasz, all too often "beneficiaries" welcome the paternalist's ideological insistence on their need for help because it places the blame outside themselves.[58] In Smith's terms, members of a corporate category may deny even to themselves that they have or could have "exclusive common affairs" in order to evade the expensive challenge of consolidating and of risking corporate autonomy. Meanwhile, acquiring concrete benefits gives them the illusion of power. When paternalism perpetuates the dependent's weaknesses with his consent, Feinberg calls it "noncoercive exploitation."[59] Considering these complex ramifications and the multilayered relationship that the ideology of helping comprises, the fact that "beneficiaries" accept the paternalist's largesse or even seek it out may make it all the more exploitative and in any case certainly does not ensure that what they receive is benign.

In a provocative historical survey, Rothman analyzes the normative assumptions of bureaucratic paternalism promulgated by its ideology, among them confidence in the greater wisdom of the state in defining the common good, the unquestioned goal of a homogeneous culture and life-style conforming to that envisioned by the paternalists themselves, assurance that the state and its clients will enjoy a nonadversarial relationship in bringing about the common good, trust in the benign workings of the system and in the selflessness of officials, and harshness towards those whom paternalism is unable to reform.[60] As many civil-liberties lawyers argue, the state uses the debilities of those it "helps" to justify negating their political rights. For instance, social workers can inspect the homes of welfare recipients whenever they deem it necessary, and the beneficiaries of government agricultural assistance must waive all farm management decisions.

Paternalism's iron hand is most dramatically illustrated in Polanyi's discussion of England's Poor Laws.[61]

A more intensive investigation of paternalism would lead us to distinguish between varying types of bureaucracies and ideologies. How do the "welfare" bureaucracies of Sweden, Harlem, and Tanzania differ? Does "paternalism" that people vote to give themselves (as it were) in a welfare state but that is nevertheless administered by bureaucrats and technocrats have less enervating effects on recipients than the paternalism of an authoritarian government? Furthermore, a particular paternalistic interaction must be located within the society at large. How does the state's paternalism towards merchants, manufacturers, or middle-class consumers compare with its paternalism towards peasants?

Perhaps the paternalistic state's most forceful ideological tool is law, best illustrated in one of the most extreme forms of state paternalism, the Soviet Union. Claiming to embody "a new conception of the role of law," Soviet law exalts the parental duty of the state to protect individuals from themselves, to discipline them, to remake their consciences fundamentally.[62] The most notable Western experiment in paternalistic transformation was launched by Robert Owen, who believed his ideal environment could succeed in refining his workers only if they relinquished all responsibility for their own characters.[63] In the paternalist systems Solzhenitsyn and Kafka describe, Jesuit rule in Paraguay, Caneville, Selznick's TVA, and the French colonial system Diamond analyzes,[64] the bureaucratic Plan's iron rationality and its craving for order are swathed in ideological benevolence and dependence.

Paternalism Contrasted with Patronage

Although anthropology has shown less interest than related disciplines in paternalism, it has developed a rich literature about patron-client relations. The terms "patronage" and "paternalism" are frequently interchanged, but patronage implies a relationship between adults and paternalism (according to the *Oxford English Dictionary*) parental tutelage over a child. The difference between treating another adult as a social inferior and treating him as a child is a profound one rooted in an appraisal of his maturity and ability to help himself, in short, his autonomy. Although for heuristic purposes I attempt to separate the two concepts, they should be considered ideal types at opposite ends of a continuum along which are transitional situations that cannot be elaborated here.[65]

The most fundamental distinction between paternalism and patronage lies in the *reciprocity* that underpins patron-client relations. The patron has needs which he relies on the client to fulfill, and when necessary the client can *initiate* services to his patron, obligating the latter to respond. This gives the client political leverage.[66] Quite in contrast, the paternalistic state has little need for a power base among its rural or indigent "beneficiaries." The very nature of what it grants emphasizes the state's vast power and the recipients' superfluousness, and therefore there is no way in which the latter can relieve themselves of their debt.

A second difference between patronage and paternalism relates to *accountability*. Since patronage rests on mutually binding obligations, the patron and client can hold one another accountable. Usually clients have discrete and objective criteria for their patron's legitimacy, hence for continuing the relationship, criteria defined by the client's own traditional values and lying entirely within their scope to measure.[67] In its paternalistic relations the modern state is far too distant ever to be measured by its "beneficiaries," and in any event it frequently confers benefits from a world entirely beyond their reference.[68]

Thirdly, *scale and distance* differentiate patronage and paternalism. In traditional patron-client relationships, the patron is accessible to his client; the latter plays off patrons, shops around for new ones, if need be, goes over one patron's head to *his* patron, or acquires more leverage by becoming a patron to others himself. The exchanges between patrons and clients are scaled to each partner's expectations and expendable capacity.[69] In contrast, the state characteristically extends its benevolence through all-encompassing programs which overwhelm individuals by its power, reducing them to "the masses."[70] Whereas traditional "clients can easily distinguish between real protection and extortion,"[71] it is extremely difficult for "beneficiaries" of paternalism to detect that the state may be exploiting their weakness because they have no grasp of its proportions.

Fourth, integral to the personalism of patron-client relations is their *continuity*, which tests reliability.[72] In contrast, the paternalism of the state, at least from the "beneficiaries'" point of view, is often arbitrary, sporadic, and temporary in its palpable benefits (if not in the dependence it creates).[73] State welfare programs come and go in response to forces no one can understand; many of them are explicitly mobile to maximize the elites' political gain. Because these programs are granted and withdrawn at the discretion of the state, when they are neither designed in response to local request nor subject to sustainable local pressures, they preclude any continuity that the local "beneficiaries" themselves might be able to affect. Hamilton has dramatically shown how the recipients of welfare in Manhattan diffuse their organizational energies in as many political arenas as possible for money and programs which, once spent, leave them powerless again. Though they gain their rewards, they remain peripheral to society's institutions of power.[74] Because paternalism fragments its "beneficiaries," violent outbursts following long periods of passiveness are their only means of political expression, and these only fragment them further.[75] In the politics of patronage (ward politics, for instance, or the vote gathering of Latin American and Filipino patrons), on the other hand, participation is methodically organized, ongoing, systematic, and cumulative.

A fifth criterion of patronage is its relationship to *the community*. Community patrons reaffirm local autonomy against the state's anonymity.[76] In contrast, instead of uniting individuals for outward initiative, state paternalism pits them one against the other for downward distributions.[77] Scott has shown us that the patron stands *with* his clients vis-à-vis the outside; sometimes the processes flows downward as well, but once this becomes his main job he has shifted his stance, now essentially being set off against them.[78] Gellner points to the fraternal quality of patronage, which "always belongs to some *pays reel* which is ambivalently conscious of not being the *pays legal*."[79] As we have seen, state paternalism is the *pays legal* with a vengeance.

While I have differentiated patronage from paternalism in terms of Smith's seminal distinction between policy making and administration, neither relationship is highly conducive to the crystallization of corporate groups out of categories. Though clients may participate in policy making, they are bound to the patron as separate individuals. There are always more clients than patrons, and the patterning of their interaction concentrates the multiple and diverse clients in singular patrons. Nevertheless, patronage may encourage the political initiatives of clients (indeed, the patron may request collective effort on their part), and when these initiatives share a focus, clients may come to recognize their common affairs, evolve internal organization and procedures, and coordinate these on their own, developing into a solid, long-standing grouping. We see this development among minor officials on many feudal manors both in Europe and in Japan.[80]

In the field of industrial management and labor unions, patronage and paternalism frequently overlap. McLaurin's history of the organization of early industrial workers in the southern United States is a classic study of how the moral economy of traditional life delayed the emergence of unions until drastic declines in wages provoked consolidation.[81] Unions' organizational impetus is typically defensive, and they tend to collapse when the grievance is removed.[82]

Japanese management has sparked the most lively interest in the effects of paternalism on workers' organization. Japanese workers are hardly even a corporate category, much less a nascent corporate group, their factory culture effectively combining the moral and even policy-making collaboration of a patron-client tie with the totalistic benefit package and sharp *vertical* incorporation of state paternalism.[83] However, without comparative or processual data showing the existence (or emergence) of workers' corporate organization, we cannot disaggregate personalism, welfare benefits, and other Japanese management strategies from their much larger cultural and historical context. Some leading scholars find the Japanese system in transition, and if so, we may be able to separate out certain variables in time.[84]

The distinction between patronage and paternalism is difficult to maintain in these and many other cases in which loyalty, obedience, even specific actions are expected of the "client" *in return for* the benefits he receives, suggesting a relationship closer to patronage in that respect. On the other hand, they are paternalistic because by extending help in the form of *material benefits* that are *irremediably disproportionate* the "benefactor" can exploit the great discrepancy between what he gives and what his "beneficiaries" could provide for themselves. This disproportion, which is exacerbated by establishing the helper's *professionalism*, guarantees that the "beneficiary" cannot get back, answer back, question, help himself, play benefactors off against each other, reciprocate, or repay, in short, regain his autonomy.

Why is it that, while the concept of patronage has engaged many leading anthropologists, the discipline has virtually ignored paternalism? If Weingrod is correct that anthropologists usually assume the clients' (or "beneficiaries" ') perspective,[85] then as long as the benefits keep flowing anthropologists may want to have no part in questioning them. Living so close to the "beneficiaries" may make it easier to confuse the economic context and "benefits" of state paternalism with *social cohesion*.

Iranian and Filipino State Paternalism Compared

My own findings in two extended field studies of state paternalism are consistent with these conclusions. The World Bank's Dez irrigation scheme in Khuzestan Province, southwestern Iran, the agricultural showcase of the shah's "White Revolution,"[86] and the Upper Pampanga River Integrated Irrigation System (UPRIIS) irrigation project in central Luzon, the Philippines, the Green Revolution ricebowl for Marcos's "New Society," were both vast (80,000–100,000 hectares), expensive, and ponderously enlightened by technocracy. Both sought quite explicitly to uplift the "backward" peasantry by providing tens of thousands of peasant farmers with year-round irrigation and in many other ways distributing subsidized welfare benefits to them. Not coincidentally, in each scheme the state at least partially implemented land reform prior to launching its transformational efforts. In both cases, the state's paternalism had political and not just social purposes. Khuzestan is Iran's oil province, dangerously situated adjacent to Iraq and containing a large Arab population. Central Luzon witnessed a vigorous communist organization effort in the 1960s, and the UPRIIS irrigation scheme, backed up by the Green Revolution and the New Society, turned these peasants into allies.

In the shah's irrigation scheme in Khuzestan, although the peasants had received title to the land in the mid '60s, those farming within the project area were moved into model towns (*shahraks*), where they became wage laborers for foreign agribusinesses or "shareholder" workers on state farms. There they were given brick homes with toilets and electricity, which contrasted with the mud huts they had built for themselves in their villages. By 1978 many other such model towns, patterned on the Dez project, had been completed.

Prior to the project, each Khuzestani village had governed itself as a miniature city-state managing its own internal affairs — zoning, immigration, administration of its school and mosque, ecological regulations, etc. — and determining its own foreign policy. Such corporate integrity offered Iranian society a potential base for stable, structured development. When they moved into the shahraks, peasants found modern state schools, "expert" government provision of all public needs, and employment bureaus connected to each of the agricultural enterprises in which all adult males, now wage laborers, were guaranteed a job (albeit low-paid and often meaningless). The state preempted all civic life and private entrepreneurial challenges. Bureaucrats administering the shahrak came there daily, in part to prevent new townsmen from taking any part whatsoever in the shahrak's affairs—for instance, to obstruct such initiatives of the workers as monitoring teachers' classroom attendance, regulating the scarce bakers' services equitably, curbing reckless driving, building their own mosques, etc.

Similar to the Dez scheme, the UPRIIS irrigation project in central Luzon "served" a rural population of approximately 30,000 families. While after land reform many peasants kept control over the means of production, the New Society's paternalism was as penetrating as the White Revolution: it substituted state programs for the services of the landlords, middleman retailers, and moneylenders and aimed to replace the traditional rice traders with state purchasing centers. Through programs planned and monitored from Manila, it upgraded schools, roads, even some health services. UPRIIS villages show many signs of prosperity: more brick houses, iron roofs, schools, television sets, etc. But the Filipino state's benevolence left as little room as did the new model towns for the initiatives of individuals or peasant groups. Although farmers in central Luzon were highly literate and relatively mobile and for decades had participated in local, regional, and national politics, the New Society kept from them any matters of import; all of these belonged to the state.

While neither Filipino villages nor even Filipino families were traditionally corporate, the country's rural areas had long enjoyed a vigorous political life under entrepreneurial local leaders. Given Filipino society's open culture and its continuous commitment to democratic governance during the past half-century, the transformation of these corporate categories (often along interest-group or sectarian lines) into corporate groups was one of its greatest needs, especially for village and provincial political development.

Thus, on the surface, the two paternalisms strikingly resembled those I have examined in the ethnographies. While raising the peasant's standard of living they confirmed the deleterious sociopolitical effects of state benevolence I have reviewed; in Iran by dismantling ancient and very strong corporate groups, in the Philippines by systematically preventing lively local-level corporate categories from shaping themselves into corporate groups. In both cases paternalism blocked self-generated collective action by making local leaders its administrators and through them dividing and ruling the population through welfare benefits. Police power was latent in each society, but far more effective was the ability of the development ideology to define any group's common affairs as the state's. It is striking how attentively paternalism often responds to small-scale needs in order to nip in the bud the very incentives which lie within the conceivable reach of peasants' initiatives. In short, in both projects state benevolence atomized the rural social forms they were meant to uplift.

But beneath these similarities, the White Revolution and the New Society differed. In the Khuzestan project the paternalism of the Iranian state—ideologically far less technocratic but in action more Draconian than Filipino paternalism—left at least the ultimate units of the peasants' social fabric intact. Though they acquiesced passively in the state's ministrations and though they were far closer to the margin of survival than the Filipinos, I never saw the Khuzestanis supplicate. Before the bureaucrats, they retained their dignity. In contrast, Filipino farms not infrequently turned beggar to the state. However illiterate and politically unsophisticated, the Khuzestanis had a simple, clear map of their political universe: as in a fairy tale, the king counted his money on his throne; a wall of deceitful advisors surrounded him; a labyrinth of rotten bureaucracies filled the void between them and the new model town. The king was, after all, king. He never pretended to seek anyone's ratification. His benevolence was transparent, even on television. Ya Allah!

State paternalism in the Philippines provided no such clear-cut boundaries. While in contrast to the White Revolution it left the means of production in the farmers' hands and the primary social units physically intact, and while it offered the hope of upward mobility for many peasants, this only heightened its attendant social confusion. Many villages ceased organizing their annual patron-saint fiestas, a Durkheimian indication of their corporate disintegration. Opportunism, suspicion, and revenge divided not just the bare social forms but individuals one against the other. The New Society coopted a large majority of the UPRIIS village leaders, many former communist war-horses serving as presidents of the state cooperatives or as captains of Imelda Marcos's village brigades. In Iran's model town, village leaders were also pressed into the state's service; in public gatherings they sullenly stood beside the bureaucrats but never in place of them.

This contrast brings us to "emic" consequences—particularly the intricacies of "beneficiaries' " consciousness—that are certainly the most difficult issues paternalism raises. Do recipients long for self-direction, and if so do they seem passive only because of paternalism's latent force? Or can the paternalist in fact make them content? Or both? Surely cultures vary in this respect, as do the different types of bureaucracies they call forth, different generations, groups at different places in the overall society, and individuals and groups over time. If paternalism lulls "beneficiaries" accustomed to autonomy, what are the circumstances and processes through which this takes place? How do groups become conscious of their dependence and revert to corporate categories? The most heated controversy about paternalism in the social sciences focuses on Genovese's conclusion that the paternalism of slaveowners in the American South *did* buy the slaves' allegiance, or at least made them complacent.[87] For arguing this he has been accused of elitism. Can a recipient of paternalistic "benefits" ever be fooled? Adams gives us a provocative description of villagers' collective opposition to the paternalism of the Senegal River Valley development scheme, based on their concern for their political integrity and not just for their economic security.[88] The complex range of "awareness" and affective bonding in paternalistic relations needs much more extensive analysis, with the help of psychological anthropologists.

Variations in the Model

With the comparison between Iranian and Filipino paternalism, we begin to move from the fundamental dynamics of paternalism to an investigation of some of its main cultural variations—in proportions (especially scale, pace, and degree of sophistication), authority, transparency, penetration, and ideology.

The proportions of New Society paternalism in central Luzon placed undertakings that had formerly been well within the peasants' technical, economic, and organizational scope beyond the reach of local initiatives. The state's response to many barely articulated interests or needs with total provisioning suffocated local action. For example, when a group of village women decided to form their own tailoring class and find a teacher, in one fell swoop the New Society offered them a free teacher with a preplanned tailoring course and all necessary supplies, down to the last free tape measure, depriving them of innumerable organizational challenges. In contrast, the absence of virtually any government agencies at all in the countryside after the Bolivian land reform challenged the peasants there to take their needs in hand themselves. As a result, today the Bolivian countryside bustles with the Indians' own local, regionwide, and national organizations.[89] The vacuum the peasants faced (25 years ago) was decisive, but so was the fact they could strengthen their corporate forms gradually.

The authority with which the Iranian and Filipino projects eroded local structures varied considerably. In the Dez scheme Pahlavi paternalism expropriated virtually 100% of the landlord estates; later one, with the same unflinching thoroughness, it took away all the land it had given the peasants. Its operations and munificence were palpable. The authoritarian character of Filipino paternalism evolved incrementally, offering commercial as well as political enticements and selectively applying land reform. Villagers who received land it left with their new holdings intact but then enmeshed in debts, obligations, admonitions, and gifts from the state. In Manila, Marcos was careful constantly to readjust his official or legal legitimacy, obscuring the fact that the *pater* was firmly in charge. This more subtle paternal authority may conceivably have undermined social forms at a deeper level than the shah's self-serving directness. That Marcos and his wife emphasized their common roots among the people created in many lower-class Filipinos a deep-seated ambivalence that precluded incorporation.

At the local level in the two projects, however, the relationship between "benefactor" and "beneficiaries" was just the reverse. The shah's bureaucrats were omnipresent; they attended to individual needs and knew not just the leaders but many new townsmen by name. This enabled their "beneficiaries," who had long ago objectified their relationship to the state, to size them up through direct experience and to sort out for themselves what one could expect concretely.[90] In contrast, the managers of the smooth and "familial" New Society had to be sought out in urban offices (greatly discouraging *groups* from presenting themselves), where they demanded from the peasants much more sophisticated begging acts—with strangers as witness. Though technocratically more accomplished, they were far less predictable, in short, more destructive of group resolve.

Finally, unlike the shah's development ideology, the ideology of Filipino paternalism even convinced the state's *opponents* of its benefits. They only complained that there should be *more*. Filipino peasants were offered a new *society*, in contrast to the shah's new Persian empire; helicopter factories symbolized the achievements of the shah's paternalism, rice harvests that of Marcos.

Probably the principal factor determining the variation in the structural consequences of paternalism—fundamentally a *cultural* one—is the "beneficiaries' " corporate strength prior to receiving the state's munificence. Whereas the granite matrix of Khuzestan's virtually autonomous villages enabled them to retain a rudimentary integrity (hence cynicism), central Luzon's very loosely structured social organization made society more receptive to paternalism's inducements at every level. The point needs to be carried farther: Although this discussion has emphasized the corrosive effects of paternalism, we must recognize and examine evidence of the opposite dynamic. Many of the instances anthropologists have documented in which external assistance has enabled groups to *strengthen* their corporate cohesion can be attributed to their prior organizational capacities. For example, central Ibo towns and villages, staunchly corporate in Smith's terms, took advantage of extensive paternalistic help to confirm their local councils' autonomy, successfully resisting government attempts to coopt them.[91]

"Economic Development" or Revolution?

Although I have shed some light on the ways in which being given to affects corporate categories and groups, considering the complexity of state paternalism and the pioneering stage of our inquiry into it no conclusions can yet be drawn about its role in sustained economic development or in the unfolding of revolution. (Indeed, inasmuch as only the *rural* population was subject to the shah's paternalism in my study, the discussion throws little direct light on the subsequent upheaval in Iran.) Disagreeing with Gunnar Myrdal or Goron Hyden, many anthropologists find the erosion of corporate groups detrimental to balanced and sustainable "development," but little has been done to elucidate this relationship. Nevertheless, since state-imposed "development" today almost always takes a paternalistic form and justifies doing so by its promises of social welfare, the possibility of its inherent contradiction challenges anthropological theory and its application.

In summary, the field studies of Iranian and Filipino paternalism bear out my analysis of the basic dynamics of state paternalism and its predation on corporate categories and groups. But this—as well as other research—suggests a diversity of paternalistic styles clearly associated with cultural differences and bureaucratic structures and styles, perhaps even specific to particular sectors of a given society. (For instance, Japanese universities have not succeeded in treating students paternalistically as industry does workers.) This indicates the wide range of important theoretical questions that paternalism raises, in addition to the critical applied challenge: how corporate categories and groups can be given help without jeopardizing—and, indeed, while strengthening—their cohesion and autonomy.

Potlatch and Paternalism

We must return, finally, to paternalism's hallmark, its ideology. Because of the pragmatic nature of patronage, that form of giving has not prompted anthropological theorists to probe the ideology of generosity; therefore we must look elsewhere, since paternalism cannot be understood without analyzing its central and distinguishing charactristic, its ideological intensity. This ideological intensity reminds us of the ostentatious boasting which envelops the "gift" in the potlatch. Without proposing a systematic comparison of these two modes of giving, I will juxtapose them briefly. In both, the "benefactor's" ideology aims at domination (which is far less extreme and hence less prominent in patronage). Like paternalism, potlatch combines the giving of material goods, often on a vast scale, with self-proclaimed generosity confirmed in the exhibitionism of public ritual.

Paternalism is a redistributive mechanism, as probably was the potlatch. In both cases, the goods are sometimes useless; indeed, goods may be sacrificed publicly without transferring them to anyone at all. Nothing more clearly demonstrates the *social* nature of surplus than paternalism, in which scarcity, value, and hence what is "beneficial" are defined *by the "benefactor."* Indeed, quite frequently he must force his "beneficiaries" to accept the gifts amassed for them

159

(which apparently never happened in potlatch). The fact that potlatch hinges on common values enables it to bind giver and receiver, who cosponsor the giving as patron and client do in patronage. Conversely, the fact that the value of what the paternalist's "beneficiary" receives is often imposed points to the depth of paternalism's interference with the latter's autonomy.[92] Paternalism is *the giver's* project alone. (Nevertheless, as Szasz has shown—at least among *individuals*—it often converts its recipients, who come to define themselves as "beneficiaries.")

Despite this contrast, for political ends both potlatch and paternalism capitalize on the symbolic content of giving. If the very act of receiving engages the "beneficiary," doing so on a large scale may enslave him. According to Lévi-Strauss, by being more generous than the receiver the giver aims to "crush him . . . with future obligations which it is hoped he cannot meet, so as to take from him his prerogatives, titles, rank, authority and prestige." But in potlatch the victor can achieve this aim only by giving *through a contest*; both parties look to a "counter-potlatch" with the tables possibly turned.[93] Lévi-Strauss compares this to the tension between two Frenchmen, strangers deciding to share their wine. Their exchange entails a risk for the one who gives first[94] because that leaves in the other's power the assessment of his move and the measure of future exchange. For this reason, we have already seen that the paternalist finds many ways to make the giver-receiver relationship *non*reciprocal. The most effective of these ways is his ideology of altruism. Altruism *requires* that nothing be returned.

The risk for the paternalist is that in approaching his "beneficiaries" he may—as in the potlatch—arouse mechanisms of segmentation among them (for instance, if they perceive a need for self-defense), thereby strengthening their cohesion and autonomy. His camouflage of charity catches those he is giving to—and indeed, others looking on—off guard. Then, when the same ideology engages the "beneficiaries" in the distribution of his benefits, he has succeeded in shifting them from corporate groups to corporate categories that carry out his designs.

Lest the insistence on his benevolence and their need still leave some "beneficiaries" wary or with a sense of repayble debt, their urge to reciprocate is put to rest by the confirmation of their superfluousness. The ideological emphasis state paternalism places today on those values that stress extremes of power and dependence — subhuman poverty versus expert knowledge and difficult, expensive technology — and on the inexorable drive to development dramatizes the "beneficiaries' " helplessness and endows the state with infallibility: it is merely the bringer of what is correct and, moreover, inevitable. How can one who is *the subject of history* reciprocate? The fact that those who lose a potlatch can weave the same kind of blankets given them keeps their door open for a comeback.

Thus, in the potlatch, the victor's boasts attempt to overwhelm just as the paternalist attempts to overwhelm. But because the former is *locked into the reciprocal terms of contest*, potlatch's ideology of giving becomes an explicit public challenge, precisely what the paternalist must avoid. Were we to follow the implications of this in terms of Smith's notion of competition, we would hypothesize that in the "classic" potlatch this public braggadocio might have been a key survival mechanism for the system as a whole: not just feeding the weak temporarily (which can be done without boasting) but then spurring them, as publicly proclaimed losers, to strengthen or renew their organizational integrity — to "get their act together." If, in potlatching societies, successful ecological management requires the decentralized responsibility of separate, self-reliant groups, then it may be adaptive for everyone that the strong, while helping the weak, discourage them from becoming dependent and challenge them to recover their autonomy. In these cultures public humiliation may ensure that the benefits of redistribution not be gained at the cost of the equally necessary benefits of segmentation (that is, at the cost of free-riders, who pose a major problem for all redistribution systems).

Paternalism inspires no loyalty in its "beneficiary," who not only has no stake in the transaction but, worse, has been used — often willingly — to collaborate in his own social negation. If Mauss is correct that a gift received has to be repaid and that assurances to the contrary amount to social deception, and if Lévi-Strauss is correct that the essential nature of society rests on the recipients' repaying what they have received, does the explanation lie partly in the threat to the autonomy of those who are given to? Can one-way help be given without jeopardizing the "beneficiaries' " integrity, without denying any social bond between them and the giver? If so, how? Does paternalism's extraordinary ideology burst forth out of its denial of reciprocity's "universal" social law?

Grace E. Goodell

The ideologies of potlatch and paternalism both utilize this "universal law," that *a gift has to be repaid*. Potlatch, binding the gift within its own fixed structural terms of segmentation, uses the law to reinforce the organizational integrity of the weak, those given to. In contrast, the ideology of paternalism would use the same "universal law" of reciprocity to destroy the cohesion of those who accept the gift.

NOTES

I wish to thank the Scaife Family Charitable Trust for the support that made this study possible. I am also very grateful to Edward Banfield, Thomas Dewar, Joel Feinberg, Ricardo Godoy, John Kleinig, Abraham Rossman, Michael Smith, and Pierre van den Berghe for their assistance on earlier drafts; and to Ellen Langer, whose research and teaching I have found very stimulating.

1. M. G. Smith, "A Structural Approach to Comparative Politics," *Varieties of Political Theory*, ed. by David Easton (Englewood Cliffs, NJ: Prentice-Hall, 1966), pp. 116–23.

2. G. Dworkin, "Paternalism," *The Monist* 56 (1972), 65. See also Donald Van De Veer, "Autonomy-Respecting Paternalism," *Social Theory and Practice* 6 (1980), 187–207. Dworkin's term "justified" is ambiguous. Does he mean that the paternalist *proves* that his interference is just through his explanation or simply that he *proclaims* it to be so? If the former, is it proof in his own eyes or absolutely? Because the objective justifiability of such an inference will often depend on the relative importance of technical considerations such as those reviewed here (and in any case it may be a long time before the consequences are apparent), the paternalist may frequently be unable to *prove* justification; he (and we) are left with a subjective evaluation of his *intentions*. Are they blameless? This is even more difficult to establish, however, since Freud has shown that we may even explain our behavior to *ourselves* (all the more so to others) in terms of motives quite contrary to our real ones. While it is important to recognize that paternalists can act out of genuinely benevolent intentions, and while we cannot assume that the consequences of their actions are integral to their intentions, the debilitating effects of paternalism over time can often be observed empirically. Why couldn't the well-intentioned paternalist see these? Similar difficulties arise when the paternalist "justifies" his action in terms of the overall interests of the social whole. While John Kleinig (personal communication) distinguishes between paternalism, professed paternalism, and patriarchalism, he offers social scientists no way of determining which applies in any given case.

In short, because it is virtually impossible to establish either objective or subjective "justification," in this essay I take Dworkin's term "justified" to refer to the fact that the actor says these are the grounds for his action, regardless of whether they are acceptable in any absolute sense. This does not mean that the paternalist is a hypocrite; he may genuinely intend to do good. It only means that, though philosophers and jurists may have to resolve the question of the paternalist's intention, I see no way at the present for *social scientists* to do so *empirically*. Perhaps this essay will bring forth questions.

3. Several justifications of paternalism advanced by philosophers (whether reasonable or not) are relevant to anthropologists, but space allows only their mention here. The first (which one often hears anthropologists themselves use in defending paternalistic "development" projects) focusses on the consent of the

"beneficiaries." A second is the *general* good which may be gained, beyond the welfare of the recipients themselves, a third the necessity to protect people against themselves (the "tragedy of the commons," for instance), and a fourth the responsibility to prevent them from missing benefits one is sure they will later wish they had. Each of these justifications comprises a tradeoff between short-run, often material gains and long-term, perhaps sociopolitical or cultural costs — an appraisal all too often left to those without a grasp of fundamental dangers to the underlying social organization.

This is not, of course, to suggest that an informed consideration would necessarily condemn paternalistic measures in specific cases, though it might modify the way they are carried out. Anthropologists have recorded instances in which paternalistic colonial "assistance" has in fact strengthened local, indigenous social structures. In any event, the moral considerations of paternalism are linked to the scientific evidence of its consequences. As John Kleinig points out (personal communication), justifying paternalism as it relates to groups is particularly difficult in cases in which individuals want what is "imposed" on them but cannot negotiate or launch it by their own efforts and therefore depend on the mechanisms of government to do so. To the extent that such government measures represent the fruits of their initiative and thus could be reversed or changed by their collaborative will, these measures are of course an expression of their autonomy and not a threat to it. This is often put to the test when such measures must be defended against countervailing policies or when the benefits extended must be maintained by local resources. The criterion, then, as Dworkin's definition suggests, is whether being given to leaves "beneficiaries" who have a particular common purpose able to *act* on their own, which in state-level societies often requires forming corporate groups.

4. See Mill, *On Liberty* [1859] (New York: Dutton, 1959), pp. 85–234; and R. Nozick, *Anarchy, State, and Utopia* (Oxford: Blackwell, 1975).

5. An entire field of Anglo-American, Canadian, and Australian law springs from these issues, especially as government regulations are said to impinge upon individual freedom of choice. See S. I. Benn, "Benevolent Interference and Respect for Person," *Bulletin of the Austrian Society of Legal Philosophy* 21 (December 1981), 99–112; Dworkin, *op. cit.*; Joel Feinberg, *Rights, Justice, and the Bounds of Liberty* (Princeton, NJ: Princeton University Press, 1980); H. L. A. Hart, *Law, Liberty, and Morality* (Stanford, CA: Stanford University Press, 1963); J. Kleinig, "Paternalism and Freedom" (MS, Australian National University, 1981); Kleinig, *Paternalism* (Totowa, NJ: Rowman and Allenheld, 1985); and Rolf Sartorius, ed., *Paternalism* (Minneapolis, MN: University of Minnesota Press, 1984).

6. Thomas Szasz, *The Myth of Mental Illness* (New York: Harper and Row, 1961). Also, these issues are summarized and many illustrations cited in T. Beauchamp, "Paternalism," in *Encyclopedia of Bioethics* (New York: Macmillan, 1978). A core legal case is reviewed in L. Guttmacher and M. Weihofen, "Mental Incompetency," *Minnesota Law Review* 36 (1952), 179–212.

7. D. Rothman, "The State as Parent," in *Doing Good*, by Willard Gaylin, *et al.* (New York: Pantheon, 1978). See also A. Davis, *Spearheads for Reform* (London: Oxford University Press, 1967); T. Dewar, "Barriers to Self-Development" (Working paper for American Enterprise Institute Public Policy Week, Washington, DC, 1981); Frances Piven and Richard Cloward, *Regulating the Poor* (New York: Pantheon, 1971); and R. Lubove, *The Professional Altruist* (Cambridge, MA: Harvard University Press, 1965).

8. See Ira Glasser, "Prisoners of Benevolence: Power Versus Liberty in the

Welfare State," in *Doing Good*, by Willard Gaylin, *et al.* (New York: Pantheon, 1978), pp. 97–170; and N. Rescher, *Welfare: The Social Issues in Philosophical Perspective* (Pittsburgh, PA: University of Pittsburgh Press, 1972).

9. For example, Piven and Cloward, *op. cit.*; and A. Weale, "Paternalism and Social Policy," *Journal of Social Policy* 7 (1978), 157–72.

10. R. Selznick, *TVA and the Grassroots* (New York: Harper Torchbooks, 1966).

11. Pierre van den Berghe, "Dynamics of Racial Prejudice," *Social Forces* 37 (1958), 138. See also his *Caneville: Social Structure of a South African Town* (Middletown, CT: Wesleyan University Press, 1964); "Paternalistic versus Competitive Race Relations," in *Racial and Ethnic Relations*, ed. Bernard Segal (New York: Crowell, 1966); and *Race and Racism* (New York: Wiley, 1967). B. Beidelman, in "A Comparative Analysis of the Jajmani System," in *Monograph of the Association of Asia Studies* 7 (Locust Valley, NY: J. J. Augustin, 1959) and others point out the paternalism in the Indian caste system but hardly subject it to theoretical analysis.

12. K. Polanyi, *The Great Transformation* (Boston, MA: Beacon Press, 1957); and E. P. Thompson, "Patrician Society, Plebeian Culture," *Journal of Social History* 7 (1974), 382–405. See also A. K. Beier, "Vagrants and the Social Order in Elizabethan England," *Past and Present* 64 (1972), 3–29. For other interesting and related studies see M. Davenport, "The Moral Paternalism of Albert Schweitzer," *Ethics* 84 (1974), 116–27; and L. M. de Bellaing, "Structure paternaliste et conceptions de l'autorité," *Cahiers Internationaux de Sociologie* 41 (1966), 63–81.

13. B. Crozier, *The Bureaucratic Phenomenon* (Chicago: University of Chicago Press, 1964), pp. 159, 265–68.

14. This cluster comprises at least four central issues: (1) *freedom*, self-actualization through commitments to one's project rather than being made another person's object, (2) autonomy contingent upon the courage for *positive action*, (3) hence, the imperative of *choice* and rejection of determinism, and (4) *responsibility* as the keystone of integrity (see K. Jaspers, *Philosophy*, trans. by E. B. Ashton (Chicago: University of Chicago Press, 1969); J. P. Sartre, *Being and Nothingness*, trans. by E. Barnes (New York: Philosophical Library, 1956); G. Marcel, *Man Against Mass Society*, trans. by G. S. Fraser (Chicago: Regnery, 1962); and others.

15. Aside from E. Wolf, who after all had a lively interest in corporate cohesion, one would have expected paternalism at least to appear in a volume like D. Browman and R. Schwartz's *Peasants, Primitives, and Proletariats: The Struggle for Identity in South America* (The Hague: Mouton, 1979); or in A. Gouldner's discussion of exploitation, "The Norm of Reciprocity," in *Friends, Followers, and Factions*, ed. Steffan Schmidt *et al.* (Berkeley, CA: University of California Press, 1977), p. 28.

16. See for example E. Norbeck, *Pineapple Town* (Berkeley, CA: University of California Press, 1959); J. Steward *et al. People of Puerto Rico* (Urbana, IL: University of Illinois Press, 1956); and E. Wolf, "Specific Aspects of Plantation Systems in the New World: Community Subcultures and Social Classes," in *Peoples and Cultures of the Caribbean*, ed. Michael Horowitz (Garden City, NY: Natural History Press). A number of other company-town studies by urban planners and analysts of model towns describe paternalism without social analysis; for example: J. Reps, *The Making of Urban American* (Princeton, NJ: Princeton University Press, 1965); A. Alanen and T. J. Peltin, "Kohler, Wisconsin: Planning and Paternalism in a Model Industrial Village," *American Institute of Planners Journal* 94 (1978), 145–59; and M. I. de Queiroz, "L'évolution de la structure sociale dans l'agriculture brésilienne, *Sociologia ruralis* 9 (1971), 277–300, the last-named essay discussing the paternalism of traditional estates. A notable exception is van den Berghe (1964), *op. cit.* An interesting

study of paternalism in American business is P. Sanford, "The Intellectual Origins and New-Worldliness of American Industry," *Journal of Economic History* 18 (1958), 47–53.

17. See for example Peter Blunt, "Social and Organizational Structures in East Africa: A Case of Participation," *Journal of Modern African Studies* 16 (1978), 45–61.

18. C. A. O. von Nieuwenhuijze, "Post-colonial Paternalism," in *Cross-Cultural Studies* (The Hague: Mouton, 1963), pp. 86–111.

19. R. G. Abrahams, *The Nyamwezi Today: A Tanzanian People in the 1970s* (Cambridge: Cambridge University Press, 1981), pp. 40, 75–79, 125, 132–34. See also G. Hyden, *Beyond Ujamaa in Tanzania* (London: Heinemann, 1980). To Hyden, the persistence of local structures in the face of the bureaucracy's drive for total power calls for even stronger state action. Three pioneering social scientists who question the benefits of Nyerere's paternalism describe state paternalism as self-serving: see Judith Heyer, Pepe Roberts, and Gavin Williams, eds., *Rural Development in Tropical Africa* (New York: St. Martin's Press, 1981).

20. A provocative study of state paternalism in African land law is M. Ault and P. Rutman, "Development of Individual Rights to Property in Tribal Africa," *Journal of Law and Economics* 22 (1979), 37–48.

21. M. Sahlins, "The Segmentary Lineage and Predatory Expansion," *American Anthropologist* 63 (1981), 339.

22. P. Hill, *Migrant Cocoa-Farmers of Southern Ghana* (Cambridge: Cambridge University Press, 1963), pp. 6–18, 38–74, 180–87.

23. See Saul Alinsky's *Reveille for Radicals* (New York: Random House, 1969) and *Rules for Radicals* (New York: Random House, 1972).

24. Rothman, *op. cit.*, p. 77; and Rescher, *op. cit.*, pp. 125–27, 150–53.

25. R. Paine, ed., *The White Arctic* (Memorial University of Newfoundland, Newfoundland Social and Economic Papers 7, 1977); Selznick, *op. cit.*; and van den Berghe (1964), *op. cit.*

26. Smith, *op. cit.*, 116. In contrast to others, Smith does not consider centralized leadership of jointly held property essential to a corporate group; shared interests — "common affairs" — can provide sufficient focus for incorporation. Nor is Smith's corporate group necessarily classless or *gemutlich*, as is sometimes mistakenly assumed. (Contrast Smith's definition of a closed corporate community with that which appears in E. Wolf's "Closed Corporate Peasant Communities in Meso-America and Central Java," *Southwestern Journal of Anthropology* 13 (1957), 1.

27. Smith, *op. cit.*, p. 123.

28. J. Embree, "Thailand: A Loosely Structured Social System," *American Anthropologist* 52 (1950), 181–93. See also H. Evers, ed., *Loosely Structured Social Systems: Thailand in Comparative Perspective* (Yale University Southeast Asia Cultural Report Series 17, 1969).

29. From psychology we learn that reactive stress can provide strong integrating force if meeting the challenge seems feasible or if the challenge is not accepted as a final authority. Thus the mainly "closed" corporate communities of Wolf's peasant villages might be more fragile than groups whose cohesion is primarily based on initiative (for instance, Dutch polder communities or overseas immigrant Chinese) or on rejection of a would-be external authority (see B. Bettelheim, *The Informed Heart* [New York: Avon, 1960], pp. 70–7, 80–2, 123).

30. Adrian Adams, "The Senegal River Valley," in *Rural Development in Tropical Africa*, R. Heyer and Gavin Williams, eds. (New York: St. Martin's Press, 1981) and C. Hamilton, "The Patron-Recipient Relationship and Minority Politics in

New York City," *Political Science Quarterly* 2 (1970), 211–27. Hamilton (pp. 217–18) documents the extraordinary decline in black political participation in areas like Harlem with the proliferation of *ad hoc* welfare programs in the 1970s.

31. M. G. Smith, "On Segmentary Lineage Systems," *Journal of Royal Anthropological Institute* 86 (1956), 48.

32. See, for instance, J. Althusius, *The Politics of J. Althusius* [1603] (Boston, MA: Beacon Press, 1964; Otto von Gierke, *Natural Law and the Theory of Society*, vol. 1, (1913), trans. E. Barker (Cambridge: Cambridge University Press, 1934); von Gierke, *The Development of Political Theory* (1880), trans. Bernard Freyd (New York: Norton, 1939); and Alexis de Tocqueville, *Democracy in America* [1834–40], ed. Phillips Bradley (New York: Vintage, 1960).

33. G. I. Jones, "Councils among the Central Ibo," in *Councils in Action*, ed. A. Richards and A. Kuper (Cambridge: Cambridge University Press, 1971), pp. 63–79.

34. Alinsky (1969, 1972, *op. cit.*) sought to meet this challenge. In a rare record of such change, R. Smith describes the transition of "free Negro villages" from the paternalistic plantation society of British Guiana to democratically elected local self-government. (See Smith's *British Guiana* (London: Oxford University Press, 1962), pp. 37–42.

35. In his analysis of paternalistic versus competitive race relations, van den Berghe (1966, *op. cit.*) dramatically illustrates how lack of opportunities to exercise initiative correlates with blurred boundaries, mutually rather than separately defined interest, and hence loss of identity. Fundamentally the same process has frequently been recorded in thought reform, which must involve the subject emotionally in the group structure of the cell in order to break down his "private inner world of values, judgments and symbols"; R. Lifton elaborates techniques successful prisoners have used to maintain their independence (see Lifton, *Thought Reform and Psychology of Totalism* [New York: Norton, 1961], pp. 145–48).

36. See, for example, R. Hadley and S. Hatch, *Social Welfare and the Failure of the State* (London: Allen and Unwin, 1981); I. Illich, *Disabling Professions* (London: Boyars, 1980); and J. McKnight, "Professionalizing Service and Disabling Help" (MS, Northwestern University, Center for Urban Studies, 1982).

37. E. Chalmers, "Parties and Society in Latin America," in *Friends, Followers, and Factions*, ed. Steffan Schmidt *et al.* (Berkeley and Los Angeles: University of California Press, 1977), p. 411.

38. Hamilton, *op. cit.*

39. I am indebted to Conrad Arensberg (personal communication) for this insight.

40. E. Genovese expounds this dynamic brilliantly in analyzing the vertical (and *personal*) identification of slaves with their masters in the paternalistic American South (see Genovese, *Roll, Jordan, Roll* [New York: Pantheon, 1974], pp. 661–63). On the plantations individuals were subject to individuals, not one class to another. In his study of French bureaucracies B. Crozier found paternalistic administrators hostile towards peer groups which buffered individuals from central control (see Crozier, *op. cit.*, p. 191).

41. L. Fallers, *Basic Bureaucracy* (Cambridge: Heffer, 1956), pp. 150–53, 173–74. See also L. Mair, *Primitive Government* (Baltimore, MD: Penguin, 1962), p. 267; and Adams, *op. cit.*, pp. 53–54.

42. The African literature includes many studies of cooptation but few of villagers' explicit rejection of it. In the case of the Kagoro chief M. Gwanna, M. G. Smith offers an example of a tribal leader coopted into the colonial system who

redefined his own position to transfer power to a genuinely representative tribal council (see Smith, "Kagoro Political Development," *Human Organization* 19 [1960], 146–49).

43. Selznick, *op. cit.*, pp. 21–23, 145–46, 217–18, 259–60.

44. See also Grace E. Goodell, "What after Land Reform?" *Policy Review* 24 (1983), 121–48.

45. Jerry Avorn and E. Langer, "Induced Disability in Nursing Home Patients: A Controlled Trial," *Journal of the American Geriatrics Society* 30 (1982), 397–400.

46. John Bowlby, *Attachment* (New York: Basic Books, 1969), pp. 28–30; Bowlby, *Separation, Anxiety, and Anger* (London: Hogarth Press, 1973), pp. 241–43; and Willard Gaylin, *Caring* (New York: Avon, 1976), p. 109.

47. E. Langer and L. Benevento, "Self-induced Dependence," *Journal of Personality and Social Psychology* 36 (1978), 886–93; and Langer, "Old Age: An Artifact?" in *Biology, Behavior, and Aging*, ed. S. Kiesler and J. McGaugh (New York: Academic Press, 1980). See also A. Averill, "Personal Control over Averse Stimuli and Its Relationship to Stress," *Psychological Bulletin* 80 (1973), 286–303; and Ricky Savage, Lawrence Perlmuter, and Richard Monty, "Effect of Reduction in the Amount of Choice and the Perception of Control on Learning," in *Choice and Perceived Control*, ed. Lawrence Perlmuter and Richard Monty (Hillsdale, NJ: Lawrence Erlbaum Associates, 1979), pp. 92–93.

48. Ervin Staub, Bernard Tursky, and Gary Schwartz, "Self-control and Predictability: Their Effects on Reactions to Aversive Stimulation," *Journal of Personality and Social Psychology* 18 (1971), 157–62.

49. H. Seligman, *Helplessness* (San Francisco: Freeman, 1975), pp. 34–36; Mark Lepper and David Greene, eds., *The Hidden Costs of Reward* (Hillsdale, NJ: Lawrence Erlbaum Associates, 1978).

50. E. Langer, "The Illusion of Control," *Journal of Personality and Social Psychology* 32 (1975), 311–28; Langer, "Re-thinking the Role of Thought in Social Interaction," in *New Directions in Attribution Research*, vol. 2, eds. John Harvey, William Ickes, and Robert Kidd (Hillsdale, NJ: Lawrence Erlbaum Associates, 1979), pp. 54–55; and Seligman, *op. cit.*, pp. 55, 151. There appears to be a link between having free options, feeling responsible for the choice one makes (hence for one's behavior based on it), and being *committed* to the action it requires. On the connection between this and many new countries' independence movements, see Isaiah Berlin, *Four Essays on Liberty* (London: Oxford University Press, 1969), p. 157.

51. Avorn and Langer, *op. cit.*, 398. In a study of socialist assistance to the poor in Cuba, M. Butterworth found that despite the state's official idealism it failed to elicit participatory local organization and initiative especially because of bureaucrats' condescension and their transparent determination to maintain control (see Butterworth, *The People of Buena Ventura* [Urbana, IL: University of Illinois Press, 1980], pp. 115–16).

52. N. Klausner, *The Quest for Self-control* (New York: Free Press, 1965), pp. 121–26, 253–56.

53. Hamilton, *op. cit.*, pp. 216–17; van den Berghe (1964), *op. cit.*, p. 251.

54. R. D. Laing, *The Divided Self* (Harmondsworth, England: Penguin, 1960), 192.

55. Hamilton, *op. cit.*, p. 216. In collective protest against higher taxes in Caneville, those who debased themselves to prove their personal duress were granted relief while those opposing the measure on the principle of overall equity were denied (van den Berghe (1964), *op. cit.*, p. 94; see also Bettelheim, *op. cit.*, pp. 171, 219, 287). P. Ollawa illustrates the same dependency "syndrome" in his study

of rural Zambia (Ollawa, *Participatory Democracy in Zambia* (Ilfracombe: Stockwell, 1979), pp. 429-30.

56. Scott, *op. cit.*

57. E. Banfield, *Unheavenly City Revisited* (Boston, MA: Little, Brown, 1968), p. 285. Many social scientists, failing to appreciate this, object vigorously to governments' announced expectations of renumeration. See, for instance, B. Kerkvliet, "Land Reform in the Philippines since the Marcos Coup," *Pacific Affairs* 47 (1974), 286-304.

58. Szasz, *op. cit.*, pp. 258-59.

59. Joel Feinberg, "Noncoercive Exploitation," in *Paternalism*, ed. Rolf Sartorius (Minneapolis, MN: University of Minnesota Press, 1984).

60. D. Rothman, "The State as Parent," in *Doing Good*, by Willard Gaylin, *et al.* (New York: Pantheon, 1978), pp. 72-78. Some fields of research increasingly document the "beneficiaries' " competence and the paternalist's relative lack of critical expertise, etc. — for instance, T. Schultz's work on peasant agricultural economics (see Schultz, *Transforming Traditional Agriculture* [New Haven, CT: Yale University Press, 1957].) On the other hand, there is no question that assistance is frequently needed; we are not discussing Gandhian self-reliance here.

61. Polanyi, *op. cit.*, pp. 78-80, 140, 224, 280-81.

62. H. Berman, *Justice in the U.S.S.R.* (Cambridge, MA: Harvard University Press, 1963), pp. 207, 283-84, 297; N. Lenin, "What Should Be Done?" [1902], in *Collected Works*, vol. 5, trans. Michael Fineberg and Edward Hanna (Moscow: Foreign Languages Publishing House, 1960); M. Mead, *Soviet Attitudes Toward Authority* (New York: McGraw-Hill, 1951), pp. 44-52.

63. R. Owen, *A New View of Society* [1813-21] (New York: Everymans, 1972).

64. H. Diamond, "An Experiment in Feudalism: French Canada in the Seventeenth Century," *William and Mary Quarterly* 18 (1962), 3-34.

65. For example, in Scott's (1976) analysis of patronage, it is the landlords' protection and the peasants' expectations of the landlords upon which his minimal-survival thesis rests and from which he draws most of his illustrations. When he discusses the state's relationship to the peasants he touches on aspects central to my distinction between patronage and paternalism — that the state takes from the peasants more than it gives; that "its social distance from the peasantry, especially in the colonial era, was measured in light years"; that its assistance is hardly reliable; and that its claims (taxes, corvée, conscription) can hardly be seen as a repayment for services received. Yet, especially after independence, when the landlords' patronage fails, the state often takes their place. Rebellious peasants may themselves make the distinction between patrons who respect them as adults (however oppressively) and the state, inasmuch as they seem to pillage the landlords' granaries but lay waste to the state's property and kill its officials. In any event, though patronage is more likely than state paternalism to lead to full participation, it is not to be confused with the political action of corporate groups.

66. James Scott, *The Moral Economy of the Peasant* (New Haven, CT: Yale University Press, 1977), pp. 22-35; J. Turner, "Can There Be Involvement Without Paternalism?" *Interchange* 28 (1980), 108-09.

67. Scott, (1977) *ibid.*, pp. 28-31; R. K. Beardsley and R. Ward, *Village Japan* (Chicago: University of Chicago Press, 1959), pp. 274-75.

68. State paternalism may, however, comprehend patron-client networks or mechanisms that are coterminous with the total political structure. (For example, political parties based on patronage may constitute a paternalistic state which is an

internally coherent system.) In these cases patronage and paternalism both obtain at the same time, though the dominant party may tend to limit redistribution to its own clients. I am grateful to M. G. Smith for these elaborations.

69. S. Silverman, "Patronage as Myth," in *Patrons and Clients*, ed. Ernest Gellner and John Waterbury (London: Duckworth, 1977), pp. 12–15.

70. Hamilton, *op. cit.*, p. 215; Grace E. Goodell, *The Elementary Structures of Political Life* (Ph.D. diss., Columbia University, 1977). See also Franz Kafka's descriptions of bureaucracy.

71. Scott (1977), *op. cit.*, pp. 36–7.

72. Ernest Gellner, "Patrons as Clients," in *Patrons and Clients*, ed. Ernest Gellner and John Waterbury (London: Duckworth, 1977), p. 3.

73. See, for instance, Chalmers, *op. cit.*, p. 410. M. G. Smith suggests (personal communication) that such impermanence and arbitrariness applies to paternalism in nondemocratic states but not to welfare benefits, which are rationally conceived products of collective experience and public choice. The former are contingent upon policy making outside of the "beneficiaries" (who are not autonomous) themselves, while in the latter (e.g., Sweden, New Zealand) society awards benefits to itself.

74. Hamilton, *op. cit.*, pp. 212–18, 220–25.

75. Hamilton, *ibid.*, pp. 216–17; Scott (1976), *op. cit.*, 114–57.

76. Silverman, *op. cit.*, pp. 12–16; Scott (1977), *op. cit.*, pp. 23–24.

77. Hamilton, *op. cit.*, p. 225.

78. Scott (1977), *op. cit.*, p. 23.

79. Gellner, *op. cit.*, p. 3.

80. See Grace E. Goodell, "From Status to Contract: The Significance of Agrarian Relations of Production in the West, Japan, and in 'Asiatic' Persia," *European Journal of Sociology* 21 (1980), 285–325. In the Philippines, for instance, patrons frequently operating elsewhere may delegate authority to long-standing client militias or villager associations, which come to acquire considerable self-direction. M. G. Smith suggests the twelve Apostles or Mohammad's followers as other examples. On the other hand, since a patron may continually add new clients, most such categories lack definite boundaries or membership.

81. M. A. McLaurin, *Paternalism and Protest in Southern Cotton Mill Workers and Organized Labor, 1875–1905* (Westport, CT: Greenwood, 1971). See also T. Ford, *Man and Land in Peru* (Gainesville, FL: University of Florida Press, 1955) and John W. Bennett, "Paternalism," in *Encyclopedia of the Social Sciences*, vol. 11 (New York: Macmillan, 1963).

82. H. B. Davis, "The Theory of Union Growth," *Quarterly Journal of Economics* 55 (1941), 612, 614–18, 625; and N. Lockwood, "Factors Affecting the Degree of Unionization Amongst Black-Coated Workers," in *Trade Unions*, ed. W. E. J. McCarthy (Harmondsworth, England: Penguin, 1972), 239, 247–49.

83. J. Abbeglan, *The Japanese Factory* (Cambridge, MA: M.I.T. Press, 1958); Abbeglan, *Management and Worker: The Japanese Solution* (Cambridge: Cambridge University Press, 1973); Beardsley and Ward, *op. cit.*, R. Cole, *Japanese Blue Collar* (Berkeley and Los Angeles: University of California Press, 1971); S. Levine, *Industrial Relations in Postwar Japan* (Urbana, IL: University of Illinois Press, 1958); and many others.

84. Abbeglan (1973), *ibid.*, 48–49; Cole, *ibid.*, 176.

85. R. Weingrod, "Patronage and Power," in *Patrons and Clients*, ed. Ernest Gellner and John Waterbury (London: Duckworth, 1977), pp. 45–51.

86. Goodell (1977), *op. cit.*

87. Genovese, *op. cit.*

88. Adams, *op. cit.*

89. D. Devine, "An Aborted Democracy," *Worldview* (May 1981), 20. Unlike most land reforms, the one in Bolivia required that each peasant pay for his land title explicitly so that he would feel it was his (J. Powelson, personal communication).

90. This is a good example of Smith's point (personal communication) that the paternalistic state can work through the mechanisms of patronage.

91. Jones, *op. cit.*, pp. 73–76. See also G. Simmell, *Conflict and the Help of Group Affiliations* [1908], trans. Kurt Wolff and Reinhard Bendix (New York: Free Press, 1955); C. White, *Patrons and Partisans: A Study in Two Southern Italian Communities* (Cambridge: Cambridge University Press, 1980), p. 172; and the illustrations already cited from Fallers and Mair.

92. This is reminiscent of the distinction J. Kleinig draws between moralistic and nonmoralistic paternalism. (See Kleinig, "Paternalism and the Public Service," MS, n.d.). In the former, the good imposed is alien to recipients' conception of their own good and thus implies the paternalist's feeling of superiority in imposing even *values*; in the second he identifies with the "beneficiaries' " own values and imposes only a way of realizing them.

93. Marvin Harris, *Culture, Man, and Nature* (New York: Crowell, 1971), p. 246.

94. C. Levi-Strauss, *Elementary Structures of Kinship*, trans. James Bell and John von Sturmer (Boston, MA: Beacon Press, 1969), pp. 59–60.

*　　*　　*

"In these polarized and emotional times we need more thinkers of excellence on both sides in order to make fair decisions concerning our future. Russell Kirk is just such an excellent thinker. I hope his The Roots of American Order *is read by fair-minded people of both left and right everywhere in our country."*

— Ray Bradbury, 1974

*　　*　　*

"One cannot be conservative in the U.S. without owing a debt to Russell Kirk. I am delighted to acknowledge mine. Russell pioneered modern conservative thought and became a major force in putting it on the map, making it respectable and responsible. Conservatives by definition are custodians of tradition. But they must be selective — there are many traditions. In the U.S. preserving the ideas and customs of the past is particularly difficult, for the main American tradition has been change. No country has changed as enthusiastically from the rural past to the urban industrial present. Yet, as Russell has unceasingly stressed, there are permanent things and they are the important things. He has constantly championed them; many conservatives have followed him. For this American society at large as well as those willing to bear the label conservative owe Russell a permanent debt."

— Ernest van den Haag,
1992

Historical Consciousness
in Antiquity

by Paul Gottfried

A *Festschrift* dedicated to an eloquent spokesman for historical conservatism should include at least some observations about historical consciousness in the ancient world. Such comments are surely
fitting; for the practices of judging political institutions by historical
experience and of searching the past for practical wisdom go back as
far as classical antiquity. Russell Kirk, the subject of our tributes,
turned to Edmund Burke in defining his own historical thinking. His
friend Peter J. Stanlis, meanwhile, traced Burke's ethics to the Middle
Ages, and more specifically to the Christian Aristotelianism taught by
the medieval schoolmen. Another scholar, Thomas Chaimowicz (in a
doctoral dissertation submitted at Salzburg in 1953), has explored
links between Cicero's *De Legibus* and *De Officiis* and Burke's views of
civic responsibility and the social bond.[1] These perceptions about
Burke are not incompatible: whereas Stanlis's works examine the
emerging natural-law tradition among ancient jurists and rhetoricians
as well as among medieval theologians, Chaimowicz takes Roman
concepts of law and society through Western civilization down to
Burke.[2]

Less congruent with Burke's historical conservatism, however, is
the opinion advanced by Leo Strauss, that historical thinking
represents a break with the Western past. In *Natural Right and History*
(1950), Strauss names Burke explicitly as a father of nineteenth-
century historicism: who prepared "an approach to human affairs
which is even more foreign to classical thought than was the very
'radicalism' of the theorists of the French Revolution."[3] Though this
remark from Strauss's Walgreen lectures of 1949 seems specifically

earmarked for Burke and his admirers, a similar one appears thirteen years earlier in *The Political Philosophy of Hobbes* (1936), about the subject of that work. There Strauss states that Thomas Hobbes performed a dangerous revolutionary act when in *Leviathan*, chapter nine, he designates history and science (Hobbes there actually groups science with philosophy) as the two fundamental branches of human knowledge. A translator of Thucydides who quoted Cicero, Lucian, and other rhetoricians, Hobbes set out to substitute "the teaching of history" for "the precepts of philosophy." Like Francis Bacon, Jean Bodin, and Niccolò Machiavelli before him, he abandoned the philosophical question of the Good for the practical use of historical example. It was the "new study of history" that became the distinguishing mark of an anti-philosophic, amoral education characteristic of the modern age.[4]

Ironically, one finds kindred observations about historical consciousness, with a different spin, in one of Strauss's least favorite thinkers, G. W. F. Hegel. In the opening pages of *The Philosophy of History* (1821), Hegel stresses the limits of the Greek understanding of historical change. The Greeks Herodotus and Diodorus Siculus had chronicled past events and the lives of great individuals without getting to the bottom of either. Only Germanic Christian civilization, which had evolved in Northern Europe since the Reformation, had a fully matured and critical historical consciousness. Only his age, Hegel believed, saw historical studies become systematic and comprehensive, as men were coming to appreciate the historicity of thought and the interrelatedness of the entire past.[5] Though Hegel, unlike Strauss, identified the "historical" with the "philosophic," both agreed that the stress on historical example and the appeal to a living past were almost exclusively modern.

Now it may be useful to point out that there is no *single* classical assessment of the value of history—any more than one can discover such for the present age. Different texts can be adduced even from the same ancient authors containing more than one opinion about the application of history. In an oft-cited passage from the *Poetics*, for example, Aristotle relegates history to a less honorable place than poetry, which is seen as more philosophic. Unlike history, Aristotle teaches in the *Poetics*, poetry at its best exemplifies what is universally true about the human condition rather than what is relevant for specific circumstances.[6] In the *Rhetoric*, however, Aristotle deems history that recounts the public deliberations of peoples to be of political, not merely rhetorical, significance.[7] And he considered political history to be sufficiently instructive to warrant his writing on the constitutional developments of more than two hundred states, of which only *The Constitution of Athens* remains extant.

By contrast, Socrates, particularly as depicted by Plato, is sublimely indifferent to history. It is thus understandable that Strauss and his epigones should focus on Plato's Socrates whenever they generalize about classical thought. Despite comments by Xenophon, who did value and write history, associating his teacher Socrates with fillial piety, it is hard to see what ancestral past Socrates sought to uphold.[8] In Plato's dialogue *Critias*, Socrates proposes imagining an ideal society at the beginning of time. Because Hesiod and other early Greeks had celebrated a past golden age, Socrates observes the same convention, without paying attention to historical records. Indeed one may compare this willfully imaginary beginning of political existence in the *Critias* to the equally arbitrary constructions of early societies undertaken by Socrates in Plato's *Republic*, Book Two. There Socrates pursues his analysis of the "true republic" by depicting a "primitive city" providing for minimal human needs. When Socrates' interlocutor Glaucon dismisses this barebones society as a "city of pigs," Socrates offers to change the model to a "sybaritic city."[9] Since these models in any case are used didactically, to teach the requirements of a just society, Socrates proceeds to conjure up a new point of origin for speculating about the nature and ends of political life.[10]

The best way to approach Socrates' and Plato's disregard of history is by considering the character of their didacticism. What they are trying to teach, first of all, is an awareness of the Just and the Good. The phenomenal world, to which history belongs, is there to provide topics and hints pointing beyond the transitory toward immovable Ideas. Thus appeals to changing, earthbound data—to the observable as recorded in chronicles—has a purely heuristic function. Such appeals are needed to further critical inquiry by moving us along the ladder of knowledge, from sense certainty toward a growing awareness of eternal forms.[11]

It is also clear that Plato's Socrates does not recognize a distinction, underlying later historical research, between a chronicler of events and a teller of myths. In the *Republic* and elsewhere, Socrates draws on both invented history and inherited myth to teach moral and theological lessons. The question of whether a particular event occurred in the historical past is no more critical from this standpoint than the question of whether a particular apparition took place in the way recounted by an epic writer or by an interpreter of oracles. Historical testimony, oracles, and legends about gods can all be made to teach true things about human nature. Why then should historians work at sifting evidence and distinguishing real from merely imagined happenings?

In the introduction to a universal history, Diodorus Siculus, in the first century B.C. raised this question while considering the changed view of the mythic past among his contemporaries. Chroniclers, who abounded in the Hellenistic world, were becoming scornful of received narratives inhabited by gods, demigods, and heroes. Ephorus the Cumaean, Callisthenes, Theopompus, and other Hellenistic historians "were distancing themselves from ancient myths."[12] All of them insisted that these narratives were resistant to proof and often in conflict. Nonetheless, Diodorus Siculus made the deliberate decision to go against the grain and to chronicle the "deeds accomplished by heroes, demigods, and other good men." In the end, he says, the "purpose of history" is, like communal sacrifice, an act of filial piety, recalling "with appropriate praise" the memorable accomplishments attributed to the gods and founders of one's city.[13]

Diodorus' introductory comments tell us two things about the status of historiography in his age. First, a trend could be discerned among "more recent" literati to examine historical materials critically, with an eye to discrediting "untrue" testimonies about the past. Second, there were those such as Diodorus who followed this trend with reservation and continued to treat at least some myth as history. Even so, Diodorus made a "conscious decision," as he himself indicates, to incorporate mythic texts into historic writings. He arrived at his decision while understanding the difference between validated historical testimony and mere legend that was inaccessible to investigation.

Without intention of invidious comparison, it should be observed that one searches through medieval and early modern Europe in vain for students of history with the technical competence of many Hellenistic historians and their Roman disciples. The contrasts here can be painfully obvious: between the rich sense of historical differences and chronological distances in Polybius, Thucydides, Cicero, and Tacitus, and the presentist conceptions of the pagan and biblical pasts reflected in medieval chronicles and art—or in Rabbinic Judaism's attempt to project on to David, Moses, Abraham, and Shem the features of later Talmudic Jewish life. An equally obvious sign of the difference in historical understanding between two ages is seen in the way their chroniclers approach specific events. Classicists can contrast with the elaborate treatment of causes, pretexts, and occasions in the opening section of Polybius' *Histories* (foreshadowed by Thucydides' discussion of the same topic) the presentation of events by Gregory of Tours, Otto of Freising, and other medieval chroniclers. Unlike Hellenistic ones, medieval historians attributed what happened to direct supernatural intervention. Medieval writers crammed whatever they associated with the past into a set framework, starting with Creation, moving through the Incarnation, and then, toward the Final Judgment. What these chroniclers brought forth is allegorical and apologetic and has little in common with ancient historiography, from Thucydides through Tacitus, except for those lapses by the ancients into mythic narrative.

But the recovery of a technically developed historical sense did not come all at once, even with the waning of the Middle Ages. Machiavelli and Hobbes, for example, may have exalted history, but both were essentially medieval in their confusion of history and myth and in their largely allegorical use of a doubtful past. Neither in *The Prince* nor in the *Discourses upon the First Ten Books of Titus Livy* does Machiavelli examine historical material, save as points of departure for lectures on political ethics. Hobbes did cite Roman rhetoricians and Graeco-Roman historians; but so had Thomas Aquinas in the thirteenth century, albeit with less emphasis on historical example. And though Hobbes commended the study of history to aristocrats, his own historical works consisted only of an autobiography in Latin verse and a highly tendentious account of the English Civil War, *Behemoth*.[14]

The true flowering of Western historiography, after antiquity, began in the eighteenth century and extended from Montesquieu, the Scottish Enlightenment, Edward Gibbon, and Edmund Burke down to the great German, French, and other continental historians of the nineteenth century. With due respect to Hegel, this flowering did not result from the Reformation, though the Protestant Reformers did try to return to Christianity's Hebraic and patristic roots. It took place simultaneously in Catholic and Protestant societies, wherever Latin rhetoric and Graeco-Roman historiography were taught. Montesquieu's Jesuit education at the Collège de Juilly, Burke's classical studies at Dublin, particularly at Trinity College, and Hegel's formal training in "the classical and humanist rhetorical program" at a Protestant gymnasium in Stuttgart all had the same effect in transmitting ancient historical methods together with ancient historical consciousness.[15]

The connection in this kind of education between rhetoric and history points to the more problematic one that existed between these disciplines in ancient times. In *What Is Political Philosophy?* (1959), Leo Strauss notes contemptuously that in Graeco-Roman culture history came from rhetoricians rather than philosophers. Ignoring the remarks devoted to Socrates and pre-Socratic philosophy in Aristotle's *Metaphysics*, Strauss then maintains that the "history of philosophy in particular was not considered a philosophic discipline: it was left to antiquarians rather than to philosophers."[16]

The close identification of historiography with rhetoric which Strauss highlights actually offended against Hellenistic historians. They consigned the chroniclers they despised to a rhetorical rather than scholarly tradition. In *Histories*, Book Two, for example, Polybius offers a scathing discourse on Phylarxus, a noted historian of Greece during the third century B.C. Polybius scolds Phylarxus for misrepresenting the events leading to the sack of the Arcadian city of Montineia by armies of the Peloponnesian Achaean League. Phylarxus as presented by Polybius had disguised the treachery of the Montineians. He neglected to mention their repeated defection from the League and their slaughter of its garrison army together with the pro-Achaean faction in their own city in 224 B.C., after the Montineians had negotiated an alliance with the anti-League Spartan King Cleomenes III.

But Polybius' main charge against Phylarxus is that the author tended to confuse historiography and drama. "Hastening to move his readers to pity . . . he evokes the dishevelled braids and hair of women and the heaving of breasts and beyond that, the tears and shrieks of men and women being led away indiscriminately with their children and aged progenitors."[17] Such embellishments are unworthy of the historian "who need not unduly excite his readers by his account, nor reach for stock phrases nor list the results of situations, as would tragedians." Rather, the historian "must note fully what truly happened and was truly said, however ordinary those things may be. For the ends of tragic drama and history are not the same but diametrically opposed." One aims at "controlling the mind through the passions and the other at teaching those avid for knowledge through authentic deeds and words."[18]

The maxim popularized by Leopold von Ranke and other "objective" historians of the nineteenth century, studying the past as it actually occurred, came originally from Polybius. Whether Ranke knew this matters little. He was replicating what by then was an ancient aspiration. Hellenistic, like later German, historians set out to record *true* happenings, a task that distinguished them, or so they insisted, from storytellers and speechmakers. In his *Anabasis*, an account of the campaigns of Alexander the Great, the second-century A.D. historian, Arrian begins by stressing his concern about "reliable" sources. He builds on the narratives produced by two members of Alexander's entourage: Ptolemy, future ruler of Egypt, and the commander Aristobulus. Neither, Arrian tells us, would have lied, both having written after Alexander's death as men of stature. Besides, their accounts meshed, unlike the divergent ones about Alexander done by encomiasts of lower social standing.[19]

Hellenistic historians engaged in distinctions between themselves and "technicians." For them, the *texnitai* were the raconteurs who ignored truth and dragged down a serious pursuit by confounding it with artistic tricks. Plainly rhetoricians belonged preeminently to this category of tricksters, and earnest Greek historians like Thucydides and Polybius shunned their association.

But rhetoric and historiography were tied indissolubly in the ancient world and recovered as a twin legacy by Western scholars and educators from the high Middle Ages on. Aquinas, Machiavelli, Hobbes, Bodin, Montesquieu, and even Burke learned Roman history predominantly from rhetoricians and from literary stylists who had historical interests. Sallust, Cicero, Quintilian, and Plutarch were for a long time more accessible sources of ancient history than the technically developed historiography of Thucydides and Polybius. Moreover, the most dramatic celebration of history, as *"vero testis temporum, lux veritatis, vita memoriae, magistra vitae, nuntia vetustatis"* came from the Roman orator Cicero. The axiom flattering to historians as well as to Romans, that Greeks taught by precept, Romans by example, can be traced to the master of Latin rhetoric Quintilian. And one of the most exhaustive ancient disquisitions on the historian's craft, *Quomodo historia scribenda sit*, was composed by another rhetorician, the second-century Greek, Lucian.

Though Romans learned to do history from the Greeks, they ignored the wall of separation that Hellenistic historians had erected between themselves and the teachers of rhetoric. Romans took pride in being both rhetoricians and historians and praised history lavishly for its truth about life and for its method of inquiry. Indeed Cicero and Quintilian raised history to a predominantly Roman acomplishment. Unlike the Greeks and other peoples, they proclaimed, Romans, who had an ancient constitution, were surrounded by the living monuments of their past. Greeks chronicled, but Romans memorialized through their ritual and social life as much as by writing annals. The orator who invoked ancestral symbols and exploits, worked, like the chronicler, to keep alive the past.

Rhetoricians participated as well in the technical evolution of history. Hellenistic historians, as can be seen from their copious remarks on research method and historical causation, aspired to reconstruct the past. This reconstruction, it was argued, required not only trustworthy testimonies but also knowledge of the real sequence in which events transpired. In *Histories*, Book One, Polybius sets forth the circumstances that he believes explains the more than half century of strife among competing powers in Italy, Spain, Illyria, Greece, North Africa, and the Middle East. Polybius invokes "the hand of Fate" to underscore the fact that events throughout the civilized world came to center on one region and "tended toward the same end." "An overview of history," Polybius adds is necessary in order that his reader might glimpse "by what means [Fate] worked toward the accomplishment of all events" treated in his work. And unlike his contemporaries who fail to provide "a comprehensive view of events," Polybius offers to relate everything to a context.[20] He will demonstrate the interrelatedness of significant events by connecting them to the supreme "achievement and contest" of his or any other time: Roman mastery of the Mediterranean.

Former generations, he goes on, had labored under the illusion that "one can only grasp history properly by seeing it in parts." Thus they became like those who were forced to study human life by viewing "the dismembered organs of a [once] vital and beautiful body." Once the observers were set before the reconstructed body, "they would all admit that they had strayed from the truth and had been like dreamers."[21] The Platonic language of conversion is unmistakably present. Polybius is saying that those who come to see historical relations aright are, like Plato's philosopher, leaving the mere dreamworld of opinion for true knowledge.

Like other Hellenistic historians, Polybius did not wish to live in the shadow of philosophy. He most certainly knew that Plato and the Platonists had patronized what he did. His "science of events" was considered by them as a lower form of study than the contemplation of eternal forms. Equally significant, Aristotle, in *Metaphysics*, Book One, had constructed a hierarchy of knowledge, in which the line of demarcation between technical and philosophic studies had been drawn, apparently, to the historian's disadvantage.[22] Philosophers were preoccupied with epistemic knowledge, which deals with the unseen causes of change. Technicians, by contrast, were seeking a limited understanding of the physical world, to control or manipulate it.

It is this challenge to the status of historians found in Aristotle's ranking of knowledge that Polybius and other Hellenistic chroniclers tried to address. They responded not by repudiating Aristotle's implicit judgment of what was subphilosophical, but by redefining their own activity. Contrary to what critics said, historians, like philosophers, were aitiologists: scholars looking for the reasons that things happened as they did. Thus Polybius offers to lead his reader "through the interrelatedness and proliferation of all things impinging on each other, indeed through their similarity and difference" to a sense of "what is useful and pleasant in history." Like the philosophical *agogē*, this journey would move from "one thing happening after the other" to a knowledge of ultimate causation.

The French classicist Paul Pédech, in a study of Polybius' view of historical causation, makes two observations relevant to our inquiry. One, Polybius develops his methodology with obvious care and applies it repeatedly in his historical writing. He takes over and tries to refine the ambiguous distinction between cause and occasion or pretext, which Thucydides had already devised in his writing on the Peloponnesian War. Polybius also introduces other concepts intended to clarify the origin and connection of events — such as point of departure and the quintessentially Aristotelian term, foundation. Though none of these conceptual labels is used with rigorous consistency, Polybius as presented by Pédech was passionately interested in showing that nothing significant occurred without design. This design was accessible to scholars — whether it arose in the minds of their subjects, like the Roman quest for domination, or from the study of interrelated, sequential events.[23]

Two, Pédech traces the aitiology constructed by Polybius and other Hellenistic historians to the manuals of rhetoricians. One of the tasks assumed by ancient rhetoricians was to prepare litigants for making courtroom speeches. In pleas and accusations the citizens of Greek cities had to convince jurors of the rightness of their account of the situation being debated. Such persuasion came to hinge on applying fixed methods of investigation devised by rhetoricians. Courtroom contestants had to defend their *history* by showing its congruence with the way events were supposed to unfold. Else their pleas and testimonies would not carry weight with the jurors.

The connection between judicial and historical investigations was fixed etymologically and genealogically. Court cases centered on those "having imputed guilt": that is, bearing or being the "cause" of a criminal action. The job of the accused was to shift the *aitia* by rhetorical means on to someone or something else. The rhetorician made himself doubly useful, providing the procedures for judicial debate and training others to use them effectively. At the same time, Pédech shows, the rhetorician contributed to the study of historical causation, but had to wait centuries before being taken back into the company of historians.

The reconciliation of the two had noteworthy consequences. It prepared the way for Roman historiography, Roman historical speculation, and the awakening of historical interest in early modern Europe. In all these cases rhetorical approaches to history and historiography had indelible effects on their readers. Rhetorical historians and historically minded rhetoricians advanced Western historical consciousness in still another decisive way: by transforming interrelatedness from a causal concept into an image of both organic unity and civilizational continuity. For Polybius the "interconnectedness of all things in relation to each other" was a problem that his science of causality was intended to address. Only history understood as *pragmateia*, a study of connected events, could make sense of human happenings and thereby enable readers to benefit from the past.

But history as rhetoric, a subject admirably treated by Thomas Chaimowicz in his work on Roman letters and their effect on Montesquieu and Burke, sacralized historical connections and historical origins. History became Cicero's "true witness" and "messengers out of the past," illuminating the present age and uplifting its inhabitants. It was also a process uniting generations, allowing those in the present to recognize a shared fate and common glory with others in the past. "What greater and higher achievements are there," Quintilian asks, "than those which can be discovered among the monuments of our civilization?" For Quintilian those monuments include "distinguished speeches and acts handed down from antiquity that are always suited to inspire our minds."[24]

These references to "*tradita antiquitus dicta ac facta praeclare*" anticipate the appeals to History that historical conservatives have made in recent centuries. Burke's *Reflections on the Revolution in France*, with its stately invocation of historical continuities and of the moral imagination, mirrors Quintilian's rhetorical defense of a living past. It is further possible to discern in Quintilian's remark the application of Aristotle's epideictic rhetoric: appeals to the sense of heroism and beauty which true communities inculcate.[25]

Quintilian's rhetorical instruction, however, stands apart from Aristotle's characterization of epideictic rhetoric by reason of its deeper historical consciousness. Aristotle cites the exemplary figure of Achilles, who taught readers of the *Iliad* that to die for one's companion is "more beautiful than life." Quintilian points to Roman republican heroes, who are presumed to have lived, to illustrate the practice of Roman virtues. Not epic figures but living ancestors provide those exemplary lives Quintilian and other Roman authors wished to celebrate.

Admittedly Romans, too, exalted mythic figures: In the *Aeneid*, Virgil constructs a national mythology intended to renew his people's moral sense by evoking a legendary past. Still, by the first century educated Romans and Greeks were more acutely aware of a real past than most literate Athenians had been five hundred years earlier. The separation of myth and history had already begun to occur; and it was important for scholars and rhetoricians to teach virtue through authenticated historical examples. Unlike Homer (or the Homeridai) many centuries earlier, Virgil did arduous research on the past before constructing his epic. He filled his great Roman achievement, moreover, with historical as well as mythic figures.[26] And Virgil's admirer, the later Roman poet Lucan, wrote the *Pharsalia*, an epic poem on the struggle between Caesar and Pompey based on historical study. A Roman patriot who died under Nero pining for the Republic and a favored author of Burke, Lucan tried to combine vivid narrative and moralizing with factual accuracy.[27]

The rhetorical appeals to History as both a continuum and the inspiration of the past reflected the cumulative achievements of practicing historians since the fifth century B.C. It was precisely because historians once considered themselves aitiologists, not rhetoricians, that eventually rhetoric and history could be rejoined in a fuller Western historical consciousness. Hellenistic historians were vital to this process; for without their consuming interest in the historically concrete, the past would have remained purely mythic: connected not by real lives but by imaginative invention. History as *pragmateia* became the precondition for history as a teacher for life and as the unifying force in a continuing civilization. It was the search to clarify and contextualize the past that turned the epic into the historical imagination.

NOTES

1. For the most comprehensive statements of Thomas Chaimowicz's view of Burke, see *Natürliche Ordnung und Kontinuität im Politischen Denken Burkes*, dissertation (Salzburg, 1953); and *Freiheit und Gleichgewicht im Denken Montesquieus und Burkes* (Vienna and New York, 1985), pp. 94–123.

2. Peter J. Stanlis, *Edmund Burke and the Natural Law* (Ann Arbor, MI: University of Michigan Press, 1965).

3. Leo Strauss, *Political Philosophy: Six Essays*, ed. Hilail Gildin (Indianapolis, IN: Pegasus, 1975), p. 138.

4. Leo Strauss, *The Political Philosophy of Hobbes*, trans. Elsa M. Sinclair (Chicago and London: University of Chicago Press, 1952), pp. 79–107.

5. G. W. F. Hegel, *Werke in zwanzig Bänden*, vol. 12 (Frankfurt: Suhrkamp, 1970), pp. 11–86.

6. Aristotle, *Ars Poetica*, Oxford Classical Text, 1351d, 1–10.

7. Aristotle, *Ars Rhetorica*, Oxford Classical Text (Oxford: Clarendon Press, 1959), 1360a.35–36.

8. Xenophon, *Opera Omnia*, II, Oxford Classical Edition (Oxford: Clarendon Press, 1986), *Commentarii* I.i–ii.

9. Plato, *Res Publica*, Oxford Classical Text (Oxford: Clarendon Press, 1965), 1.373.

10. *Ibid.*, 1.372.

11. This argument is made effectively if not always clearly in N. R. Murphy, *The Interpretation of Plato's Republica* (Oxford: Oxford University Press, 1967).

12. Diodorus Siculus, *Bibliotheca Historica*, Teubner Edition (Leipzig, 1906), 1.10–15.

13. *Ibid.*, 1.20.

14. An illuminating though not entirely convincing portrait of the essentially medieval Hobbes can be found in F. C. Hood, *The Divine Politics of Thomas Hobbes* (Oxford: Oxford University Press, 1964).

15. On the classical educations of the above-cited figures, see Joseph Dedieu, *Montesquieu* reprint (Geneva: Slatkine Reprints, 1970), p. 5; Stanlis, *op. cit.*, pp. 186–88; and John H. Smith, *The Spirit and its Letter: Traces of Rhetoric in Hegel's Philosophy of* Bildung (Ithaca, NY: Cornell University Press, 1988).

16. Leo Strauss, *What Is Political Philosophy, and Other Studies*, (Glencoe, IL: The Free Press, 1957), p. 58.

17. Polybius, *Historiae*, Teubner Edition (Stuttgart, 1962), 2.56. 7–8.

18. *Ibid.*, 2.56.11.

19. Arrian, *Anabasis*, Teubner Edition (Leipzig, 1903), prooemium 1–3.

20. *Historiae*, 1.4.2–4; 1.63.9; 1.64.1–10.

21. *Ibid.*, 1.4.8–10.

22. Aristotle, *Metaphysica*, Oxford Classical Edition (Oxford: Clarendon Press, 1973), pp. 981–82.

23. Paul Pédech, *La méthode historique de Polybe* (Paris: Belles lettres, 1964), pp. 33–52. Another relevant study of Polybius' formative role as a historical theorist is in K. F. Eisen, *Polybios interpretationen. Beobachtungen zu Prinzipien griechischer und römischer Historiographie bei Polybios*, dissertation (Heidelberg, 1966).

24. Quintilian, *Institutio Oratoria*, Teubner Edition (Stuttgart, 1910), 12.2.29–30.

25. Aristotle, *Ars Rhetorica*, 1359a.1–5.

26. See Viktor Pöschl, *Die Dichtkunst Vergils* (Innsbruck and Vienna: R. M. Rohrer, 1950).

27. On the relationship between Lucan's poetry and political principles, see Georg Pfligensdorffer, "Lucan als Dichter des geistigen Widerstandes," *Hermes*, 87 (1959), 344–77.

*   *   *

"I am glad to hear that Dwight Macdonald has approved Beyond the Dreams of Avarice, *as he is one of the small number of left-wingers whose brains I respect and whose personality I like. I have dipped into it myself again and again, and usually find something that meets with my agreement. It pleased me to read your appreciation of Wyndham Lewis — a just and well-balanced one, I think. Much of what you say about this country supports my own gloomy views, and I think it is very true to say of any country, that a decline in private morality is certain to be followed in the long run, by a decline in public and political morality also."*

— *T. S. Eliot, in a letter to*
Russell Kirk dated October 31, 1956.

Millenarianism and Revolution

by Gerhart Niemeyer

Two words, each with a wide variety of meanings, are mentioned in this paper's title. Relevant questions become possible only as one learns to use especially the word "revolution" in more precise ways, since not all revolutions seem to lend themselves to linkage with "millennium." A rough phenomenal survey yields six types of revolution:

1. An uprising of a particular person leading an armed force with the aim of making himself ruler in the place of the actual ruler. (The history of China knows of many such cases of revolutions aimed at change of rulers but not of systems.)

2. An uprising of a subject social class against a ruling class, attributed by Aristotle to the absence of a common principle of justice (the poor rising against the rich, or vice-versa).

3. An uprising of a subject people offended by the imposition of a foreign divinity or symbol of worship. (For example: the Maccabee rebellion, or that of Bar Kochba.)

4. Jihad, a war waged by Muslims with the object of effecting a religious change in the lands of other peoples.

5. A seizure of political power by a person or group of persons claiming authority by virtue of direct divine revelation. (For example: Cola di Rienzo in 1347, the Bohemian Taborites in 1420, and the Anabaptists in Münster in 1534. Consider also the film "The Emperor Jones.")

6. An uprising of an organized and armed movement aimed at total change of a social and political system. (For example: the English Puritans in the sixteenth and seventeenth centuries, the French Jacobins in 1792, and the Russian Communists in 1917.)

Obviously no religious motives are at work in the first two types of revolution, while millenarianism may not play a role in all of the remaining types. But then, millenarianism may not arise in all types of religions.

As for "millenarianism" the word refers to a period of a thousand years which is mentioned in Revelation 20:1–7:

> Then I saw an angel come down from heaven with the key to the Abyss in his hand and an enormous chain. He overpowered the dragon, that primeval serpent which is the devil and Satan, and chained him up for a thousand years. He hurled him into the Abyss and shut the entrance and sealed it over him, to make sure he would not lead the nations astray again until the thousand years had passed. At the end of that time he must be released, but only for a short while.
>
> Then I saw thrones, where they took their seats, and on them was conferred the power of judgment. I saw the souls of all who had been beheaded for having witnessed for Jesus and for having preached God's word, and those who refused to worship the beast or his statue and would not accept the brand-mark on their foreheads or hands; they came to life and reigned with Christ for a thousand years. The rest of the dead did not come to life until the thousand years were over; this is the first resurrection. Blessed and holy are those who share in the first resurrection; the second death has no power over them but they will be priests of God and of Christ and reign with him for a thousand years.
>
> When the thousand years are over, Satan will be released from his prison. . . .

This passage in turn goes back to Daniel 7, where a vision of four beasts is reported, the fourth "fearful, terrifying, very strong; it had great iron teeth, and ate its victims, crushed them, and trampled their remains underfoot. It was different from the previous beasts and had ten horns." Then,

> While I was watching,
> thrones were set in place
> and one most venerable took his seat.
> His robe was white as snow,
> the hair on his head as pure as wool.
> His throne was a blaze of flames,
> its wheels were a burning fire.
> A stream of fire poured out,
> issuing from his presence.
> A thousand times ten thousand stood before him.
> the court was in session
> and the books lay open.

While the beast was put to death, and the other beasts were deprived

185

of their empire "but received a lease of life for a season and a time,"

> . . . I saw, coming on the clouds of heaven,
> as it were a son of man.
> He came to the most venerable
> and was led into his presence.
> On him was conferred rule,
> honor and kingship,
> And all peoples, nations and languages became his servants.
> His rule is an everlasting rule
> which will never pass away,
> and his kingship will never come to an end.

If until then we had not been fully aware of the thoroughly political content of this vision, an authoritative explanation is added identifying the four beasts with four kingdoms on earth, with the fourth one insulting the Most High and planning "to alter the seasons and the Law." But he is destroyed,

> and the splendors of all the kingdoms under heaven will be given to the people of the holy ones of the Most High, whose royal power is an eternal power, whom every empire will serve and obey.

The two passages together form one spiritual symbol with two variations. It is a vision of a heavenly rule transcending the reality of cosmos and earthly empires. The circumstantial terms of the scene, the "most venerable," "on the clouds of heaven," "eternal power," "the Abyss," do not belong to nature or history; they stand in sharpest contrast to the "four kingdoms" as well as to "all peoples, nations, and languages." The Christ of the Book of Revelation is the risen and ascended Christ; the rule of the "Son of Man" is an "everlasting rule," which, unlike earthly kingdoms, is "over all peoples," and "for eternity." The symbol tacitly assumes the tension between human, historical reality and the transcendent and eternal God, but the scene envisages the resolution of this tension, and it is not of this world. This applies to both Daniel and Revelation. In the latter, however, we find the variation: a thousand year reign of Christ with his Saints. While it comes toward the end, it is said to end *in* history and to be followed by another period in which Satan will again be free. Thus it is not an eschatological but an apocalyptic symbol. The thousand years are still a part of history, even though they have an uncosmic character in that there is a divine ruler of earthly peoples and no earthly kingdom or empire still exists. A puzzling feature of the symbol specifies a thousand-year period but mentions no change of generations. One might explain this away by surmising that the text, after all, does mean a heavenly rule of the heavenly Christ with heavenly subjects. But the release of Satan within this same population hardly fits in with this. There is, then, no getting around the fact that in these texts transcendent and supernatural elements are inseparably linked with cosmic and historical ones, and that we have here a vision of a cosmos radically changed and history without any human faults.

The two texts are a part of a voluminous literature mostly stemming from the period of 200 B.C. to 200 A.D.[1] Under the depressing experiences of historical and human disasters the former authority of prophets is now replaced by that of "seers," who may borrow the names of prophets or apostles as supposed authors of their writings. Here we find the notion of "two aeons:" "It is for this reason that the Most High has created not one aeon but two" (2 Esdras 7:50). The first aeon will push its godless and anti-human evil to ever greater degrees of misery and will eventually perish in a series of thunderclap catastrophes. But the new aeon will be free from all evil, shining in joy, peace, and splendor. Between the old and the new aeon there will be a divine judgment, not just of one people but of the whole world. The entire drama will be accomplished by a divine agent: in Daniel "the Son of Man," in Revelation the risen Christ using angels as his generals and heralds. It is a vision both fantastic and very powerful, and thoroughly futuristic. "Why then, Ezra, are you so deeply distressed at the thought that you are mortal and must die? Why have you not turned your mind to the future instead of the present?" (2 Esdras 7:15–16) This transcendent hope, fully as powerful as that of Gnosticism (with which it shared the stage for a while) meant to push orthodox and traditional religion aside. But, having little hope that it would be given a hearing, it published its ideas by way of an "underground literature," and underground its influence continued, only to break out into the open during the fourteenth, seventeenth and nineteenth centuries, becoming in our days a worldwide persuasion of large masses. In spite of its almost conspiratorial character, it has impressed very solid leaders from time to time. Thus, for example, Papias, Irenaeus, Lactantius accepted its imagery of an earth that eventually would produce, without human labor, unheard-of abundance, while the heathen would be subject to the faithful.

187

What is even more astonishing is that, 1600 years after Papias, in 1724, an outstanding pastor of Swabian Protestantism, Johann Albrecht Bengel, began again to speculate on the text of Revelation, particularly the number 666, and drew from this not only the vision of "better times to come," but also his certainty about the numerical order by which such events could be precisely foretold. He predicted glorious things for the year 1809, although he did allow for the possibility of a mathematical mistake, in which case the scheme would have to be reexamined. Together with two Alsatian predecessors (Spener and Petersen) and a Swabian friend, Friedrich Christoph Oetinger, the movement of German Pietism was launched, with Oetinger even including the Kabbala as an authoritative source. Oetinger loved to immerse himself in massive images of coming glory, "to eat at one table with Christ, to drink from the fruits of the vine, bodily to sit on chairs while smashing nations like clay pots."[2] Practically all of Protestant Swabia followed these two seers, a fact possibly not without effect on three young men who by the end of that same century did their theological studies in the Tübingen *Stift*: Schelling, Hölderlin, and Hegel. It is further remarkable that at this late date, these men were fully aware of Augustine's admonition not to use Revelation 20:7 for speculations on the future but to accept the Catholic Church as the already-realized "reign of Christ with his saints."[3] Not without much intellectual and emotional effort were Bengel and Oetinger able to put behind them the traditional attitude of looking on past and present, and to adopt as theirs an inner eye wholly fixed on the future.[4]

Millenarianism, then, knew itself to be revolutionary doctrine; it has been called "conspiratorial writing" comparable to the revolutionary pamphlet literature of the French Revolution and afterwards. Still, Bengel and Oetinger started no conspiratorial organization nor inflamed a revolutionary movement. If one wants to find an indirect link between the Swabian millenarians, Jacob Boehme, and other religious speculators, one would have to raise more general questions concerning "order" and "disorder," "balance," "reality" and the loss of it, and a general crisis of culture. These kinds of questions have given us, in modern scholarship, such concepts as "Gnosticism — the Nature of Modernity" (Eric Voegelin), "The Mind as its Own Place" (Marion Montgomery), and "Metaphysical Rebellion" (Albert Camus). Drawing the scope of research still wider one might look into the kind of religions that produce something akin to millenarian symbols, in all probability finding no millenarianism within religions of intracosmic divinities. For in these religions not only the gods but also the kingdoms are part of the cosmic order, and when a terminal catastrophe is envisaged not only men and their kingdoms but also gods go down. In that kind of world, the terms "transcendence" and "immanence" look quite out of place. Gods, to be sure, are of a higher order than humans but they, too, are subject to fate. "Transcendence" arises as a symbol of mystic philosophy whose mystical experiences also transcend the cosmic gods.[5]

Religions worshipping a divinity beyond the cosmos experience a characteristic tension between this world and the transcendence, a tension which, in times of great tribulation, presses toward some kind of resolution. Thus the Book of Daniel was written at the height of the Maccabean wars. It is therefore remarkable that its author takes hardly any notice of this great event: "Those of the people who are wise leaders will instruct many; for some days, however, they will stumble from sword and flame, captivity and pillage. And thus stumbling, little help they will receive, though many will be scheming in their support." (Daniel 11:33–34) Thus the writer of the first mature apocalyptic text and creator of the first encompassing millenial symbolism dismisses the Maccabean revolution as merely a part of the problem, looking for resolution only on another, higher plane.

Medieval millenarianism has some revolutions to report: Fra Dolcino, Cola Rienzo, the Spiritual Franciscans, later the Hussites of Mt. Tabor, the Anabaptists of Münster, Thomas Müntzer. The Taborites did wage war, not only in Bohemia but also in Central Germany, off and on for almost 15 years. The others were of short duration and remained local; they should be called uprisings rather than revolutions. The Brethren of the Free Spirit, a millenarian group not centrally organized but consisting of local groups in loose touch with one another, persisted for more than two hundred years and had a late revival in the Ranters of the English Civil War. They were indeed revolutionary, but not politically or militarily active.[6] Still, millenarian thinking did engender some activist movements and events, from the thirteenth century on. One may suspect that a new element of thought played some role in this: the notion that history is a knowable and even calculable whole culminating in something like God's kingdom on earth. This came from the publications of the

Calabrian Abbot Joachim of Fiore, whose ideas were given wide publicity by Gerardo of Borgo San Domingo's book, in 1254.[7] The place of the "thousand years" was here taken by the "Third Age" (of the Spirit, following two previous Ages, one of the Father, and one of the Son). This was also the last Age of history, peopled by monastic groups of autonomous men who needed neither authority, nor teaching, nor law, nor king, nor church, and also no property. The presence of Joachimite ideas in the Taborite movement and also in that of Thomas Müntzer has been conclusively established. Thus the end of the Middle Ages produced a first edition of the millenarian vision combined with a mathematical "knowledge" of history.

II

Should one expect something like a "second version" of a similar combination of elements at the turn from the eighteenth to the nineteenth century? Protestant millenarianism of the seventeenth and eighteenth centuries engendered no activist revolutions, while a kind of millenarianism, both activist and military, appeared both in the French Revolution, in Babeuf's Conspiracy, and in other socialist organizations. That added element of a "knowledge" of history was clearly present. As early as 1750 Turgot had formulated a rough "theory" of history, approximately at the same time at which Voltaire formulated his postulate of *histoire en philosophe* (in his *Essay sur les moeurs et l'esprit des nations*). History was seen as the result of observable causes, its sequence of ages both logical and predictable, its movement headed toward ultimate fulfillment. Between Turgot and the next generation of pretenders to a "knowledge" of history, there occurred the French Revolution, in the wake of which emerged Condorcet, believer in "the infinite perfectibility of mankind"; Saint Simon, visionary of the new age of non-political and non-military societies; Fourier, author of a complete scheme of History, with a total of 32 ages and 80,000 years, with the present constituting the fifth and worst age; Owen, who foresaw a new "age" to be brought about through a new religion and new form of economic production; Auguste Comte, who conceived of history as three "ages" of the mind, culminating in scientific certainty of morality and a society without contradiction. Each of these thinkers, to whom could be added many more, put before the world the radical distinction between the old aeon, about to end, and the new aeon free from disunities, disharmonies, and human flaws, the contrast being presented not as a vision but of "scientific" analysis. The common characteristic of all these schemes was the idea that the new aeon would be the work of men unaided by any superhuman agency. To some extent such "optimism" (the word stems from this period) was induced by the French Revolution which such observers as Kant and Wordsworth greeted with a kind of holy enthusiasm. But then, the entire century had already been filled with the enthusiastic conviction, based on Locke, that a science of society was possible and could solve any moral problem. Again, however, we find that none of these bodies of ideas produced more than this or that experiment (with no experiment lasting more than a brief time), rather than a mighty revolution.

In German Romanticism alone, rational philosophical analysis deliberately combined with spiritual fervor to engender a revolutionary animus capable of turning into "massive" action. Again, a novel and powerful philosophy of history is at work, that of Hegel. True, Kant and Fichte had both envisaged a new world, one of perpetual peace, the other of complete freedom, and no revolutionary masses rallied around them, which goes to show that not every philosophy of history can bear revolutionary offspring. Nor did Hegel's, immediately. Hegel taught, essentially, a message of reconciliation: the reconciliation (*Vermittlung*) between the world of singularities and the universal Absolute, and the reconciliation of Christian faith (Lutheran) and systematic philosophy. Speculating on God, Hegel defined God's essence as knowledge: "God is not only eternal being (substance) but also the Knowledge of Himself (subject). . . . God is real only in so far as He knows himself; along with His Consciousness his existence appears and disappears; with this reference of being and knowledge to God as the absolute Object, to itself the absolute Subject, the Bible is in agreement. . . . [8] Thus mystical visions and allegorical symbols were left behind, in favor of the precise "Concept," while philosophy as a whole was changed from the "love of truth" to the "certainty of science," all this amounting to a break with Christianity, even if that was not Hegel's intention. Hegel looked on his own system as the final and terminal achievement, the ultimate fulfillment of all philosophy, so that his philosophical system was charged with the enormous power of Christian eschatology, combined with the almost as enormous power of chiliastic vision.

Hegel himself intended this power only for the contemplative use of his system. It was a revolution undertaken by the mind, in the mind, for the mind, culminating in the "final age" of "absolute knowledge," the human mind sharing God's self-knowledge. Thus, while no revolutionary masses gathered around Hegel's house there was, indeed, a gathering of revolutionary minds who, however, did become conscious of their own intent only in the ten years after Hegel's death. Then, however, they began to "live" his message by way of two negations: on the one hand, they proceeded to purge Hegel's system from all remnants of religious transcendence through a radical "critique of religion"; on the other hand they turned to "critique" (destructive attacks) of political and social circumstances as well as on each other. In the words of Karl Löwith: "Feuerbach and Ruge, Ruge and Marx, Marx and Bauer, Bauer and Stirner are pairs of hostile brothers, which any particular moment might begin to fight each other as enemies."[9] Looking at this scene, two of that period's shrewdest observers could already discern the potential of coming violence: Jacob Burckhardt and Heinrich Heine. Burckhardt predicted a time of "long voluntary subjection under individual *Führers* and usurpers. People no longer believe in principles but will, periodically, probably believe in saviors. . . . For this reason authority will again raise its head in the pleasant twentieth century, and a terrible head."[10] In 1835 Heine published his *Geschichte der Religion und Philosophie in Deutschland*, at the end of which he speaks of "revolutionary energies which only wait for the day on which they will erupt and fill the world with horror and admiration." He can see Kantians "with sword and axe," "armed Fichteans," and "revolutionary philosophers of nature," all determined to "extirpate the last roots of the past," and then continues: "such transcendental idealists will be more intransigent than the early Christians who became willing martyrs in order to obtain eternal salvation, while the transcendental idealists consider martyrdom a mere appearance and cannot be reached by anyone in the fortress of his own thoughts."[11]

III

Hegel's movement from "love of truth" to "certainty of science," from mystical and analogical symbols to "the Concept," includes the drawing of the eschaton into history. Hegel's disciples knew that

Hegel had in effect abolished transcendence but then called for a thorough combing of the system for residual bits of the banned stuff, particularly of Christianity. The ensuing "critique of religion" had no quarrel with Hegel's conception of history as the coming-to-be of reason, culminating in mankind's deliverance from blindness and ignorance, which deliverance must take political form. Like other Hegelians, Marx retained the "meaning of history" and the millenarian vision but filled this with the contents of the post-Hegelian critiques of residual transcendence. This in itself was a further revolution — against the revolution embodied in Hegel's system. Marx replaced the classical notion of man as a creature of reason by man's essence defined as labor, the physical transformation of nature's matter into means of sustaining human life. This enabled him to deny that man has a Creator; rather, man "creates himself," through labor. The labor-essence, finally, provided Marx with a human agent of mankind's redemption; the proletariat, first a "Suffering Servant" in whom all humanity is annihilated, then a mighty Avenger of all historical wrong and Destroyer of all social elements of evil, whose victory constitutes the ultimate realm of freedom. Thus Marx's revolution against the revolution combines historical materialism, Promethean humanism, a radically new concept of man, an economic analysis of historical wrong, a non-political view of power and revolution, an identification of proletarian self-emancipation with the universal salvation of mankind — truly a most incendiary package of novelties. This revolution within the revolution is a negation, but not in the sense of "negation of the negation" which cancels negation so as to begin new order. Rather, it doubles the revolutionary negation, conceiving more thorough and comprehensive destruction. Such a dialectic of the revolutionary No can be empirically observed in many apocalyptic movements, from the sixteenth to the twentieth century.

Hegel's negative thinking had remained less than total. His term *aufheben* combined the meanings of "extirpation," "preservation" and "elevation." Marx's materialist reductionism resulted in his pushing the post-Hegelian meaning of "critique" to "destruction," and "the weapons of critique" to "the critique of weapons," as stated in his *Introduction to the Critique of Hegel's Philosophy of Law*. Only one step further and he had discovered the idea of "radical revolution" that does not leave "the pillars of the house standing." His progression from one level of critique to the next made him turn first against Hegel in the name of Bruno Bauer, then against the Bauer brothers in the name of Feuerbach, then against Feuerbach in the name of History. In the name of History he also called on the proletariat to do not "what this or that proletarian, or even the whole of the proletariat at the moment considers its aim," but "what *the proletariat is*, and what, consequent on that *being*, it will be compelled to do."[12] This incendiary package, however, would not explode without "revolutionary consciousness," a notion incompatible with Marx's denial of any freedom of consciousness in history.[13]

This was a truly apocalyptic message even though Marx had utterly rejected all ideas of divinity, Creation, and divine Salvation. One can trace the chiliastic elements at several points of Marx's arguments. By way of a preface, an apocalyptic assumption: "*Die Geschichte aller bisherigen Gesellschaft ist die Geschichte von Klassenkaempfen.*" The English translation, rendering "*bisherig*" as "hitherto existing," misses the language of two aeons Marx is using in the opening sentence of the *Communist Manifesto*. "*Bisherige Geschichte*" says, "everything up to here," dismissing it all as the first aeon, and "here" means, "at the time and place where the new aeon is about to begin." Next, we mention three operative concepts. First, the "realm of freedom" is to occur in history but will not be subject to the forces of decline and decay that have spelled the doom of all historical forms of the past. There will be no further revolutions, even though revolutions in the past have attended the transition from any given type of society to the next. Harmony will be both complete and unchanging: these are characteristics of God's "everlasting kingdom." Here lies the difference of Marx's utopia from that of Plato's *Republic*, where human error and fault invariably bring about a slide into lower forms of order. Marx's realm of perfection has Daniel and St. John's Apocalypse for its ancestors. Secondly, mention has been made of the requisite "revolutionary consciousness." At first Marx suggested that this will come to the proletariat from revolutionary philosophers, i.e., from himself. Later, however, he insisted that "revolutionary consciousness" would form in the course of the proletariat's struggle, which means that it would develop in a way that cannot be known and certainly cannot be controlled by men. This mysterious growth of the required kind of consciousness is first cousin to Divine Providence and guidance. Finally, Marx recognizes that the new aeon requires a new man. His most definite description of the new man is one "for whom labor is the prime want of life"; that is, the man who works without inducement or compulsion. This would imply the identification of socialized labor with freedom. But it is Marx himself who rejects this idea, in the third volume of *Capital*, chapter XLVIII: "The realm of freedom actually only begins where labor . . . ceases. . . . Freedom in this field can only consist in socialized man, the associated producers, rationally regulating their interchange with Nature. . . . But it nonetheless still remains a realm of necessity. Beyond it begins that development of human energy which is an end in itself. . . . This latter is clearly a common-sense statement based on previous experience. The "man whose prime want in life is labor" stands for something akin to a transfigured human being, certainly a transformed man not known to sense-experience, a first cousin to "the saints" of religious chiliasm. The fact that this transformed man, now dubbed "the new Soviet man," is held the indispensable core for any realization of Communist society shows to what extent the Communist vision is heir to the Bible's Thousand-Year Kingdom.

Marx's message is structured by symbolic forms created by Hegel, while its content stems from Marx's further revolution against transcendent elements still lingering in Hegel. But Marx himself trusts that the needed "revolutionary consciousness" will somehow just come to a class of alienated and dehumanized wage-slaves, enabling them to transcend self-interest into their "historical mission." Half a century after these ideas were formulated, Lenin revolted against Marx almost as radically as Marx had earlier revolted against Hegel. In *What Is to Be Done?* Lenin accepts as his dogma that the Suffering-Servant class, the proletariat, by itself cannot have any other but a trade-union consciousness. A trade-union consciousness, fixed on present needs, is motivated by the past, while a revolutionary consciousness must be rooted in the Communist future. Lenin created the Communist Party as the instrument through which revolutionary consciousness could be deliberately "made" or at least adequately manipulated and protected against the corrupting influences of the present-day world. To that extent Lenin purged Marx's legacy from one of its residual millenarian elements. To that extent also, however, is Lenin's elevation of the Party to the rank of humanity's saving agent a twice-perverted demonic design.

There can be little doubt that Gorbachev was engaged in still another one of these purges of residual transcendence, and that he was right in calling this initiative "Leninist." *Perestroika*, the introduction of price incentives and managerial freedom, amounted to dropping "the new Soviet man" into the waste-paper basket. Where Lenin decided that the socialist revolution would have to be "made," Gorbachev discovered that a socialist economy cannot wait for "the new Soviet man" and that Russia's *homo oeconomicus* needed to be "made." He thus appealed from Marx's man "whose prime want in life is labor" to Marx's common-sense statement that labor will always remain in the realm of necessity, in conflict with human freedom. The effective removal of "the new Soviet man," however, leads to the conclusion that the Communist "realm of freedom" will be subject to forces of decline and decay just like other historical forms of life. And, with the disappearance of the notion of an "everlasting" socialist society from Soviet thinking and feeling, could the Communist Party long survive on that pedestal, above the nation, the culture, the economy, the state, above good and evil, above even Marx's "Laws of History," where Lenin's utterly perverted chiliasm had placed it? Criticism of Stalin, which faulted the results of the show-trials of the 'thirties, left huge question marks next to every part of the past seventy years in Soviet history. How could it be possible, then, to maintain the Party's place as authority-above-all-authorities? One may assume that Mr. Gorbachev had no intention to remove the halo surrounding the entire Soviet Union as the trailblazer of mankind's destiny. But all the same his work resulted in doing away with the last traces of supernatural chiliasm that still stood in the way of dealing in a common-sense way with the business of running the Russian empire. The question of what this revolution-against-the-revolution would ultimately mean for the Soviet Union's relation to the rest of the world is one for which a millenarian analysis alone holds no answer, but which is unfolding gradually each day now in the months after the empire's collapse.

IV

Some conclusions may be drawn. Chiliasm is a perennial body of beliefs on the margin of Christianity. It has strongly appealed to a great number of people and has shown its power to arise anew at the beginning of modern times. One hesitates to call it heretical even though it knows itself opposed to orthodox religion. Still, unlike

Gnosticism, it has not declared war on the cosmos nor claimed "knowledge" about a wholly unknowable god. It has not exalted man above a fallen godhead, as did the Gnostics; it does not contain any idea of superman. But its dogma of a future divine kingdom on earth, without any trace of evil, dangerously rejects the limitations of human existence in the cosmos. It also tends to fuse the idea of a thousand-year rule of Christ with the vision of God's eternal kingdom beyond history. Among the political rebellions in its wake, one may dismiss all those attended by extraordinary displays of the ruler's splendor and his love of power as examples of self-seeking rather than God-inspired belief. On the other hand, there were the author of the Book of Daniel and the Swabian chiliasts of the eighteenth century who were interested in the message rather than in revolution, in hope rather than action.

Where modern revolutionary action on a large scale materializes with elements of chiliastic thinking, however, these elements resemble Biblical chiliasm in that they retain, along with the program of human action, something unknown and unmanipulable which also is at work. Marx ultimately looked upon "revolutionary consciousness" as something of a mystery, as he also envisaged a type of man not known to human experience. Even more, the "everlasting" quality of his realm of freedom belongs to the category of divine realms rather than human societies. In the same way in which the apocalyptic literature mixes divine and human elements, Marx knew of man's "common-sense" existence as well as existence in a higher-ranking society, even though he has no word like "holy" for the higher rank. Insofar as revolutionary ideology deliberately claims this "higher-than-human" rank into the orbit of human control and manipulation, we are in the presence of perversion of both spirit and reason, which perversion does deserve the name of "illegitimate."

NOTES

1. Other related parts of the Bible are: Joel 2:1–11; 4:1–21; Isaiah 13 and 24–27, Ezekiel 38–39, Zephaniah 1:14–18, Mark 13, Matthew 24, Luke 21. Further, there are apocryphal or simply non-canonical books, among them: Enoch, Slavonic Enoch, Testaments of the Twelve Patriarchs, Sibylline Oracles, The Assumption of Moses, 2 and 3 Baruch, 4 (2) Esdras, and the Apocalypses of Peter, Paul, and Thomas.

2. Walter Nigg, *Das Ewige Reich* (Erlenbach-Zürich: E. Rentsch, 1944), p. 293.

3. Augustine, *The City of God*, p. xx.

4. Only in the South was German Pietism millenarian: there is no millenarianism in the Northern Pietism of Francke and Zinzendorf.

5. A contemporary book, *Millenial Dreams in Action* (Sylvia L. Thrupp ed., The Hague: Mouton and Co., 1962) includes in "millenial dreams" native movements, some of them magic in character, others pertaining to the category "periods of cosmic renewal," thus sacrificing the one poor element of precision attached to "millennium" by the text of the *locus classicus.*

6. For these movements, see Norman Cohn, *The Pursuit of the Millenium,* 2nd ed. (New York: Harper and Row, 1961).

7. Karl Löwith, *Meaning in History: The Theological Implications of the Philosophy of History* (Chicago: University of Chicago Press, 1949), p. 146.

8. G. W. F. Hegel, in his review of C. F. Goeschel's *Aphorismen über Nichtwissen und absolutes Wissen,* quoted in Jürgen Gebhardt, *Politik und Eschatologie* (Munich: C. H. Beck, 1963), p. 58.

9. Löwith, *Von Hegel zu Nietzsche* (Stuttgart: W. Kohlhammer, 1958), p. 80.

10. Burckhardt, quoted in Löwith, *Meaning in History,* p. 24.

11. Löwith, *Von Hegel zu Nietzsche,* p. 57.

12. Karl Marx and Friedrich Engels, *The Holy Family* (Moscow: Foreign Languages Publishing House, 1956), *passim.*

13. Marx and Engels, *The German Ideology* (New York: International Publishers 1960), *passim.*

*   *   *

"It is easy to enumerate Russell Kirk's contributions to the conservative cause in the past half-century: The Conservative Mind, *the founding of* Modern Age, *his "From the Academy" column which appeared for more than two decades in* National Review, *and a prodigious torrent of books and other writings. All this is extraordinary, laudable — and obvious. Less remarked upon have been the qualities of mind and soul that have infused his tireless defense of the permanent things.*

"Three, to me, stand out. Dr. Kirk has been unwaveringly committed to scholarly pursuits and the demands of a life of letters; he has never let political passions consume his energies. He has cheerfully persevered in his fundamental convictions, surrendering not to the torments and allures of "the drift of things." And he has been willing, even in his seventies, to spend time with students yearning for instruction in liberating truths. Like another conservative elder, Ronald Reagan, he has maintained a vivifying rapport with the young.

"In each of these ways Russell Kirk has not merely articulated conservatism for our generation. He has exemplified it. In doing so, he has given heart as well as intellectual nourishment to many who once felt alone. As we evaluate his multifaceted accomplishments, let us remember and celebrate not only the influential substance of his writings but the generous and stalwart content of his character."

— George H. Nash, 1992.

Religious Freedom and "Compelling State Interest"

by William Bentley Ball

I fear that Dr. Kirk, when he reads this *Festschrift*, will not welcome a personal anecdote involving him. But the tie-in between the story about him which I shall relate and the subject of this chapter is too significant to be left out.

Some years ago I was defending in court a small, non-tax-aided Christian college which a state educational hierarchy had decided to shut down. The college was profoundly religious and existed solely to be a religious ministry of a church. The state's pretext for the shutdown (its closure edict being delivered while the students were on Thanksgiving vacation) did not allege any deficiency in the college, physical or intellectual. The pretext was solely the college's refusal to obtain state "approval"—in effect, a license or permit to exist. "Approval" meant that it would have to have submitted itself to total state governance. In particular, the college had been asked by the State Board of Higher Education to agree to subscribe to an infinitely long list of state-concocted standards ("minimum" standards, in the state's Aesopian phrasing). These would govern every aspect of the life of the institution. In effect, the college had been pressured to sign a blank check, giving to government plenary jurisdiction over both an intellectual enterprise and a religious ministry. The college's painfully considered refusal was to be at the price of its ceasing to exist.

Moving for an injunction to restrain the state, the college went to trial. The supreme issues were, to me, obvious: under what circumstances may government put a stop to religious endeavors? How far does the power of government extend in relation to the exercise of religion? And, in the realm of the intellect, is government the sole, or a superior, educator? The Supreme Court of the United States, in 1963, in *Sherbert v. Verner*, had held the answer to these questions, so related to spirit and mind, to be this: government may indeed restrict the exercise of religion, but it may do so only in the name of a "compelling state interest" and if no less restrictive means exist for achieving that interest.[1] Was there, in our case, a compelling state interest in the closure of this college (due to its refusal to subject itself to total state jurisdiction)? And, if so, did not any means exist, short of shutting the college down, by which the state's interests (even though "compelling") could be realized? Those questions, in turn, led to the deeper question: *What* was the state's interest? Was it simply in having regulations, for their own sake, obeyed? Was it *education*? Obviously, the state would have to say that it was the latter, that its regulations existed for the end of good education and that a reasonably close cause-effect connection existed between the regulations and good education. Also, the state would have to show that that "good education" which it sought to effect by its regulations was of so immense and immediate importance as to justify destroying a college and a ministry in its name.

This unusual case called, above all, for the factor of *enlightenment*. The State Board of Education's witnesses, pedigreed employees of the bureaucracy, could not supply that by their arbitrary insistence that all education must conform to their prescriptions. Their testimony showed they could not explain key parts of those prescriptions. Nor did they seek to say of what "good" education consists. Therefore, if the "compelling state interest" issue—the very heart of the case—was really to be aired in court, a witness was needed who could go beyond and outside of the opaque mandates of the state regulators, who would turn their many dogmatic conclusions into questions, who could inform the Court (out of an immense background of knowledge and experience) of the meaning of education—in short, for a witness who could enlighten this proceeding. I knew that that witness should be Russell Kirk.

This personal anecdote ends with the fact that Dr. Kirk consented to study my case, concluded that he could supply the evidence crucially needed, flew, at real risk, in hazardous night weather, to appear as an expert witness, and gave testimony which educated the court, informing it on the true nature of education. His testimony conclusively showed that the state's "minimum standards" were, to a considerable extent, not conducive to good education, but were mere, arbitrary, open-ended assumptions of power. Finding (as one with decades of experience in higher education) that this small college was performing responsibly in meeting the intellectual and religious needs of its students, Kirk saw no justification for its being forced into a governmental mold (whose success, in terms of provable educational results, he seriously questioned). Kirk destroyed the State's pretentious case.

Here, then, in this anecdote, is a laboratory example of the "compelling state interest" question in one of the forms in which it has been arising in American courts during the past four decades. The visible elements are (1) a litigant's religious or intellectual claims, (2) action by government to impose regulations overriding those claims, (3) government's asserting, as its justification, a "compelling state interest" for its doing so, (4) government's claim that no less-restrictive alternative is available to it than its contemplated action.

Since, in our overly litigious American society, cases are daily moving through our courts, in which freedom of religion is said to be threatened by governmental action, it is of more than passing importance to examine the concept of "compelling state interest." Is it a meaningful term? Is it merely a label which may be applied to justify any governmental aggression? If it may be regarded as a hurdle which government must cross in order to restrict religious activity, may courts set the hurdle high in some kinds of cases, low in others? May courts kick the hurdle aside and sanction actions of government without reference to the magnitude of its interest when compared with the importance of the liberty whose exercise it opposes? Most important of all: if it is a concept which is protective of religious liberty, is it being applied by our courts today with vigor, or is it being abandoned? Our starting point in answering these questions is a closer look at the *Sherbert* case.

The Supreme Court, prior to its 1963 decision in *Sherbert*, had ruled in numerous conflicts between government and religion. As early as 1879, it suggested the "compelling state interest" concept and later applied it to overrule religious claims involving polygamy,[2] compulsory vaccination,[3] military training,[4] and child labor.[5] From 1940 forward, however, the Court, giving increased scope to its recognition of religious liberty in cases involving religious solicitation,[6] taxation,[7] and wartime promotion of national cohesion,[8] foreshadowed the high standard it would state in *Sherbert*.[9]

In *Sherbert* the Supreme Court was faced with the claim of one Adele Sherbert, a Seventh-day Adventist, that the State of South Carolina had unlawfully denied her unemployment compensation benefits. The State's defense was that unemployed persons who refuse employment cannot collect such benefits. Employment had been offered Sherbert, but she had refused it. Sherbert said that the employment involved Saturday work, that Saturday was her Sabbath; hence she could not accept the employment. To force her to violate her religion, she contended, in order to enjoy a state benefit to which she would otherwise be entitled, violated her religious liberty. The State of South Carolina looked at the matter very differently. Its unemployment compensation statute, like those of almost all the states, contained no wording making exceptions or exemptions relating to work on religious days or for any reasons related to religion. By an ancient and respected tradition in the law, enactments of legislatures are presumed constitutional, and a heavy burden is placed on anyone who attacks that presumption.[10] And for good reason: the legislature is that branch of government closest to the people and thus most attuned to the people's needs and wishes. The legislative process is futile if courts are free to carve out exceptions to legislative enactments. And South Carolina argued, further, that the statute served a public interest; and that, if the Court were to rule that there could be exceptions such as that called for by Miss Sherbert, administrative difficulty and increased costs of the program were likely.

The Supreme Court's response was, first, that state laws which, on their face or in application, burden the exercise of religion[11] "must be justified by a compelling state interest in the regulation of a subject within the State's constitutional power to regulate." The Court illuminated the concept of "compelling state interest" as follows:

> It is basic that no showing merely of a rational relationship to some *colorable* state interest would suffice; in this highly sensitive consitutional area, "[o]nly the *gravest abuses, endangering paramount interests*, give occasion for permissible limitation." [Emphasis supplied.][12]

The Court further stated that even though a compelling state interest is found, it must appear that no less restrictive means exists for government's achieving of that interest. The Court had no difficulty in finding that Miss Sherbert's practice of her religion would be seriously burdened by the State's denying her benefits except on the condition that she violate her religious convictions. And it had no difficulty in declaring that no compelling state interest justified the State's denial of benefits. The costs to South Carolina in terms of administrative inconvenience and possible new drafts on the unemployment compensation fund apparently bore, in the Court's view, a mere "rational relationship" to some merely "colorable" state interest. Those costs did not fall within the class of "gravest abuses, endangering *paramount* interests" of society. (Since the Court found no compelling state interest, it had no call to discuss "less restrictive means.")

This test of the constitutionality of governmental actions affecting religion thus involved two affirmations (1) that religious freedom is a "fundamental" liberty; (2) that only a "paramount" societal interest may ever justify limiting it. If it is "fundamental," freedom of religion must *in itself* be regarded as a "compelling state interest." Legally, it must always be presumed inviolable. Only some rare societal interest, of the most immense urgency and magnitude, should be deemed by the courts as possibly superior. That being so, *most* societal interests — that is, most statutes, ordinances or administrative regulations which threaten adverse effects upon religious liberty may not override that liberty. That government action limiting religious liberty is basically justified by a mere "public" interest will not validate it constitutionally. Those are the plain teachings of the *Sherbert* decision.

Rounding out an understanding of the *Sherbert* "compelling state interest" doctrine, it is important to ask two questions: In the phrase "compelling *state* interest" what is meant by "state?" Second, in litigation between government and a citizen who contends his or her First Amendment rights are threatened by governmental action, how does the court find out whether a compelling state interest is really involved?

It is vital to understand that "state," in the phrase "compelling state interest," must be taken to mean "societal" rather than "governmental." The interest of the bureaucracy in the conduct of its affairs or the maintaining of its powers is absolutely irrelevant. When the National Labor Relations Board, in 1977, sought to fasten its jurisdiction upon the Catholic parish schools of Philadelphia, the Labor Board, in the court contest which ensued, sought to impress the court with the importance of the Board's being able to exercise jurisdiction over all employers and the danger of weakening its authority by a ruling limiting its authority.[13] But the majesty of government and its prestige, bulk greatly though they may in the public eye, must, under the teaching of *Sherbert*, be disregarded by the court, since it is never the interest of government, *qua* government, which should be deemed to constitute the "state" interest (*i.e.*, the societal interest). Unhappily, in some religious cases, courts have bowed to the prestige of government and ruled against the non-government challenger of governmental action[14] — who may indeed lack such prestige and is often a lone individual or small group resisting the governmental will.

How, under the *Sherbert* test, does the court go about finding out whether there is, or is not, a supreme societal interest which justifies governmental action injuring religious exercise? The answer is not to be found in the say-so of either party. The court dare not merely take the word of, say, a religious litigant, that God told this litigant to ignore or defy the civil law. Rather he must *prove* his claim that his position is based upon a sincere and well-rooted religious belief and that his liberty to exercise that belief will be substantially limited by threatened governmental action. That is, in the setting of a litigation, he must offer actual evidence of these things — the testimony of witnesses, documentary evidence (*e.g.*, copies of articles of faith, doctrinal statements, etc.). The religious party to the controversy thus makes his *prima facie* case.

What, then, of the government's case in light of the *Sherbert* test? Its mere stating of its claim of compelling state interest and lack of less restrictive means — like the religious party's mere stating of its claim — will not, under *Sherbert*, suffice. Like the religious party, the governmental party must *prove* its claim. The burden of proof thus shifts to government, and it, too, must come up with *facts* if it is to make its *prima facie* case. These facts — through witnesses, documents, and other evidence — will operate to demonstrate the magnitude of the societal interest which the government contends necessitates its action.

The requirement, under *Sherbert*, that each side "make its case" through factual proof is, as shall be seen, extremely significant. It is also entirely reasonable. It does not guarantee just results, but it is the best means we have in the effort to obtain just results. As the Court has recently stated, " 'the function of a standard of proof, as that concept is embodied in the Due Process Clause and in the realm of factfinding, is to instruct the factfinder concerning the degree of confidence our society thinks he should have in the correctness of factual conclusions'."[15] For a particular reason it is important to examine why it is necessary that the *state* be made to bear an actual burden of proof when it threatens to collide with First Amendment liberties. Suppose that, while the court would require the religious party to a litigation to prove the sincerity and *bona fides* of the religious claim and the certainty of injury to religious exercise if the challenged governmental action were allowed (Parts 1 and 2 of the *Sherbert* test), the state were let off the hook—*not* held to a requirement that it *prove* compelling state interest and absence of alternative means (Parts 3 and 4 of the *Sherbert* test)? Would this not amount to a license given the state to override fundamental freedoms? Rightly, our courts ought not stomach allowing a religious claimant to prevail in litigation against the state on that claimant's mere assertion that "God wants it that way." Is it imaginable that our courts should, on the other hand, allow government to prevail against the religious claimant on the government's mere assertion that "the government wants it that way?" As the Court has said in some other kinds of cases, government should be required to make its case by "clear and convincing evidence" where the interests at stake "are both particularly important and more substantial than mere loss of money."[16]

I have thought it important briefly to discuss the *Sherbert* case and detail its implications for two reasons. First, *Sherbert* states a high and reasonable standard of review for the courts of the land in cases involving religious liberty. Second, this standard—with its potent restrictions upon governmental action and its high regard for rights of religious practice, observance, and proper immunities—is today being judicially overridden in favor of a jurisprudence of secular utility—a novel jurisprudence undeniably totalitarian in tendency.

What has been described as the "high watermark" in religious liberty decisions of the Supreme Court[17] came nine years after *Sherbert*. The case was *Wisconsin v. Yoder*,[18] in which the Court held that, due to the Free Exercise Clause of the First Amendment, Amish children could not be forced to attend high school in violation of Amish religious beliefs. The Court rested its decision squarely on *Sherbert*. It examined with care the "quality of the claims" (the religious claims) made by the Amish, stressing that, "to have the protection of the Religion Clauses [of the First Amendment], the claims must be rooted in religious belief."[19] Finding that "the traditional way of life of the Amish is not merely a matter of personal preference, but one of deep religious conviction, shared by an organized group, and intimately related to daily living," and that "Old Order Amish daily life and religious practice stem from their faith . . . [which requires that] they 'be not conformed to this world',"[20] the Court found that "[t]he impact of the compulsory attendance law on the . . . practice of the Amish religion is not only severe, but inescapable, for the Wisconsin law affirmatively compels them, under threat of criminal sanction, to perform acts undeniably at odds with fundamental tenets of their religious beliefs."[21]

With the religious claim and with religious injury established, the stage was set for examination of the compelling state interest issue. Wisconsin claimed that its interest in its system of compulsory education was so compelling that "even the established religious practice of the Amish must give way."[22] The Court stated the standard to be observed:

> The essence of all that has been said and written on the subject is that only those interests of the highest order and those not otherwise served can overbalance legitimate claims to the free exercise of religion.[23]

The Court would hence not accept Wisconsin's broad, purportedly self-evident claim of compelling state interest. Rather, the Court said:

> Where fundamental claims of religious freedom are at stake, . . . we cannot accept such a sweeping claim; despite its admitted validity in the generality of cases, *we must searchingly examine the interests that the State seeks to promote* by its requirements for compulsory education to age 16, *and the impediment to those objectives* that would flow from recognizing the claimed Amish exemption.[24] [Emphasis supplied.]

This requirement of "searching" examination is of the highest importance. The State was put upon its proof, and the Court's opinion in *Yoder* is largely an examination of the *facts* adduced upon the trial. The "say-so" of parties is rejected. And because Free Exercise rights are at stake, government will not get by with broad allegations, and the Court will not attempt to supply government's case. The Court's opinion contains twenty references to the trial record, and it repeatedly notes the failure of the State to have furnished factual proof of a compelling state interest.[25]

Given the facts of *Yoder*, the *Yoder* decision was inevitable — given

the "compelling state interest" test of *Sherbert*. That *Yoder* represented a
"high-water mark" in the Court's religious liberty decisions,[26] however,
is the troublesome fact which must now be faced by all who now venture to resist moves of government inimical to religious freedom. This
change has come about, not by a single, express overruling of *Sherbert*,
but by omission, by indirection, and by new teaching.

1. Departure from Sherbert

A sharp step down from the *Sherbert* standard came ten years after
Yoder in a case of the most dubious background, badly suited to being
a religious liberty test case, and, tragically, identified with the Amish.
The Amish do not "go to the law"; they do not sue, and the Amish
community was not involved in the suit aberrantly brought against
the United States by one Edwin D. Lee. Lee was an Amishman who
operated a lumber-finishing business. He claimed that, as an
Amishman, he was protected by the Free Exercise Clause from having to pay the employer's share of social security taxes and to withhold
his employees' share. His attorneys did not seek a trial in the case, and
the sole facts presented to the Supreme Court were found in a meager
written stipulation agreed to by the attorneys for each side. The
Supreme Court ruled in the Government's favor. Looking at Lee's
religious claim, the Court rejected the Government's contention that
payment of the taxes "will not threaten the integrity of Amish religious
belief or observance." "[C]ourts are not arbiters of scriptural interpretation," said Chief Justice Burger, speaking for eight members of
the Court. He concluded that compulsory participation in the social
security system violated Amish religious beliefs and interfered with
Amish Free Exercise rights. Thus having addressed the first part of
the *Sherbert* test, the Court had set the stage for addressing the second
part, the "compelling state interest" issue. The Court stated:

> The state may justify a limitation on religious liberty by showing that it is
> essential to accomplish an overriding governmental interest.[27]

Here the Court cited both *Sherbert* and *Yoder*. Is "overriding governmental interest" simply another way of saying "compelling state interest?" To suggest that it is not, and that the omission of the word
"compelling" (and substituting the word "overriding") was a calculated
weakening of a constitutional protection may seem captious, hyper-

sensitive reliance on formalism. But that it is such is not free from doubt, and uneasiness with the *Lee* decision arises from what else the Court had to say in its opinion. The Court went on to inquire whether accommodating the Amish beliefs would "unduly interfere with fulfillment of the governmental interest." That interest, said the Court, was the maintaining of the social security system (with universal participation in it). This definition of state interest is broad indeed. It specifies *uniformity of participation* as an interest above all other interests, even the interest represented by a First Amendment claim. It suggests applications reaching far beyond the social security situation; uniformity could be made the basis, too, for requiring all children to attend public schools.[28]

Having identified that interest, the Court stated that "it would be difficult to accommodate the comprehensive social security system with myriad exceptions flowing from a wide variety of religious beliefs." And the Court concluded with a broad new prescription:

> Because the broad public interest in maintaining a sound tax system is of such a high order, religious belief in conflict with the payment of taxes affords no basis for resisting the tax.[29]

Leaving to one side the extreme, and obviously dangerous, ramifications both of that sentence and of the "uniformity" requirement, the student of the teaching of *Sherbert* is driven to inquire as to the *factual basis* of the Court's ready conclusion that exempting Mr. Lee posed a mortal threat to the American social security system. That is, we naturally ask what burden of proof the Court compelled the Government to bear that this threat was posed by Mr. Lee's claim and that a supreme societal interest was at stake in the case. For the proof needed, the Court could not refer to a trial record. No trial in the case had taken place. The Court therefore relied on Government briefs and on its own research (*e.g.*, mainly a Senate study which broadly stated that "[W]idespread individual voluntary coverage under social security . . . would undermine the soundness of the social security program."). The conspicuous failure of the Court to spell out the how or why of that conclusion — that is, to be specific about the compellingness of the governmental interest in denying exemption to Mr. Lee or to other Amish — set the stage for a case in which that specificity would be demanded.

Mr. Lee's case was totally unsuited to being the test case for a staggeringly important constitutional ruling. As I have inferred, his attorneys did not press for the making of a trial record (which would or should have involved forcing the Government to try to prove its case that the social security system would be threatened by the tolerance of the exemption sought by Lee). Plainly the Government ought to have been made to produce documented justification of its claims respecting the vulnerability of the system. In 1982, when *Lee* was decided, every nonprofit organization in the United States was exempt from the social security program and had been so for a half a century. In spite of this vast exemption, the program had thrived.

In 1987 there was presented to the Supreme Court precisely the case needed in order to substitute facts for opaque generalities with respect to the supposedly "overriding" interest of government in permitting religiously based exemptions to participation in the social security program. The new case, furthermore, would raise, in a far more basic way than did the *Lee* case, the profound relationships between taxation and religious freedom. The case was *Bethel Baptist Church v. United States*.[30] In 1984 Bethel was faced with a crisis. The Congress, in 1983, had amended the Social Security Act to impose its tax and program on all nonprofit organizations, including churches. In 1984, following a protest by thousands of small churches over this first-time-ever taxation of churches, the Congress amended the law in order to permit (within a short statutory period) any church to opt out of the social security program. But, as Bethel was quick to note, if a given church opted out, its employees would (under the amendment) be treated as "self-employed" and required to pay double the social security tax which they would pay absent the "opting out." Also, though now called "self-employed," they would be denied those tax deductions (*e.g.*, for automobile, etc.) to which other self-employed persons are entitled under the Internal Revenue Code. The employees of Bethel Baptist Church all deemed themselves to be, and were, engaged, whole-soul and full-time, in a religious ministry. Bethel was hence faced with a crisis: if it did not "opt out" the church would be taxed; if it did "opt out" those who followed a religious vocation through employment in the church's various ministries (including conducting its schools and its child-care program) would be taxed on that account. Bethel therefore sued in federal court, advancing the plainest imaginable claims of religious profession and threatened injury. These claims (Part I of the *Sherbert* test) could scarcely be denied. The critical thrust of the litigation would therefore need to be the compelling state interest issue.

Unlike Edwin D. Lee, Bethel Baptist Church was prepared to litigate the issue in depth. The papers it filed in the United States District Court, where it launched its case, hammered at the Government's door, demanding that the Government come forward with proof, if any it had, that exempting Bethel or its ministers from payment of the taxes would have any effect—even the slightest—on the national social security program. Bethel offered to present detailed evidence that no such result could ensue.[31] Bethel also filed requests with the court that the Government be made to furnish specific documents and respond to pointed questions which, so Bethel claimed, would demolish the Government's pretense that a reasonable religious exemption would in any way endanger the social security system. Bethel, in other words, directly relying on *Sherbert*, demanded that the court require Government to prove the Government's "compelling state interest" contention. The District court refused these requests by Bethel; indeed, it refused to allow a *trial* in the case. It granted the Government's motion for summary judgment, citing *Lee* as precedent authority.[32] Bethel appealed to the U.S. Court of Appeals for the Third Circuit which affirmed, holding fast to the same "protect taxation" line taken by the District court. Bethel sought review by the Supreme Court; the Supreme Court declined review.

It is not the purpose of this essay to push further into matters of taxation and non-taxation, since the sole point of inquiry which I have proposed to explore in this essay respects the concept of "compelling state interest." Not, therefore, to expatiate further on the totality of the threat which the taxing power holds to religion,[33] but only to conclude discussion of that power in relation to "compelling state interest," mention must be made of *Bob Jones University v. United States*[34] and *Texas Monthly, Inc. v. Bullock.*[35]

Bob Jones University, a pervasively religious institution, had a policy whereby it forbade interracial dating and intermarriage between students or staff; it had earlier barred all non-white applicants for either enrollment or employment. Both policies were found, upon trial, to be firmly rooted in a sincerely held interpretation of the Bible. The IRS, in 1976, revoked the long-existing tax-exempt status of the

University, stating that the Internal Revenue Code did not allow tax exemption for racially discriminatory organizations. The Supreme Court, in ruling in the ensuing litigation brought by the University, added remarkable new content to the concept of "compelling state interest." It held that the tax-exempt status of a religious body could be revoked on the ground that such status offends *"national public policy."* The "national public policy" here was a national rejection of racial discrimination. That the subjecting of religious bodies to taxation, and (as also here) the related non-deductibility of gifts to such bodies, may greatly injure, if not destroy, them in the carrying out of their ministries, appeared, in the Court's opinion, to be matters of little moment. But, though weighing Bob Jones's religious claim but lightly in the *Sherbert* scales, it added a new kind of "compelling state interest" to the government's side of the *Sherbert* scale: not tangible proof of tangible harm to a supreme societal interest, but to an indefinable thing called "national public policy." It had been the essence of prior jurisprudence that exercises of speech, press, religion, or assembly could be restricted or denied when colliding with specific statutes or administrative regulations sustainable in the name of a compelling state interest, or when offending a specific constitutional provision. Bob Jones University had been charged with no breach of any statute or constitutional provision. No such basis was alleged for denial of its tax-exempt status. Instead the Court read into the Internal Revenue Code the concept that all "charitable" organizations must conform to a thing outside the Code: national public policy.

"National public policy" is uncomfortably close to the *ragione di stato* doctrine of the seventeenth century: rights may be subtended for "reasons of state."[36] The decision in *Bob Jones University v. United States* may seem remote in intent and spirit from the balefully totalitarian jurisprudence which has held so much of mankind in its grip in our century, but it is not hyperbole to say that it states precisely the principle of *Gleichshaltung* imposed by the Third Reich.[37] If "national public policy" may now be invoked to justify the oppression of exercise of a religious liberty, there are no limits to what may be called "public policy" and no place to go, except (ultimately) to the nine justices of the Supreme Court (five of whom will suffice for decision). This new doctrine is remote indeed from what the Court had given us to understand in its decisions from 1940 forward on religious liberty. True, the courts, under *Sherbert*, *could* declare the most trivial of public interests to be "compelling." But to do so credibly, they would (if following *Sherbert*) have to demonstrate, by evidentiary findings, a cause-effect connection between the contemplated societal interest and contemplated governmental action, as well as demonstrate why that interest was so great as to call for sacrifice of a First Amendment freedom. But in *Bob Jones* the Court treated the contemplated governmental action (revocation of tax-exempt status) as a built-in part of the Internal Revenue Code. This renders *Bob Jones* a decision quite different from those in *Sherbert* and *Lee*. In those cases the Court merely inquired whether a statute of national scope could be applied against religious exercise. The Court then answered its question in terms of the importance which it found attached to the particular national program and the danger it deemed that recognizing the particular religious claim would pose to that program. In *Bob Jones* the Court found no danger to the national tax-collecting program which would be posed by the continuance of the tax-exempt status of racially discriminatory religious bodies. Instead it found that the statute itself, the Internal Revenue Code, *had* to be applied irrespective of harm to religious liberty, because built into that statute was a national public policy.

Bob Jones thus opens wide doors to further limitation of religious rights. If "national public policy" is now moved into our jurisprudence to render irrelevant contests over "compelling state interest," the threat of destructive taxation of religious endeavors is very great. Many federal statutes, *e.g.*, the Environmental Quality Improvement Act,[38] contain express declarations that they are enacted as expressions of national policy. If at some future time population control were deemed essential to preservation of an environment conducive to a good "quality of life,"[39] a religious institution which refused to hire employees who did not pledge their opposition to contraception and abortion, could be subjected to federal income taxation — and why not to other penalties?

Rounding out the Supreme Court's recognition of total power to tax religion (and hence, we cannot fail to note, to tax it out of existence) is its 1988 decision in *Texas Monthly, Inc. v. Bullock, supra*. A Texas statute had contained a sales-tax exemption for religious literature, but not for other literature. While the Court invalidated the exemption on Establishment Clause grounds, the Court also concluded that the Free Exercise Clause does not require exemption from a governmental program unless inclusion in the program actually burdens Free Exercise rights. The Court, referring to *Lee*, found no evidence "that the payment of a sales tax by subscribers to religious periodicals or purchases of religious books would offend their religious beliefs or inhibit religious activity." In noting this summary dismissal of the religious claim we must take into account the fact that the claimant was not a religious party but was the Comptroller of Public Accounts of the State of Texas. His interest was the routine interest of a public official in defending a statute which it was his duty to administer. *Texas Monthly*, then, like *Lee*, was an inadequate vehicle for testing so significant a question as the constitutionality of taxing religious expression in the form of publications. It was an extremely unfortunate case, because the Court utilized it as the occasion to virtually overrule its 1943 decision in *Murdock v. Pennsylvania* (see note 7), in which it had held that dissemination of religious beliefs through the sale of religious tracts could not be made subject to a license tax.

> To the extent that language in [*Murdock*] is inconsistent with our decision here, based on the evolution in our thinking about the Religion Clauses over the last 45 years, we disavow it.[40]

This statement is ominous indeed. This regressive thinking is seen further in two decisions of the Supreme Court (not in the field of taxation) which plainly replace *Sherbert's* "compelling state interest" standard with a principle of mere utility.

In *Goldman v. Weinberger*,[41] the Court was faced with the claim of Capt. S. Simcha Goldman, an Orthodox Jewish rabbi, that his religion called for his wearing of a yarmulke indoors while on duty, while the U.S. Air Force contended that its established rules, based on considerations of military regularity, forbade this. Here, plainly, were pitted against one another religious and governmental claims. Goldman said that the Air Force's prohibition violated his rights under the Free Exercise Clause. He described the yarmulke as "an expression of respect for God . . . intended to keep the wearer aware of God's presence." Understandably relying on *Sherbert* and *Yoder*, he argued that no compelling state interest had been proved to justify the Government's position. The Supreme Court, in a decision in favor of the Government, avoided the *Sherbert* test. That is, the Court not only did not hold the Government to *proving* that a compelling state interest justified its forbidding Goldman's practice; it did not even apply the *Sherbert* test. The Court referred briefly to (substantial) evidence supporting his religious claim which Goldman had presented—but dismissed it, in large part, as "quite beside the point." The complementary aspect of the *Sherbert* standard—government's proof of compelling state interest—was not part of the *ratio decidendi*. The Court instead relied upon the "considered professional judgment of the Air Force" and concluded that the First Amendment did not require the military to accommodate religious practices that "would detract from the uniformity sought by the dress regulations."[42]

In *Goldman* we thus see the "compelling state interest" requirement omitted and the substitution for it of a mere "public interest" (in this case, a public interest in maintaining military uniformity, without the allowance of exceptions). Utility, in other words, is placed on the balancing scales with religious liberty, and the Court's hand weights down utility's side of the scales.

In *Lyng v. Northwest Indian Cemetery Protection Association*,[43] we see a further substitution of the principle of utility in place of the requirement of proof of compelling state interest. There the Court held that the Free Exercise Clause does not bar the federal government from permitting timber-harvesting in, or constructing a road through, a small mountain area which for two centuries had been utilized by Indians as a place, sacred to them, for religious rituals and practices. *Lyng* posed, in the clearest way, the applicability of the *Sherbert* standard of review. Looking first to the religious claim, the Court readily agreed that "[i]t is undisputed that the Indian respondents' beliefs are sincere and that the Government's proposed actions will have severe adverse effects upon the practice of their religion."[44] Later in its opinion the Court expanded on the harm to the Indians' religious life. "The challenged governmental action would interfere significantly with private persons' ability to pursue spiritual fulfillment according to their own religious beliefs"[45]—indeed that "the logging and road-building projects at issue in this case could have a devastating effect upon traditional Indian religious practices."[46] The Court, ruling against the Indians' religious claims, all but scrapped the requirement that religious liberty may not be violated by governmental action which does not represent a compelling state interest. This rejection was express, as compared with the mere avoidance of the compelling state interest requirement in *Goldman*:

> Respondents contend that the burden on their religious practices is heavy

enough to violate the Free Exercise Clause *unless the Government can demonstrate a compelling need* [for its actions]. We disagree. [Emphasis supplied.][47]

Again,

> Whatever may be the exact line between unconstitutional prohibitions on the free exercise of religion and the legitimate conduct by government of its own affairs, *the location of the line cannot depend on measuring the efforts of a government action on a religious objector's spiritual development.* [Emphasis supplied.][48]

Their "spiritual development" was scarcely what the Indians were talking about in their pleas to the courts, and the use of the deprecating phrase was not necessary to the thrust of the point now made by Justice O'Connor (writing for the Court). The point was a new and adverse turn for the fortunes of religious liberty. The "compelling state interest" doctrine of *Sherbert* was now to be drastically altered. Only government activity which would "have a tendency to *coerce* individuals into acting contrary to their religious beliefs requires government to bring forward a compelling justification for its otherwise lawful actions." By that reasoning, provided that government did not pressure the Jews of Beth El Temple into taking actions contrary to their religious beliefs, government could constitutionally raze Beth El to create a municipal flower garden.

2. Present Dangers, Open Questions

It is neither advisable nor possible to bracket the Supreme Court's decisions on the free exercise of religion within a single, short statement. The Court has no philosophy and few, if any, philosophers. Variation within its ranks is characteristic of the Court. Justice Scalia, who denounced the views of the majority in *Texas Monthly*, joined the majority on *Lyng*. Justice Brennan, who wrote the opinion in *Texas Monthly* was a heated dissenter in *Lyng*. If you are a Seventh-day Adventist (or a convert thereto) denied unemployment compensation because you will not work on the Saturday you are offered employment, the Court will be at your side. If the government is about to tax your ministry out of existence, the Court will be on the government's side. So matters stand. Nor for the future are sure-fire predictions possible. Changes of mind take place among Court members, and disabilities and death take place with politics always ready to fill vacuums they create. But the present trend in Free Exercise decisions, utilitarian and pragmatic, in which secular considerations prevail over sacred, is dramatically clear. In such decisions as *Lee, Bob Jones, Goldman, Texas Monthly,* and *Lyng,* we witness the Free Exercise Clause radically diminished in significance. The Court's refusal to hear cases in which petitions for review have posed major Free Exercise questions,[49] reinforces that conclusion. The Court's growingly narrow and constrictive view of the Free Exercise Clause of the First Amendment contrasts sharply with the almost unlimited breadth it accords the Free Speech and Free Press Clauses of the First Amendment.[50] Almost unlimited freedom for obscenity and for defamation are now held by the Court to be absolutely required by the necessities of human freedom. Yet, less than a half century ago, the Court had held *all* the First Amendment freedoms to be "conjunctive" freedoms and had indeed said, not that Free Exercise was less significant than Free Speech or Free Press, but that the latter freedoms were *as important as* Free Exercise — a nuance different from the view the Court now takes of Free Exercise.[51]

Historically, there can be no doubt that to call Free Exercise "the first freedom" was an accurate phrase to state the invaluable character which universally attaches to religious liberty. Until recently, Free Exercise has been treated as a "preferred" freedom and a "fundamental" right, not as editorial fill-in in Court opinions but in decisional results. The Court had never before held the First Amendment to grant religions *"exemptions,"* but simply (as with freedom of speech) to declare a *right.* Today the Free Exercise of Religion, in diminished status, appears often to be treated as the Free Exercise of Whim — skeptically, quizzically, as a secondary freedom entitled to come into its own if and after secular interests are satisfied. It is remarkable, when Free Exercise is seen in the majesty of its historical setting, that when it spoke of "national public policy" in *Bob Jones,* the Court did not at least ask itself whether the Free Exercise Clause does not represent "national public policy" — of the highest possible nature.

The trend toward giving secular interests prevalence over religious liberty interests has been facilitated by the almost total scrapping, by the Court, of the "compelling state interest" test (with its accompanying safeguards respecting proof) best expressed in *Sherbert.* It may now be of value to assay the causes.

The trend toward judicial secularism is possibly due in part to the Court's broadening of the definition of religion to embrace a wide range of ideologies whose protection was not contemplated by the drafters of the Free Exercise Clause.[52] Thus diluted, the Clause's protection of theistic religion may be weakened. Again, religious cases have come to the Court which lacked adequate records. Among such were cases like *Lee* where, if the Court had desired to carefully employ the test of "compelling state interest," it would have found no well-developed trial record with which to work. In some other cases the appellate court whose decision, adverse to religious liberty, was brought for review by the Supreme Court, itself skillfully contradicting a well developed trial record, had held the state to have proved a compelling state interest, thus diminishing the chances that the Supreme Court would give the case plenary review.[53] But most of all, the trend toward judicial secularism mirrors the materialism of an American society whose values are increasingly responsive to pressures in its media, its schooling, and its politics to favor secularism. These values tend to ease Free Exercise from its high station in the First Amendment. While Free Exercise was intended by the Constitution's frames as a free-standing right, not dependent for its protection as a form of speech, today the Supreme Court appears to bespeak a skepticism respecting it. In its effort to assure us that freedom of religion is not absolute, the Court makes absolutes of public interests opposing religious exercise.

That, however, could not continue to happen if the Court were to revert to the traditional test which it had stated in *Sherbert*, with its dual protection of religion and of the common good and its essential and sensible feature respecting factual proofs.

3. Postscript/Postmortem

As the reader can see, I had ended my examination of the compelling state interest doctrine with foreboding. In April 1990 I was on the phone with our editor to ask for additional space because on April 17 the Supreme Court fulfilled my dire prophecy. In *Employment Division v. Smith*,[54] the now-famous case involving the religious use of peyote, the Court expressly threw out the compelling state interest doctrine and thereby has opened wide the door to unlimited government power over religion. The Court's opinion, by Justice Antonin Scalia, holds that, provided a legislative enactment is one of general application (*e.g.*, a state statute requiring all children to attend public school), it must be enforced in spite of any religious objections. If a statute meets those conditions, any mere "public interest" it expresses will override any religious interest. To the foregoing the Court made two miniscule exceptions: (a) a governmental act *expressly* singling out a religious practice for attack (*e.g.*, outlawing the mass), (b) a governmental act which is forbidden by some provision of the Constitution *other than* the Free Exercise Clause. But (a) never occurs, while (b) honors freedom of religion only when it is piggy-backed on, say, freedom of speech.

I have spelled out my objections to this in an "op-ed" published April 22, 1990 in *The Los Angeles Times*. There I wrote:

> The Supreme Court ruled last week that since Oregon could prohibit the religious use of the hallucinogenic drug, peyote, it could deny unemployment compensation to persons discharged for such use. Thus stated, the decision appears unremarkable. In fact, the court's opinion opens up a constitutional fault of San Andreas proportions.
>
> Many times before, the Supreme Court, and all lower courts, have issued rulings telling us that our First Amendment freedoms are not absolute. When my speech is sufficiently incendiary, or when your assembled followers become an unmanageable mob, the common good may require me to shut up, and you to disband your crowd.
>
> So, too, with religion. A century ago, the Supreme Court said that if a religion calls for human sacrifice, the First Amendment's free exercise (of religion) clause does not protect such a practice. Polygamy could be made a crime, even though, to Mormons, it was religiously required. Child labor laws could prohibit a Jehovah's Witness from using her small child to hawk religious tracts on city streets. In all of these cases, the common good — protection of life, protection of the family, protection of children — was deemed a barrier to the religious practice in question.
>
> But the Supreme Court, from the early 1940s on, had insisted that the freedoms of religion, speech, press and assembly were "preferred" freedoms — fundamental and precious — unlike, for example, freedom of contract or economic liberties.
>
> What practical difference does it make to say that First Amendment liberties are "preferred"? An enormous difference. A law restricting an "ordinary" liberty — such as the local zoning ordinance that forbids you to put a garage on your side yard — will be upheld by the courts if they can find that the ordinance has some possible reasonable basis for this restriction on your use of your property. But suppose an ordinance forbids citizens to circulate leaflets attacking the city government. Constitutionally (so we have always understood) that's a wholly different ball game. Your free press rights to circulate the leaflets can't be denied unless the government can prove that a "compelling state interest" (a *supreme* societal interest) justifies the leaflet ban. Just finding some "reasonable basis" for restricting your press rights won't do.

Further, the Supreme Court had held that it is up to government to prove with credible facts that its interest is "compelling." That rule made sense. Those who assert precious First Amendment liberties are usually at a disadvantage when government seeks to infringe upon those liberties. Government, in such contests, usually has the edge economically, in attorney manpower — and sometimes politically. As Charles Dickens noted in *Bleak House*, legal processes have enormous potential for "wearying out the right." Hence, where our most basic liberties are concerned, it is essential that our courts not only invoke the standard of "compelling state interest" but that they make government prove it.

Last Tuesday, all of that changed. In the peyote case, involving American Indian religious practices, the Supreme Court expressly jettisoned the "compelling state interest" test. It held that in this and future cases, no "compelling state interest" need justify government action against religion. With two narrow exceptions, generally applicable prohibitions of conduct which government deems to be "socially harmful" must be upheld against objections based on religion. The first is the imaginary case posited by the court in which government expressly bans the performance of a specific religious act. The court here mentions (oddly, in this peyote case) "participating in the sacramental use of . . . wine." The second is where religiously motivated action has involved not only the free exercise clause but some other constitutional protection, such as freedom of speech or press. This second "hybrid situation" exception takes religious liberty from its high place in the Bill of Rights, giving it scope only if it is attached to some other right.

Where does this lead?

It moves the principle of religious liberty, as given in the First Amendment, to the back of the constitutional bus — maybe off the bus. The court deems free exercise to be a free-standing right only in the improbable situation in which government singles out some religious practice as forbidden. If a prohibitory law is "generally applicable," too bad for religious interests that get in the way of it. Hence, the wage-and-hour prohibitions of a labor relations act could be applied to work done by clergy under vows of poverty. And since the court's reasoning is broad enough to include mandatory as well as prohibitory laws, religious schools could be required to be carbon copies of public schools.

The court's opinion is strikingly cold in reference to religion. It has not a good word to say for the traditional glory of American religious liberty. The tone is entirely one of limitation and curbing, as though the free exercise of religion were a danger to be closely confined or is of little greater significance than the rampant exercise of whim. The court has used a trivial circumstance as the vehicle for a catastrophic decision. It is tragic that it utilized this case to create a precedent that will govern future cases involving churches, religious schools, clergy, ministries — indeed the future religious life of the nation.[55]

Readers should take note that the *Smith* opinion is supported by three justices of the Supreme Court — Scalia, Kennedy, and Rehnquist — who are widely touted as "conservative." It is to be hoped that admirers of Russell Kirk will look again to Kirk's definition of "conservative" as one having "belief in a transcendent order, or body of natural law, which rules society as well as conscience." The destruction of the compelling state interest standard is the work, not of conservatives, but of statists.

NOTES

1. *Sherbert v. Verner*, 374 U.S. 398 (1963).

2. In *Reynolds v. United States*, 98 U.S. 145 (1879) and related cases involving the Mormons, the Court said that practices, though religious, such as polygamy or human sacrifice, may always be suppressed by government.

3. *Jacobson v. Massachusetts*, 260 U.S. 174 (1905).

4. *Hamilton v. Regents of the University of California*, 293 U.S. 245 (1934).

5. *Prince v. Massachusetts*, 328 U.S. 158 (1944).

6. *Cantwell v. Connecticut*, 310 U.S. 296 (1940).

7. *Murdock v. Pennsylvania*, 319 U.S. 105 (1943).

8. *West Virginia State Board of Education v. Barnette*, 319 U.S. 624 (1943).

9. *Braunfeld v. Brown*, 366 U.S. 599, decided in 1961, appeared inconsistent with the trend. It involved the application, upheld by the Court, of Sunday closing laws to commercial activities of Orthodox Jews. The Court reasoned that the burden on the Jews, though severe, was only "indirect" and hence did not implicate the Free Exercise Clause. As shall be seen, the "indirect burden" concept of *Braunfeld* continues, at the hour, to trouble religious litigants.

10. *Adkins v. Children's Hospital*, 261 U.S. 525, 544 (1923).

11. The constitutional provision is the Free Exercise Clause of the First Amendment: "Congress shall make no law . . . prohibiting the free exercise [of religion]. . . . " This limitation upon the powers of Congress was extended to the States in 1940 in the case of *Cantwell v. Connecticut, supra*.

12. *Sherbert, supra,* at 406.

13. *Caulfield v. Hirsch* (E.D.Pa. No. 76-279 Civ., 1977).

14. See, *e.g.*, *State of Texas v. Corpus Christi People's Baptist Church*, 683 S.W.2d 692 (Tex. 1984).

15. *Cruzan v. Director, Missouri Department of Health*, 497 U.S. 261 (1990).

16. *Addington v. Texas*, 441 U.S. 418, 424 (1979).

17. J. Choper, in "The Supreme Court, 1988 Term." 57 U.S.L.W. 2227 (October 18, 1989).

18. 405 U.S. 205 (1972).

19. *Id.* at 215.

20. *Id.* at 216.

21. *Id.* at 218.

22. *Id.* at 221.

23. *Id.* at 215.

24. *Id.* at 221.

25. *E.g.*, " . . . it was incumbent on the State *to show with more particularity* how its admittedly strong interest in compulsory education would be adversely affected by granting an exemption to the Amish." *Id.* at 236. (Emphasis supplied.) "Against this background it would require a *more particularized showing from* the State . . . to justify

the severe interference with religious freedom such additional compulsory attendance would entail." *Id.* at 227. (Emphasis supplied.)

26. This level continued to be maintained by the Court until 1982, an example of strict fidelity to the *Sherbert* test being seen in *Thomas v. Review Board*, 450 U.S. 707 (1981). *Thomas*, like *Sherbert*, involved a Seventh-day Adventist's claim for unemployment compensation, but here it was based solely on religious beliefs against working on production of armaments.

27. *United States v. Lee*, 455 U.S. 252, 257 (1982).

28. I am aware that the Supreme Court, in its famous decision in *Pierce v. Society of Sisters*, 268 U.S. 510 (1925) held invalid a state law imposing such a requirement. But I am likewise aware that eminent scholars have attacked the *Pierce* decision as "judicial law-making." See Bork, R., *The Tempting of America*, 48–49 and my article to the contrary, W. Ball, "The Tempting of Robert Bork," *Crisis*, V.8, No. 6, at 28 (June 1990).

29. *Lee, supra*, at 260.

30. 629 F. Supp. 1073 (M.D.Pa. 1986); 822 F.2d 1334 (3rd Cir. 1987); cert. denied 485 U.S. 959 (1988).

31. The affidavit of Peter J. Ferrara, a recognized expert on the social security system, stated, in part: "It is, therefore, my considered judgment that excluding Bethel Baptist Church and employees from mandatory coverage will not disrupt the administration of the Social Security System, nor will it affect in any significant way the revenues enjoyed by that system or the ability of the system to pay promised benefits and indeed may even ease any long-term financial problems of the system. This same result would likely obtain even if all other religious institutions which object, on religious grounds, to mandatory coverage were to be similarly excluded."

32. "Summary judgment,", *i.e.*, a form of disposition of a case when a court adjudges that no questions of fact exist in a case and that one of the parties is clearly entitled to judgment as a matter of law. Here the District Court believed that the Supreme Court's prior judgment in *Lee* governed the *Bethel* case as precedent.

33. The Supreme Court, in 1970, in *Walz v. Tax Commission*, 397 U.S. 664, held that the state could exempt a house of religious worship from real property taxation. That decision was not based on Free Exercise rights of churches but held merely that the allowance of exemption of such properties from taxation did not violate the Establishment Clause. A fundamental and highly perceptive commentary on religious taxation is to be found in D. M. Kelley, *Why Churches Should Not Pay Taxes*.

34. 461 U.S. 574 (1983).

35. 489 U.S. 1, 109 Sup. Ct. 890 (1989).

36. See, C. J. Friedrich, *The Age of the Baroque*, 31.

37. See, R. Grunberger, *The 12-Year Reich*, 337, 481–501.

38. 42 U.S.C. §4321.

39. This is now a recurrent theme in the literature of the global environmentalists. See, *e.g.*, the report of "Worldwatch," *The New York Times*, January 14, 1990, p. 24.

40. *Texas Monthly, supra*, at 903.

41. 475 U.S. 503 (1986).

42. *Id.* at 510.

43. 494 U.S. 872, 108 Sup. Ct. 1319 (1990).

44. *Id.* at 1324.

45. *Id.* at 1325.

46. *Id.* at 1326.
47. *Id.* at 1324.
48. *Id.* at 1326.
49. See, *e.g.*, *Sheridan Road Baptist Church v. Michigan Department of Education*, 481 U.S. 1050 (1987) (state certification of religious school teachers); *Church of St. Paul and St. Andrew v. Barwick*, 479 U.S. 985 (1986) (landmarking of houses of worship).
50. See, *e.g.*, *Hustler Magazine v. Falwell*, 485 U.S. 46, 108 Sup. Ct. 876 (1988).
51. *Thomas v. Collins*, 323 U.S. 516, 530 (1944).
52. See, *e.g.*, *Torcaso v. Watkins*, 367 U.S. 488, 495 (n. 11: Taoism, Buddhism, Secular Humanism, etc. held "religions") (1961).
53. See, *e.g.*, *State of Texas v. Corpus Christi People's Baptist Church*, 683 S.W.2d 692 (Tex. 1984).
54. 494 U.S. 872, 108 Sup. Ct. 1444 (1990).
55. *The Los Angeles Times*, April 22, 1990, p. M7.

*   *   *

"All of us concerned with the humane traditions of Western culture are indebted to Russell Kirk, whose sweeping erudition has been carried with such gentleness, humility, dignity, and charm."

— David L. Schindler, 1992.

*   *   *

"Without fear of contradiction one refers to Russell Kirk as the doyen of a conservative wisdom that twenty-five years ago was dismissed as idiosyncratic but is today near the center of public discourse. Mr. Kirk would be appalled by the suggestion that his views have triumphed. And that for at least three reasons. First, because he insists that he is not advancing 'his views' so much as he is giving voice to the reflected experience of a civilization. Second, because in our public life the voices that are ignorant of, or hostile to, that civilizational experience are still dominant. And third, in Russell Kirk's understanding, wisdom is not the militant stuff of cultural, never mind political, triumph. Wisdom is the deep deposit of living tradition, the apprehension of 'the permanent things,' another generation's ever surprising discovery that it need not, cannot, should not, begin the human enterprise from scratch."

— Richard John Neuhaus, from his essay "Kirk on That Savage God" in The Religion & Society Report, *September 1988.*

Journalism as Parable

by Ian Boyd, C.S.B.

It would be easy to sketch a dark and forbidding picture of Chesterton's journalism and of the Chesterton tradition in journalism. Oddly enough, much of the information for such an uninviting picture can be derived from Chesterton's own writing. He is the most searching critic of the viewpoint which is usually attributed to him. His attitude towards his own profession was a curiously ambivalent mixture of admiration and disdain. On one occasion, he will write of the romance of journalism, "the great lights burning on through darkness to dawn weaving the destinies of another day."[1] In that romantic vein, he will insist that newspapers are the greatest exercise in anonymity since the building of the Gothic cathedrals. But on other occasions, he will describe the modern journalist as "a man who writes things on the backs of advertisements," and he will wonder aloud whether there are any institutions in the modern world that do harm on so gigantic a scale as the press. He makes a sharp distinction between journalism and those who practise the profession of journalism, but his praise of journalists is often touched with irony. "In truth," he writes in *G. K.'s Weekly* (March 28, 1925), "nothing is more notable than the superiority of journalists to journalism. The inside of Fleet Street is far larger than the outside. . . . it is generally a very small and unrepresentative part of each man that gets into the paper he writes." Thus he describes the old journalist who debases journalism by writing trifling gossip about the more or less imaginary love affairs of the famous, but who, in his own time, "has perhaps given advice to great Editors and newspaper-proprietors in some crisis that has affected the whole world." Judging only from the old journalist's writing, one would never guess that he had "assisted in some great public work, such as the blackmailing of a Prime Minister, the buying up of a dangerously truthful journal or the hurried departure of some distinguished person to South America."

Perhaps the most damaging thing that is said about the Chesterton tradition in journalism is that it is irrelevant to his true achievement as a writer. That accusation has been made by some of the people who admired Chesterton most. Even his wife, the devoted Frances, seems to have had scant respect for her husband's efforts to keep *G. K.'s Weekly* in existence: she regarded that work as a foolish distraction from his real work as a man of letters. "He is so dissipating his energies," she wrote to Father John O'Connor, "and his own work gets thrust more and more into the background." In her view, "his own work" was emphatically not his journalism; *The New Witness* and *G. K.'s Weekly* have often been regarded as irrelevant to Chesterton's central work which is thought to be essentially literary. It is said that if polemical journalism did not kill him, it did shorten his life and did prevent him from writing more literary criticism such as *The Victorian Age in Literature*; the Browning and Dickens criticism; more novels, such as *The Man Who Was Thursday*; more short fiction, such as the Father Brown detective stories; more verse, such as his rollicking comic songs and his serious epic poem, *The Ballad of the White Horse*; more drama, such as *Magic*, or those "lost" plays that, in vain, Bernard Shaw kept on urging him to write; and, above all, more of the serene and non-controversial religious treatises, such as *Orthodoxy* and *The Everlasting Man*. This work, it is said, is the work on which Chesterton's reputation really rests, and his preoccupation with ephemeral journalism kept him from writing more of it.

The political and social movement which Chesterton's journalism was meant to support has also received a good deal of hostile and dismissive criticism. Distributism is said to be one of those sad populist movements that hold such a fatal attraction for middle-class faddists and cranks. It is said that, an economic theory, it paid scant attention to the complex problems of modern economic life which it claimed to solve. As a social theory, it had the reputation of presenting an unrealistic programme of romantic mediaevalism, of advocating a return to a mediaeval past which existed only in the imagination of the Distributists themselves. Although never accused of being sympathetic to the fascists, the Distributists were said to be involved in a marginal right-wing movement of the twenties and thirties; and some of their writing, including some of Chesterton's own writing, was said to have about it an unmistakable whiff of anti-Semitism. In a word, it has been said that the journalism for which Chesterton sacrificed his life and his literary reputation was not worthy of such a sacrifice.

Another serious criticism concerning the Chesterton tradition concerns an element of religious narrowness and propaganda which it is said to embody. This impression seems to have been derived partly from the tone of some of the writing and partly from some of the favourite themes dealt with by the group of journalists who gathered around Chesterton and Belloc — particularly around Belloc. George Orwell, whose own first journalistic writings appeared in *G. K.'s Weekly*, complained that Chesterton devoted his later journalistic career to an absurd exaltation of Catholic culture over Protestant and pagan culture. For Orwell, an ignorant idealisation of all things Catholic made Chesterton's journalism almost unreadable. "Chesterton," he writes, "was a writer of considerable talent who chose to suppress both his sensibilities and his intellectual honesty in the cause of Roman Catholic propaganda."[2]

No-one who has read Chesterton's journalism is likely to consider such criticisms a fair description of what they have read. In fact, much of the criticism turns out to be, not only untrue, but even the direct opposite of the truth. Perhaps the major error contained in such criticism concerns the very nature of Chesterton's work. There is an implication in such criticism that it is both possible and desirable to separate Chesterton's literary work from his journalistic work. The literary work is supposed to contain most of what is of permanent value in his writing; the journalism is supposed to represent everything in Chesterton's writing that was ephemeral and slipshod. Yet, when Chesterton's writing is carefully examined, it turns out to be all of a piece. The sort of literature that his journalistic work is supposed to have kept him from writing turns out to be itself a kind of journalism. What, after all, are most of Chesterton's books except collected journalism? Much of his best literary criticism, the best of his satiric verse, as well as the best of his fiction, were all published in the despised magazines and newspapers as part of his everyday journalistic writing. Because some of this work was later gathered into books, its journalistic origin is often forgotten. Almost all the so-called literary writing is best understood when it is returned to its journalistic context and seen as part of a journalist's effort to make sense of the rapidly changing political and social environment which he was attempting to influence by his writing.

But if the literary writings have many of the characteristics of journalism, it is also true to say that the journalistic writings have many of the characteristics of literature. In some important articles that he published in *G. K.'s Weekly* in 1929 during one of the many crises in that magazine's short history[3] Chesterton distinguishes between two kinds of journalism. The first he calls scientific or practical journalism. Such journalism, he explains, sets out to provide solid and exhaustive scientific analysis about the economic and social ills of modern society. The second he calls artistic journalism. Such journalism seeks to awaken the imagination of its readers so that they will be capable of seeing, for the first time, a world which has become overly familiar to them. In this journalism, Chesterton explains, the journalist makes use of parable and allegory, "a considerable element of fable and fantasy and all that the serious may call nonsense" (January 19, 1929), as he attempts to shock his readers into an awareness about the grotesqueries of modern life that they no longer wonder about. In Chesterton's own words, the task of artistic or literary journalism is to make readers "see what they have seen," for as he explains, "what is seen too often is no longer seen at all" (January 19, 1929). Although some of the journalism in the Chesterton tradition, especially the journalism of his brother, Cecil Chesterton, attempted to be journalism of the first kind, Chesterton's own journalism is almost always journalism of the second kind. A good deal of the misunderstanding about it derives from a failure to recognise the sort of journalism that it really is.

It is, therefore, helpful to see Chesterton as a writer who continued the journalistic tradition of Carlyle and Ruskin and the other Victorian sages whose writings sought to educate a people dazed and bewildered by intellectual and social changes that they could scarcely cope with. In his valuable Introduction to a selection of Chesterton's journalistic writings, *The Man Who Was Orthodox*, A. L. Maycock cites a passage from Ruskin in which that author says that for a hundred people who can feel there is only one who can think, and that for ten thousand who can think there is only one who can see.[4] Applying this comment to both Ruskin himself and to Chesterton, Maycock describes them as authors who possess a poet's gift, "a rare power of intuition which is called in scripture the gift of wisdom—an immediate apprehension of truth that outstrips the exercise of reason, coming like a sudden blaze of light and with a quality of revelation."[5] Maycock cites a few sayings from Chesterton's journalism: "The meanest man is immortal and the mightiest movement is temporal, not to say temporary"; and, on the subject of suffering, "The King may be conferring a decoration when he pins the man on the cross, as much as when he pins the cross on the man"; and again, on the connection between moral anarchy and the modern bureaucratic state, "When you break the big laws, you do not get liberty; you do not even get anarchy. You get the small laws." Maycock then goes on to comment on the significance of this sort of writing:

> A man might remember his first readings of such passages as decisive events in his life. They produce precisely that effect of shock or surprise which, as Chesterton repeatedly insisted, is necessary to awaken us to see things as they really are, to see the world with a proper astonishment and a proper gratitude.[6]

Many of the difficulties in interpreting Chesterton's journalism can be resolved when it is recognised and read as imaginative and visionary utterance rather than as sober scientific investigative reporting. The clearest comment about what he meant by Distributism, for example, is found in *The Return of Don Quixote* (London, 1927), a novel that was partly serialized in *G. K.'s Weekly*. The novel is subtitled, "A Parable for Social Reformers" and is pointedly dedicated to W. R. Titterton, one of the most enthusiastic and literal-minded of Chesterton's Distributist followers. Chesterton once wrote that he doubted whether any truth could be told except in parable, and the meaning of this particular gentle parable is easy to interpret. What the novel satirizes is precisely the romantic mediaevalism which is supposed to represent Chesterton's own political dream. The novel warns about the dangers inherent in the politics of political nostalgia because of the way in which such political movements can blind people to the pressing problems of contemporary life and open them to exploitation by political extremists and unscrupulous ideologues. Instead of strident and humourless railing about political corruption, Chesterton's journalism is more likely to contain subtle and self-deprecating questions about the political movement which he himself had founded. The most intelligent criticism of Chesterton's journalism is, therefore, contained in Chesterton's journalism itself. As John Coates points out in *Chesterton and the Edwardian Cultural Crisis*, the only book which examines Chesterton's writings in their journalistic context, the fact of Chesterton the journalist wears an ironic Cervantic smile. In Coates's opinion, Chesterton's journalism presents a cautious, humane and balanced view of human limitations and of Original Sin; it refuses to adopt authoritarian nostrums; it never rejects democracy or the liberal traditions of tolerance; it is inherently moderate and it distrusts over-neat, schematised and too narrow statements of even its own positions,[7] and it establishes a relationship with its readers which is based on affection, trust and freedom, as well as on an element of good-natured teasing and self-mockery. A failure to recognise these qualities in the journalism means a failure to understand it.

The genuine faults of Chesterton's journalism are best understood as failures in his usually generous and genial imagination. Such a time of imaginative and emotional breakdown occurred a few years before the First World War when, under the stress of a darkening political situation and the threat to his brother at the time of the Marconi Scandal, he briefly became the narrow and angry writer whom obtuse critics have claimed that he always was. Intermittently during those years, in the articles, for example, which he wrote for the Socialist and Syndicalist *Daily Herald*, the criticisms of the Chesterton tradition in journalism were sadly justified. It is significant that most of the passages that come close to serious anti-Semitism are confined to this period. He began his journalistic career protesting the treatment of Jews in Tsarist Russia and warning an indifferent Edwardian public about the dangers of the proto-Nazi and racialist Eugenics Movement; he ended his career protesting the Hitlerite persecution of the Jews in Germany, a persecution which he regarded as a continuation of the earlier evil in a new form. In Chesterton's journalism, as John Gross once pointed out, nothing obscures his fundamental decency for long.[8]

Nevertheless, there remains a stubborn conviction that more is involved in the Chesterton tradition of journalism than a bland liberal decency. Chesterton himself always insisted that popular ideas usually turn out to be more true than false. If he is right, there must be truth in the popular opinion that Orwell expressed when he said that Chesterton's journalism really is a form of political and religious propaganda. What exactly it is propaganda for is difficult to say. As a lifelong Liberal, Chesterton was nevertheless an incisive critic of political liberalism; and, although he insisted that whatever he was, he was never a Conservative, he combined a deeply Conservative respect for tradition with a deeply radical contempt for those who betrayed the tradition; a foe of Conservative nostalgia, his contradictory heroes were Samuel Johnson and William Cobbett — both Tories, but Tories of a very different kind. As a Distributist, Chesterton seems to have remained curiously detached from the political movement that he founded. His religious position was similarly complex. Beginning with a near-Deist, Unitarian upbringing, he became an Anglican, and remained an Anglican for most of his journalistic career. Yet, as an Anglican, he never practised the faith for which he was a spokesman. His conversion to Roman Catholicism was the great event of his later life. Yet, as a Roman Catholic, although he practised his religion, he engaged in surprisingly few Catholic controversies in his everyday journalism. Like Father Brown, he is unabashedly Catholic; but he says almost nothing about specifically Catholic doctrines, preferring instead to defend humble material realities, the apparently profane side of everyday life which is embodied in such things as right reason and civility.

And yet, although all these things are true, Orwell's angry criticism does express the fundamental truth about Chesterton's journalism. More than anything else, Chesterton is a spokesman and an apologist for Catholicism. His political, social and literary writings are integral parts of a single religious view of life. Chesterton the journalist is in truth Chesterton the religious teacher.

How a journalism which avoids directly religious comment can nevertheless be profoundly religious is perhaps the best of the Chestertonian paradoxes. T. S. Eliot once said that Chesterton was, in his day, the leading spokesman for Catholic social and political ideas; but, in Eliot's view, in order to re-assure the British public, Chesterton concealed his revolutionary purposes behind a Johnsonian fancy-dress, in much the same way that, in Chesterton's novel, *The Man Who Was Thursday*, the enormous President Sunday concealed his revolutionary designs by holding the meetings of his fellow Anarchist conspirators on a balcony in Leicester Square. He concealed by exposure. But this tactic was not dishonest. The religious tradition to which Chesterton belonged, both as an Anglican and as a Roman Catholic, was a sacramental tradition. According to that tradition, the

Incarnation was the turning-point of human history, because this unique embodiment of the Divine in human events meant that all subsequent human history acquires a religious significance. Christ was a sacramental sign of God's continuing presence in history through the Christian community which is called the Church. The work of the Christian journalist is, therefore, a work of interpreting contemporary events as sacred signs of this on-going revelation by the Incarnate God. In the sacramental tradition, God himself is regarded as a cosmic novelist who speaks through parables and allegories. Yet these sacred stories are also human stories whose religious significance will be understood only by those who understand that the unique Gospel event is endlessly re-enacted throughout history in the lives of ordinary people.

This sacramental faith provides the key to everything that is puzzling about Chesterton's journalism. The love of allegory and symbolic utterance, and the belief that the deepest truths can be told only by parable turn out to be religiously significant. The Distributist social vision to which Chesterton devoted so much of his journalistic career also acquires a deeper significance. The reverence for the common man is not sentimental populism, but the expression of a religious faith that the common man is the privileged sacramental sign of Christ. The attempt to teach a vulnerable and inwardly confused people about their human dignity can now be seen as an attempt to provide them with an understanding of the religious significance of an aspect of their lives which they had regarded as merely human. Such journalism avoids narrowly religious controversies, because it seeks to emphasize those aspects of material life which are often regarded as profane, but which often contain the deepest and most neglected of religious truths.

NOTES

1. G. K. Chesterton, cited by A. L. Maycock in *The Man Who Was Orthodox* (London, 1963), p. 16.

2. George Orwell, "Notes on Nationalism," *The Collected Essays, Journalism and Writings*, ed. S. Orwell and I. Angus, volume III (London, 1968), pp. 365–68.

3. G. K. Chesterton, "A Fact in Reconstruction" and "The Place of Nonsense in Sense" in *G. K.'s Weekly* (January 12 and January 19, 1929).

4. A. L. Maycock, *The Man Who Was Orthodox*, p. 40.

5. A. L. Maycock, *The Man Who Was Orthodox*, p. 40.

6. A. L. Maycock, *The Man Who Was Orthodox*, p. 40.

7. John Coates, *Chesterton and the Edwardian Cultural Crisis* (London, 1984), p. 243.

8. John Gross, *The Rise and Fall of the Man of Letters* (London, 1969), p. 222.

The Family Adams

by Anne Husted Burleigh

Every autumn I become nostalgic. Each year when whirring insect voices sing their chorus, when cool nights signal October's approach, something tells me that it is time to prepare for settling in, time to find old roots, to reaffirm ties with those who have gone before. And I long to return to Quincy.

Every season means something special. But autumn always stirs in me the memory of the Adams family mansion — affectionately called the Old House — at Quincy, Massachusetts. My attachment to the Old House began over two decades ago, in late fall of 1965, when my husband and I went to Quincy so that I could absorb "atmosphere" in preparation for writing a biography of John Adams.

All of Quincy belongs to the Adamses — the birthplaces of John and John Quincy; the tombs of John and Abigail and John Quincy and Louisa Catherine; Quincy Bay where the family fished and boated — but in particular the beautiful eighteenth-century gambrel-roofed house which John Adams called "Peacefield" or "Stonyfield" and which later family members called simply the "Old House." Adams bought the house before he returned home from Europe for the last time. He and Abigail had decided that their modest little saltbox inherited from his father no longer suited their improved circumstances, that a returning ambassador and his family deserved a grander house.

Yet when they did return to Quincy, the new house, to their dismay, was much smaller than they had remembered it. Abigail soon put carpenters to work to build an east wing — a gracious parlor on the first floor to house her French furniture and, on the second story above it, a large study. John Quincy and Charles Francis changed it still further, building a separate stone library on the west side of the house to accommodate the papers and books of his father and grandfather. The fourth generation improved the plumbing and kitchen. The last member of the family to live in the house, Brooks Adams, died in 1927, whereupon the house became a national historic site.

It is a lovely house, a charming house, a living house. Every other restored house I have ever seen (with the possible exception of Monticello) pales by comparison. Most other houses exhibit furniture of the period, books and ornaments such as the owner would have had. Not the Old House. Here is a tea table of Abigail's, there a knife box of Louisa Catherine's, here a desk of John's, on the desk a book inscribed from John Adams to his grandson. John's favorite wing chair still reposes in the study. John Quincy's trees still thrive.

The farm is gone, of course. Only a few acres surrounding the house remain to serve as buffer against the bustling town of Quincy that engulfs the little estate. But on that golden autumn day when I first saw the house, I was enraptured. The painted gray clapboards gleamed gently in the sunlight; summer's vines still tumbled over the trellis fronting the porch.

I had to go back, and every fall my obliging husband took me back. But after four years the book was published, and so we did not return. Every fall, however, I thought of Quincy. Then came the Bicentennial, an opportunity to take our eight-year-old son on a gala trip into history. This time we returned to Quincy in late March. I was not disappointed. Though it was not yet spring and the day was cold, the sun bounced from the old glass of the windows; crocuses bloomed behind the house.

I wondered whether I would still find the interior of the house so appealing. I did. The house still exuded its intimacy, its feeling of being gracious but scaled down in the kind of New England warmth that somehow has never been equalled for me in the old houses of Virginia. Moreover, this time I could show our son the delights of the house — the settee where, for example, a gnarled, wasted but still intellectually vigorous John Adams sat at 90 to have Gilbert Stuart paint his portrait; the walking stick in the hall upon which he rested his hand in the Stuart painting; the fine secretary desk that he had brought from Holland; the japanned highboy in the upstairs hall; the closets where he stored his books.

As we wandered through the light-filled, airy rooms, I thought how much this latest trip meant after an interval of some eight years.

In the intervening years I had left John Adams for a time, had gone on to other projects and then had returned to the Adams family—this time in the person of Henry, the teacher, historian, novelist, author of a nine-volume history of the United States during the administrations of Jefferson and Madison: a biography of Albert Gallatin; two novels, *Democracy* and *Esther*; and the classic, *The Education of Henry Adams*.

Henry Adams had fascinated me. I had even considered writing a book about him. The march from John to John Quincy to Charles Francis to the fourth generation, that is, John Quincy II, Charles Francis II, Henry and Brooks encompassed some of the most intriguing themes I had ever studied. Consequently, when I returned to the Old House for this visit, I came with a wider frame of reference than simply John Adams himself. I could see in the house now not only John but his descendants.

This visit to the Old House brought to focus my questions about the place of the Adams family in American history. I wondered: Could the Adams men—all fiercely independent, non-partisan, duty-bound, devoted to country—be termed successful in this American democracy? Why had not they ever achieved (at least until they became the subject of a television series) the fame and recognition in keeping with their stature? Had the principles of liberty, or limited, balanced government espoused by John Adams in the eighteenth century become by the fourth generation of Adamses as hopelessly out of tune with the times as Henry Adams said they were? I believe—had to believe—that those principles were not dead, that the necessity for men to live according to those principles of freedom was just as valid in 1776, in Henry Adams's turn of the century, or in 1976. But I had the sinking feeling, as did Henry Adams, Tocqueville, and others, that America had turned her back on those principles and, indeed, that it was perhaps in the very nature of democracy to destroy the liberty it once had revered. I had begun to wonder not what the Adamses meant to America but what America had done to the Adamses.

It was not a happy reflection for a bicentennial observance. Yet, as I stood in the garden of the Old House, all these questions came to me.

Two weeks later we were in Washington. There was something I wanted to see, something that before I concluded my years with the Adamses I had to see and judge for myself.

Henry Adams, as all the Adams men, had married well. His wife Marian Hooper, daughter of a well-to-do Boston physician and surgeon, had been an intellectual companion and a gracious and renowned hostess in Washington society. But "Clover," as she was called by her family, suffered from periods of depression. After the death of her father, with whom she was very close, she committed suicide. Henry was crushed. Clover for twelve years had been everything to him. Now he would spend the rest of his life trying to understand this cruel twist of events.

To commemorate his wife, Henry commissioned the French sculptor Augustus St. Gaudens to make a bronze statue to be placed in Rock Creek Cemetery. Though it never had a name, the statue gained the popular title of "Grief." St. Gaudens, however, considered that title inappropriate; he preferred to call his work "Peace of God." I had seen pictures of this statue, had read Henry's one brief reference to it in *The Education*. Now I had to see the real thing.

Our cab entered Rock Creek Cemetery, wound around several tiny lanes, and stopped before a clump of high shrubbery. We could see no statue yet, but we alighted. Telling the driver to wait, we hastened down a patch, turned the corner around the bushes into a small garden. There was St. Gaudens's statue. I was taken aback. I could not justly describe it then. I cannot now. Seated in front of a great upright slab was the figure of a woman draped and veiled, her hand brought up to her chin but not really supporting it. The figure was massive, almost frightening under its shadowy veil. Yet the hand and arm bore a graceful, delicate air. The face, though strong, was distinctly feminine. It did not weep; neither did it brood. John Hay, friend of Henry Adams, said it showed "infinite wisdom; a past without beginning and a future without end; a repose, after limitless experience, a peace, to which nothing matters. . . . "[1] I could not say.

Later, I read again the brief remarks Henry wrote about the statue. It was not a portrait statue, he said. Moreover, "the interest of the figure was not in its meaning, but in the response of the observer . . . . Like all great artists, St. Gaudens held up the mirror and no more." Whatever the observer brought within himself when he came to view the statue, the statue itself reflected. Henry often sat and observed those who came to the statue. The layman saw nothing much; the clergyman saw atheism, despair, denial. But this was not surprising. For Henry Adams, the American mind "shunned, distrusted, disliked, the dangerous attraction of ideals, and stood alone in history for its ignorance of the past." Because "the American layman had lost sight of ideals," he could see nothing; because "the American priest had lost sight of faith," he could see only denial. Both types, said Henry, truly represented America.[2]

And so again I was facing my dilemma. What was the future of American democracy? Could it withstand forever the assaults from within and without that had battered it continually almost since its inception? Could liberty ever rest comfortably in a democracy, or would liberty and democracy forever be opposed? What of values, standards, distinctions of goodness, intellect, or achievement? Were they doomed, as Henry Adams thought, to be sacrificed before the altar of equality?

Could such men as the Adamses, who resisted every encroachment upon their independence, every appeal to party or faction, ever become powerful voices in a democracy? Could these aristocrats of intellect, education, and character ever become more influential than Jeremiahs preaching their message to a heedless populace? Was the Old House at Quincy a symbol of the principles the Adamses stood for, or was it just another antique house where some famous people once lived? Did the St. Gaudens statue really mean nothing or, if something, that life was not worth much?

I recalled a chilling exchange in Henry Adams's novel *Democracy* in which the beautiful young heroine Madeleine Lee questioned Mr. Nathan Gore of Massachusetts. "Do you yourself think democracy the best government, and universal suffrage a success?"

> Mr. Gore saw himself pinned to the wall, and he turned at bay with almost the energy of despair:
> "These are matters about which I rarely talk in society; they are like the doctrine of a personal God; of a future life; of revealed religion; subjects which one naturally reserves for private reflection. But since you ask for my political creed, you shall have it. I only condition that it shall be for you alone, never to be repeated or quoted as mine. I believe in democracy. I accept it. I will faithfully serve and defend it. I believe in it because it appears to me the inevitable consequence of what has gone before it. Democracy asserts the fact that the masses are now raised to a higher intelligence than formerly. All our civilisation aims at this mark. We want to do what we can to help it. I myself want to see the result. I grant it is an experiment, but it is the only direction society can take that is worth its taking; the only conception of its duty large enough to satisfy its instincts; the only result that is worth an effort or a risk. Every other possible step is backward, and I do not care to repeat the past. I am glad to see society grapple with issues in which no one can afford to be neutral."

"And supposing your experiment fails," said Mrs. Lee; "suppose society destroys itself with universal suffrage, corruption, and communism."

"I wish, Mrs. Lee, you would visit the Observatory with me some evening, and look at Sirius. Did you ever make the acquaintance of a fixed star? I believe astronomers reckon about twenty millions of them in sight, and an infinite possibility of invisible millions, each one of which is a sun, like ours, and may have satellites like our planet. Suppose you see one of these fixed stars suddenly increase in brightness, and are told that a satellite has fallen into it and is burning up, its career finished, its capacities exhausted? Curious, is it not, but what does it matter? Just as much as the burning up of a moth at your candle."

Madeleine shuddered a little, "I cannot get to the height of your philosophy," said she. "You are wandering among the infinites, and I am finite."

"Not at all! But I have faith; not perhaps in the old dogmas, but in the new ones; faith in human nature; faith in science; faith in the survival of the fittest. Let us be true to our time, Mrs. Lee! If our age is to be beaten, let us die in the ranks. If it is to be victorious, let us be first to lead the column. Anyway let us not be skulkers or grumblers. There! Have I repeated my catechism correctly? You would have it! Now oblige me by forgetting it. I should lose my character at home if it got out. Good night!"[3]

This speech of Nathan Gore's had haunted me. It exemplified everything that I did not want American democracy to mean. For Mr. Gore democracy was a necessary development in the evolutionary path of history; it had to happen when it did, but neither would it likely survive. It was a mere product of historical necessity, not of men's ideals or actions.

Hoping all the more to find answers to my questions about the future of American democracy, I turned to the Adamses themselves. As I read and re-read parts of their lives and works, I was struck by several characteristics that marked them as Adamses. First of all they pledged themselves to pursue their duty, regardless of the outcome to themselves. Second, they were conscious of their role in history both individually and as members of a family that had always assumed positions of leadership. Third, they sought not fame so much as recognition. Fourth, they feared the effects of democracy on the nation that they had helped bring into being. It seemed to me that an examination of these characteristics would clarify what the Adamses had meant to America—or, as I feared, what America had done to the Adamses.

In the first place, devotion to duty marked these men more strongly than any other feature. John Adams, for instance, never refused a call to service to his country even when it meant a separation of years from his family. In his old age he wrote to his friend, Benjamin Rush, "My conscience was clear as a crystal glass without a scruple or a doubt. I was borne along by an irresistible sense of duty."[4] His son, John Quincy, was so groomed for public duty from his earliest youth that after the age of ten, when he accompanied his father to France, he scarcely had a boyhood. At a mere fourteen he knew French so well that he became private secretary to Francis Dana, new minister to Russia; only after a year and a half, at the conclusion of an overland trip in winter made alone from St. Petersburg to Finland, Stockholm, Copenhagen and Hamburg to The Hague, did he finally rejoin his father. His anxious mother back in Quincy had not heard from him for two years. Such an adolescence could not breed softness or self-indulgence. John Quincy learned to rein in his passions and his high temper behind what his son Charles Francis was to call an "iron mask."[5] Educated to a disregard for personal whim, he devoted himself so completely to his country that he denied himself almost any private life. As a result, his wife and sons unquestionably suffered. Indeed, old John Adams later advised his son that "children must not be wholly forgotten in the midst of public duties."[6]

John and John Quincy and those who followed had a moral zeal that sprang from their New England Puritanism. Devotion to duty was a kind of self-abnegation, a justification, a proof to themselves that they were righteous. It was partly for this reason that the first three generations kept such extensive diaries — in writing, their thoughts and actions were laid bare, a witness to the purity of their motives, a record by which God and posterity could judge them. The Adamses prided themselves on following the independent course their consciences dictated even at the expense of their political well-being. Both John and John Quincy, in their efforts to exhibit public virtue, to prove that they were immune to attractions of power, retained and tolerated in their administrations men who were their political enemies. Complete independence of party was a key mark of their characters. Consequently, they could be statesmen but not politicians.

Their devotion to duty, however, was in no way entirely of psychological motivation. They were inspired by a passionately deep love of country, of principle, of devotion to liberty to which personal desire must always take second place.

John Adams, at the close of his Presidency, wrote to Benjamin Rush what amounted to his credo,

> I do not curse the day when I engaged in public affairs. I do not say when I became a politician, for that I never was. I cannot repent of anything I ever did conscientiously from a sense of duty. I never engaged in public affairs for my own interest, pleasure, envy, jealousy, avarice, or ambition, or even the desire of fame; if any of these had been my motive, my conduct would have been very different.[7]

In addition to having in common their finely tuned concept of duty, the Adamses were aware of themselves in history, both as individuals and as a family. From the first two Adamses the family inherited a tradition of combined meditation and action, of contemplation and service. It was an awesome heritage. To have two Presidents in one family immediately imposed upon each of the Adamses a standard of achievement that from the cradle settled heavily upon them. To some, the fact of being an Adams beckoned as an incentive, but to those whose natures were unsuited to rigorous self-discipline and the conflict of public life it proved an intolerable burden.

Charles Adams, second son of John Adams, a lovable, generous, sociable fellow, died a drunkard's death at age thirty, leaving a wife and two small children.

Thomas Boylston Adams, youngest son of John Adams, never managed to succeed in public life. He developed a drinking problem, becoming in later life merely a kind of caretaker for his aged father.

George Washington Adams, oldest of John Quincy's three sons, was romantic and gracious like his mother, Louisa Catherine. With his poetic and literary interests, he did not take to the legal career his father had laid out for him. Drink became his solace. Eventually he became involved with a young servant girl, by whom he fathered an illegitimate child. Faced with the scandal of a child and a mountain of debts, he committed suicide.

Yet despite these tragedies, there were those in the family who could discipline themselves to put aside their own desires for the sake of duty. For those Adamses the family tradition forced extension of themselves to new heights. Charles Francis Adams was such a man.

However, as a young man he, too, had chafed under the Adams yoke. "I am growing more and more attached to the idea of private life," he confided to his diary, "and can only lament the necessity of the name of which I am so proud."[8] Only when he realized that neither of his older brothers would assume the Adams obligation, that his father focused all hopes upon him, did he acquiesce in a legal and political career. He began to emulate his grandfather, John, who he thought "was the most extraordinary character who figured in the American revolution,"[9] and his father, John Quincy, whom he described as "uncommonly eloquent after dinner today, and laid himself out more forcibly than usual. When he does so, how immeasurably he rises above all others. There is no comparison."[10]

Nonetheless, Charles Francis, like his son Henry after him, thought himself inadequate to the challenge of the Adams standard. He felt under great pressure to prevent the family name from deteriorating. "My pride," he said, "is such as not to allow me to think for a moment that the family name shall be set down as degenerating."[11]

Henry, one of the most fascinating of the Adamses, all his life felt guilty because he had not done his part to take the Adams name into the seats of political power. A brilliant historian and man of letters, he still felt that because public life had never been available to him, he had never truly accomplished anything worthwhile. His *Education of Henry Adams*, an elegantly styled autobiography which has become a standard in American literature, is a sort of apology for having failed to exceed what he thought were the mediocre pursuits of teaching and writing.

If the Adamses were conscious of themselves and their family as playing a part in history, then the natural outgrowth of this awareness was ambition for recognition. And the Adamses were ambitious — not for fame in the sense of being widely known, not for money or power — but rather for appreciation, for receipt of their just due. Ambition in the Adams definition meant a desire of being emulated, of being looked up to as meritorious. Moreover, ambition for recognition moved hand in hand with devotion to duty. To be recognized as having performed valuable service in behalf of one's country would harmonize not only with the Adams name but with self-justification; it would stand as proof that duty had been performed.

Charles Francis spoke as a young man of his "ambitious feelings," his "desire of distinction and knowing so well that I am called upon particularly to act as becomes a member of a high family."[12] He described the familial attitude toward recognition when he recorded the feelings of both himself and his father during the 1824 Presidential campaign. The Presidency was John Quincy's just due. "A life," said his son,

> spent in the public service and almost exclusively devoted to it, ought to obtain so high an honour. His competitors are so much his inferiors, also, that it is mortifying to suffer a defeat. This is what my father would feel and this only. His high spirit will ill bear to see a man whom he despises governing a nation partially and feebly. But if so, it must be, I am resigned.[13]

Though the Adamses aspired to recognition in the here and now, they concerned themselves equally with what posterity would think of them. For that reason, they took great pains to clarify the historical record, to make sure that history should judge them and their period fairly. John Adams spent much of his retirement laboring over this very task. He doubted that history would ever treat him kindly, or that the Revolutionary and early federal period would ever receive a correct accounting. Always plagued by self-doubt, he "never could bring myself seriously to consider that I was a great man or of much importance or consideration in the world"; he realized unhappily that "the few traces that remain of me must, I believe, go down to posterity in much confusion and distraction, as my life has been passed." Then, having said that, he characteristically chided himself, "Enough surely of egotism!"[14]

Yet, even though the Adamses aspired, almost agonizingly at times, to recognition, their sense of duty forbade them from seeking it by means other than independent action. Both John and John Quincy desperately wanted the Presidency; but their sense of honor would not permit them either actively to seek it or to act in a consciously politically advantageous way. In other words, their search for recognition derived not from lust for power but from a desire to be judged both by contemporaries and posterity as dutiful and virtuous.

The Adamses never received the recognition to which they aspired. There were times, of course, when their actions coincided with popular feelings; at such times they gained a certain adulation. Nonetheless, they were not politicians. Their personalities were ill-suited to pleasing crowds. What is more, their concept of democracy was generally misunderstood by the public. Though they loved their country, they expressed misgivings about the future of American democracy. In plain fact, they were not in the real sense of the word democrats at all. To be sure, they were republicans, advancing limited, constitutional government based upon fixed laws equally applied; their government was to be balanced in form so as to prevent any of the rival factions of society from encroaching upon the rights of anyone. Liberty was of primary importance to these men; widespread suffrage was not. In other words, liberty rather than equality formed the keystone of a happy and prosperous society. The one had impelled the American Revolution, the second the ill-fated French Revolution.

When John Adams expounded these views in 1776 and in the 1780's and the 1790's, he was not alone. Most of his collegues agreed with him; they had inherited from colonial America a tradition of ardent allegiance to constitutional liberties. Consequently, the temper of the late eighteenth century weighted the scales in favor of liberty rather than equality.

Each generation of Adamses beginning with John and proceeding to John Quincy to Charles Francis to Henry received its education in the tradition of classical eighteenth-century liberalism. But almost before the Revolution had drawn to a close, the democratic drive for equality in suffrage, in property, in education, in manners, in every facet of life began to overtake the fervor to preserve and protect liberty. The duty of government came to be seen by more and more people not only as protection of liberty but as fostering — even forcing — equality. As the years passed, then, the Adamses who had been so much in the mainstream of the Revolutionary and early federal concept of liberty began to find themselves increasingly out of step with popular opinion on the proper role of government.

John Quincy was the last President who had been educated in the eighteenth-century principles of the Founding Fathers. Even then, time was short; John Quincy could not be elected to a second term. When Andrew Jackson became President, he ushered in a democratic world that was completely different from that of 1776.

Charles Francis could not succeed in election to the Presidency. And Henry could not find even a niche in public life. By the fourth generation Henry considered the family to be an anachronism. Henry did not think that even his brother Charles Francis II, historian and president of the Union Pacific Railroad, could successfully pit honor and integrity against a wheeler-dealer tycoon, Jay Gould, whom Henry saw as part of the democratic tradition.

As strongly as ever the Adamses felt a necessity to perform their duty in the family tradition and at the same time craved recognition for their achievements. Yet, they realized that their country, in its move away from the prinicples of the Revolutionary period, was thwarting their efforts to provide it with leadership. Understandably, then, they suffered periods of great bitterness.

During his Vice-Presidency, a time of frustration and trial for him, John Adams lamented the "deplorable condition" of the country, "which seems to be under such a fatality that the people can agree upon nothing."[15] Charles Francis during the 1824 Presidential campaign of his father wrote, "This country though the purest under the sun is going to ruin. I am in perfect despair for republics. . . . "[16]

In their old age, however, both John and John Quincy forgot the bitterness engendered by the presidencies, bandaged old wounds, and, with typical resilience, went on to new pursuits. John spent his retirement writing letters and philosophizing. John Quincy never retired at all but began a new career more successful than the first — as representative to Congress, a post which he held until at age eighty he collapsed on the floor of the House and died a few hours later.

It is surely a function of age to put aside old griefs and grievances, to get on with the high business of stripping life to its truths. Since age does not have to concern itself with the inconsequential, it ought to rise to new understanding of life. Religion, for that reason, ought to achieve a peak of maturity.

It was in depth of religious faith that Henry seemed to part company with prior Adamses. All before him had relied, even more so in old age, upon faith. John Adams, for all his attention to eighteenth-century reason, inherited from Puritanism an active, living faith. John Quincy, if possible, felt an even stronger presence of God in his life. But Henry, though he was a son of the eighteenth century, of the Founding Fathers, of Quincy and the Boston State House, as he said, was likewise a son of the nineteenth century, of science, of Auguste Comte and Charles Darwin. If as an old man he had attained a degree of faith, his *Education* does not reveal it. His *Education* imparts a futility, a sadness that what former generations possessed he could not grasp. In his eyes not only the principles of his fathers and the society they had helped to create but even their religion had, by his generation, dried up. He himself puzzled over the demise of faith in himself and his brothers and sisters. His own father Charles Francis had been a religious man. But between the third and fourth generations there evidently had been no transmission.

Said Henry, about himself,

Of all the conditions of his youth which afterwards puzzled the grown-up man, this disappearance of religion puzzled him most. The boy went to church twice every Sunday; he was taught to read his Bible, and he learned religious poetry by heart; he believed in a mild deism; he prayed; he went through all the forms; but neither to him nor to his brothers or sisters was religion real. Even the mild discipline of the Unitarian Church was so irksome that they all threw it off at the first possible moment, and never afterwards entered a church. The religious instinct had vanished, and could not be revived, although one made in later life many efforts to recover it.[17]

Sadly enough, Henry knew what he was missing. Of all periods in history he most admired the thirteenth century, the age when he thought society through the unifying force of religion was most cohesive, with all elements most in tune. Henry would have loved nothing better than to have recovered medieval unity, to have found the one truth among a multiplicity of conflicting facts. But he could not make a leap of faith. He hoped merely that could he return to earth after death he might "find a world that sensitive and timid creatures could regard without a shudder."[18]

What Henry apparently did not realize is that he was trying to do the impossible. Achieving faith through the study of history is a fruitless pursuit. Although the *effects* of faith can be seen in history, God's hand in time appears only to the eyes of a believer. In other words, the student is an outsider looking at faith in history. Though he may study faith, though he may see how powerfully faith has worked in history, if he does not believe, he remains an outsider. One *studies* theology; one *lives* faith. Thus Henry Adams followed a thankless course. Despite his brilliant career, his magnificent, beautifully written historical works, he failed to make the leap of faith, to take the risk of believing that marks the heroic man and that marked his predecessors. He remained for me a sad character, a figure from a Henry James novel. And so, captivating though I found him, I never could write about him.

I now had looked back over the Adams men. I had surveyed their sense of duty, their commitment to the Adams tradition, their ambition for recognition, their thoughts on democracy. I had seen that though they had had strong doubts about the future course of democracy, though they had seen America move away from rather than toward their principles, all but the last of them, in spite of periods of disillusionment, had retained a vital religious faith. How were they able to remain faithful? I began to see that I could answer my own question. The Old House in Quincy, the St. Gaudens statue—I could see now that they did have meaning. But my question, what had America done to the Adamses, became meaningless. For what did it matter? What did it matter that America had never appreciated the Adamses? What did it matter that they had not been politicians? What did it matter to the fact of *their* greatness that America had rejected their principles, that America for the most part had preferred equality and uniformity? It mattered for America, of course; it still made the future of America tragically uncertain; but it did not diminish the Adamses.

What mattered were their *ideas*. They themselves were dead and buried; the intricacies of their diplomatic labors, their presidencies were long forgotten within the pages of a history text. But their ideas, contrary to what Henry thought, were not anachronisms. Accepted or not, their ideas on freedom were harmonious with human nature. Consequently, their ideas carried a ring of truth.

"The fundamental article of my political creed," wrote John Adams,

> is that despotism, or unlimited sovereignty, or absolute power is the same in a majority of a popular assembly, an aristocratical council, an oligarchical junto, and a single emperor. Equally arbitrary, cruel, bloody, and in every respect diabolical.[19]

I could now answer my question of how, despite what could be viewed as abandonment by their country of their most cherished ideals, in other words, of *them*, the Adamses could keep their faith. Men, the Adamses knew, are strange beings. They are earthbound; they have sins and imperfections that will forever cause them to abuse their freedom, to relinquish what they hold dear, to search for the easy life, to be lured by the siren song of a multitude of earthbound things. Yet they are more. The whole man does not live only here; a part of him extends into infinity. And that part that lives in the other sphere is able to gain at least some understanding of the eternal.

When a man departs from earth, no one may remember him; no one may remember what he looked like or what he did. But that man will have thought something; he will have had an idea. Thus, even in earthly life he will have projected himself into the spiritual. For a brief moment he will have transcended his boundaries to catch a glimpse of the infinite. Moreover, his idea is the one real link he has with both his ancestors and posterity. Deeds once done are irrecoverable; but posterity may one day rethink a man's idea and, in doing so, actually possess it. Hence, ideas not only link man to God but they link man to man and generation to generation. I think the Adamses believed that. I think that for that reason they did not despair that their ideas would die with them. No matter how shabbily America treated them, no matter how far America departed from their ideas or what would be the future course of America, they knew that nothing could destroy their ideas.

They knew that their idea of liberty was a great one — great because it coincided with the part of man that is of the spiritual — his freedom. They knew, too, that earthbound man is always changing, always becoming, as the philosophers say. On earth, then, he will never realize fully the spiritual; he will never become completely free. Yet knowing that he does have a bond with the eternal vision of liberty moves him to strive toward realization of his ideal. One of Henry Adams's contemporaries, Robert Browning, put it this way:

Ah, but a man's reach should exceed his grasp,
Or what's a heaven for?

I understood now that hereafter the Old House would embody for me the striving of the Adamses to translate their ideas into actuality. Simply because man does in a small way share God's vision of the ideal, the Adamses were bound to strive for perfection. They did not succeed wholly; no one ever does. But heroes strive; commonplace men accept their bounds. And from time to time the hero receives his reward: he sees with uncommon vision. If a man is a seer, as the Adamses were, he may be able to share his vision with others. The Adamses did share their vision of the ideal. They gave voice to a vision so powerful that no matter what the world did to them, their vision remained for posterity. The Old House represented to me all their striving to save that vision for those to come.

On the other hand, the St. Gaudens statue meant to me something further. John Quincy, it is said, in the moments before he died, uttered, "This is the end of earth." There was silence. Then he said, "I am content." The statue was like that. It was the end of striving, the end of earth. St. Gaudens's own title, the "Peace of God," served well. For in the serene face was contemplation of a vision already realized.

NOTES

1. Elizabeth Stevenson, *Henry Adams, a Biography* (New York: Macmillan, 1956), p. 223.

2. *The Education of Henry Adams*, introd. James Truslow Adams (New York: Modern Library, 1931), pp. 328–29.

3. *Democracy, an American Novel*, introd. Van Wyck Brooks (Greenwich, Connecticut: Fawcett Publications, 1961), pp. 49–50.

4. *The Spur of Fame, Dialogues of John Adams and Benjamin Rush, 1805–1813*, ed. John A. Schutz and Douglass Adair (San Marino: The Huntington Library, 1966), p. 191.

5. *Diary of Charles Francis Adams*, 6 vols. Vols. I–II, ed. Aida DiPace Donald and David Donald (New York: Atheneum, 1967), I, p. 315.

6. *Diary of Charles Francis Adams*, I, xxv.

7. *Spur of Fame*, p. 83.

8. *Diary of Charles Francis Adams*, I, p. 330.

9. *Ibid.*, II, p. 118.

10. *Ibid.*, II, p. 116.

11. *Ibid.*, I, xxx.

12. *Ibid.*, I, p. 184.

13. *Ibid.*, I, p. 281.

14. *Spur of Fame*, p. 61.

15. *The Works of John Adams, Second President of the United States: with a Life of the Author*, ed. Charles Francis Adams, 10 vols. (Boston: Little, Brown and Company, 1850–1856), IX, p. 567.

16. *Diary of Charles Francis Adams*, I, p. 330.

17. *Education*, p. 34.

18. *Ibid.*, p. 505.

19. *The Adams-Jefferson Letters: The Complete Correspondence Between Thomas Jefferson and Abigail and John Adams*, ed. Lester J. Cappon, 2 vols. (Chapel Hill: University of North Carolina Press, 1959), II, p. 456.

*   *   *

"Mr. Kirk is assured a place of prominence in the intellectual histories for helping to define the ethical basis of conservatism. He has tried to pull conservatism away from the utilitarian premises of libertarianism, toward which conservatism often veers, toward a philosophy rooted in ethics and culture. While the fundamental conflict between these two viewpoints is unresolved, both sides recognize and salute Mr. Kirk's contributions to the debate."

— W. Wesley McDonald,
from his essay "Russell
Kirk: Conservatism's
Seasoned Sage" in The
Wall Street Journal,
November 19, 1984.

Lamennais and Tocqueville

by Robert Nisbet

A year before Tocqueville and Beaumont departed Paris in April 1831 for their nine-months visit to America, a new newspaper was launched in Paris, edited by Lamennais with the assistance of two youthful followers, Lacordaire and Montalembert, both to have lustrous careers in the burgeoning liberal Catholic movement in France. The newspaper was christened *L'Avenir* by Lamennais, and he was quick to set forth to readers what would be the guiding principles and aspirations of the paper. These included, for all to see clearly: 1. The restoration of the ancient autonomy and political significance of the commune, the local community in France; 2. Freedom of association—religious, social, and economic association; 3. Decentralization of the national government, to restore to provinces as well as local governments a significant role in the governing of France; 4. Freedom of education; more particularly of private schools in order to end the state's monopoly of education; 5. Separation of the judiciary from the executive branch of government; and 6. The complete separation of church and state, the better to allow the church the corporate freedom it had known historically.

It is almost inconceivable that Tocqueville would have been unaware of the launching of *L'Avenir* in 1830. He was twenty-five years old and already, as a magistrate in the government, keenly interested in not only governmental affairs but in the varied currents of opinion regarding government (of which there were in the Paris of the 1820s and 1830s a very considerable number). The year 1830 was, of course, the year of the July Revolution and the fall of the Bourbon dynasty. Tocqueville had already become very much a liberal, influenced by among others Royer-Collard, Guizot, and, as I shall suggest as a strong possibility in this essay, Lamennais.

Lamennais was one of the most lustrous intellectuals in Paris by the year in which he founded *L'Avenir*. His spectacular career in the Church had earned him celebrity status if nothing else had. Born Hugues Félicité Robert de la Mennais in 1782, in St. Malo, of industrious if not prosperous parents, Lamennais (as he was to be known throughout most of his life) early elected the Church for his career. Ordained as a priest in 1816, he made his innate brilliance known to the Catholic world in the following year when his *Essai sur l'Indifference* was published. It was an immediate success among French Catholic conservatives, led by Bonald. It should have been so greeted, for Lamennais, in brief, proposed the restoration of the Church of Rome to its medieval power and glory, to its ultramontane authority in Europe. In the course of the proposal he presented a philosophy of Western European history which saw, from the Reformation on, the nation-state assuming more and more of the functions that had once been ecclesiastical and more and more of the powers that had once belonged to the family, local community, church, guild, and monastery swept into the very maw of the new territorial state. It was, Lamennais argued, in the context of the state's supersession of civil society that the heresies of individualism, egalitarianism, and popular sovereignty had made their appearance and had grown strong in Europe, even before the French Revolution.

I shall come back shortly to Lamennais's ideas. For the moment it is important to mention the highlights of his incandescent career. No one stood higher in the esteem of the Vatican after Lamennais's *Essai* was published. When he made his first pilgrimage to Rome, he was received by Pope Leo XII, who actually had a picture of Lamennais on the wall of his private sitting room. During the year or two following, it was widely rumored that Leo had even offered him the red hat of cardinal, member of the Sacred College. This was in 1824, following his pilgrimage and audience with the Pope.

Yet a decade later Lamennais, after receiving the warnings of two encyclicals addressed largely to his views, was excommunicated. This was after his thunderbolt *Paroles d'un Croyant* (1834) had come off the press with its challenge to the Church and State alike to democratize, to become responsive to the needs and desires of the people. In this little book, "small in size, large in perversity," declared Leo XII's succesor, Gregory XVI, Lamennais not only reaffirmed the ideas which formed the masthead of *L'Avenir*, but declared too his unwillingness to remain any longer a member of the unreformed Church. Thus the excommunication.

Lamennais never returned to the Church he had once loved and given fealty to. His death instructions, duly acted upon when he died in 1854, said: "I wish to be buried among the poor and like the poor; nothing shall be placed on my grave, not even a simple stone; my body shall be carried direct to the cemetery, without being presented in a church previous to burial." When he lay on his deathbed, he instructed followers to stand vigil against any efforts by priests serving the Church to enter his bedroom and dispense, or to claim later to have dispensed, last rites. To his last breath Lamennais remained totally defiant of the Church.

It was an astonishing development, one with few if any modern parallels. His fame and influence in France, and indeed in Europe, remained high almost to his death in 1854, aged 72. If, with his excommunication from the Church, he lost most of his Catholic audience, he gained the attention of not only intellectuals and politicians of the day but also an impressive number of workers. It is said that as the pages of his *Paroles* came off the press, the printers cheered them, one at a time.

He was an active thinker and writer throughout his life. Politics also interested him, and, along with Tocqueville, he served some years in the legislature. When the Revolution of 1848 broke out, Lamennais and Tocqueville were both elected to the constitutional commission, entrusted thereby with the foundations of the new French government. In his *Recollections* of the Revolution, Tocqueville describes briefly his association with Lamennais: how, in a fit of despair at the commission's refusal to take his ideas on decentralization seriously enough, Lamennais resigned, with Tocqueville deputed by the commission to go after Lamennais and beg him to rejoin the group. Lamennais would not rejoin. Refusal to compromise had been the essence of his life from his ecclesiastical years onward. Decentralization, localism, separation of powers, and freedom of association were his passion as well as mission. Even during the period of his popularity with and devotion to the Church, the profoundest single article of his conviction was the absolute necessity of restoring decentralization in French government and of freedom for intermediate associations, including the Church, to assert their functions and authorities without interference by the political state.

*   *   *

I want to turn now from the dramatic personal life of Lamennais to his ideas. He was twenty-three years older than Tocqueville, who was only twelve when Lamennais's *Essai sur l'Indifference* was published. It is highly unlikely that Tocqueville read it, but it is entirely possible, as Andre Jardin suggests in his excellent, recent biography of Tocqueville, that he was affected by some of the breezes and currents stirred up first by Lamennais's singular devotion to the Church and then by his gradual but remorseless defection from Papal dogma. Coincidence may have been the essence, but the fact is that the young Tocqueville met his crisis of faith and then his lifelong status of skeptic at about the same time that Lamennais, in a series of publications (including *L'Avenir* and its constitutive principles and also *Paroles*) announced to the world his own crisis with Rome.

On what basis, we are obliged to ask, did Lamennais, after years of devotion to Roman Catholic Christianity, come to break with the Church? The answer appears to be: through the development of ideas of power and liberty which were first adumbrated in behalf of the Church alone — but then, as though by iron logic, were extended to other groups and associations in society such as labor unions, cooperatives, and political parties which the Church, especially after the accession of Gregory to the Papacy, did not choose to countenance.

In Lamennais's *Essai sur l'Indifference* there is a philosophy of Western history based upon the perception of the Christian Church as in a state of decline from the Middle Ages on, a decline which Lamennais attributes to the increasingly secularized state in the post-mediaeval period. The Reformation, from Lamennais's point of view in the *Essai*, was at bottom little more than the final triumph of the national state over the once-ultramontane Church. With the emphasis by Luther and Calvin upon individual faith there went, as Lamennais saw, a desire to weaken the corporate structure of the Church and to strengthen the civil order. With the continuing supremacy of Gallicanism in France and Erastianism in England — in each of which lay the doctrine of the supremacy of the state over the Church — the modern state grew ever larger on what it took from the Church. Even before the Revolution in France, Lamennais argued, the European state was beginning to show the effects of engorgement of ancient authorities and liberties. Just as Tocqueville would assert in Part II of *Democracy in America*, Lamennais, in the *Essai*, declared that much of the rampant individualism of his time was the consequence of the state's pulverizing effect upon all that lay intermediate between it and the individual. The Revolution in 1789 merely capped, in Lamennais's and Tocqueville's common judgment, a process of politicization that had been going on for hundreds of years.

The Revolution marked the triumph of the political order over all economic, social, and religious groups in France. The centralization and relentless politicization of society which had begun irreversibly in the Reformation, reached its apogee in the France of the Jacobins. The major victim was of course the Church; but so were the guilds, universities, schools, monasteries, and the aristocracy victims of the Revolution. Even the patriarchal family, along with its old principles of entail and primogeniture, suffered the calculated blows of the Revolutionary legislators.

The crisis in Lamennais's life — the crisis that in the end wrecked his Catholic mission — came about between 1817, when the *Essai* was published, and 1830, when he founded *L'Avenir*. Specifically it was caused by Lamennais's continued reflection upon the logic of his opposition to the centralization of political power. That is, if such centralization was inimical to the Church, why should it not be seen as inimical to other associations in society, such as cooperatives and labor unions? More dangerously, why, if centralization is evil in the state, is it not evil in the religious sphere, in the Church of Rome? The period of authoritarianism under Pope Gregory during this period of intense reflection was bound to have acted as a catalytic on Lamennais's thought processes.

Thus prior to and inexorably leading up to his excommunication from the Church, there were the announced goals of *L'Avenir*; but these were directed entirely against the French state, not yet to the Church. It was when he published his *Paroles d'un Croyant* in 1834 and challenged the Church alone with the State to adopt the principles of pluralist democracy that his career with the Church had to be terminated. Throughout his life prior to about 1830, Lamennais saw the Church as no mere religious autarchy, for all its massive panoply of

Papal Christianity, but rather as the potential inspiration of an intellectual, social, and moral rejuvenation of Western Europe. In the beginning he thought the state his only enemy. It was the climax of his life when he concluded that the monistic Church is not more compatible with a free society than is the monistic state—or, for that matter, any other structure of authority in society. "Centralization," he wrote, "induces apoplexy in the center and anemia in the extremities."

Like Tocqueville, Lamennais saw the twin menaces of modern life to be, on the one hand, a rampant individualism, and on the other, the centralization of power. Also like Tocqueville, Lamennais recognized the linkage between those two forces. For the centralization of state power to reach its maximum, it was necessary that the population be ground down into particles as small and helpless as possible, down into individuals, lone and isolated. Complementarily, for individualism to reach the state of prosperity its advocates desired, it was necessary for human beings to be separated as far as possible from the traditional structures of the social order: family, local community, church, class, etc. And this was a process in which the atomizing power of centralization of the state was crucial.

"Despotism," wrote Tocqueville in 1840,

> which by its nature is suspicious, sees in the separation among men the surest guarantee of its continance, and usually makes every effort to keep them separate. Equality places men side by side, unconnected by any common tie; despotism raises barriers to keep them asunder.

Nearly a decade before Tocqueville's words were published, Lamennais, still within the Church, wrote:

> From equality is born independence, and from independence isolation. As each man is circumscribed, so to speak, in his individual life, he no longer has more than his individual strength for defending himself if he is attacked; and no individual strength can offer a sufficient guarantee of security against that incomparably greater force which is called sovereignty and from which arises the necessity of a new liberty, the liberty of association.

Interest in free, intermediate associations as socializing forces for individuals and as buffers against the power of the state, the democratic state included, is thus more nearly a conclusion reached (by Lamennais) in the light of European and particularly French affairs than it is the result of Tocqueville's short visit to America and his discovery there of the large number of free, intermediate associations.

In truth, by the time Tocqueville came to write Part II of *Democracy*, his own attention was much more closely fixed upon his own France than it was — despite the full title of his work — *in America.*

It was Lamennais's great contribution, one joined in due time by Tocqueville's own, to remind his readers and listeners that society precedes state and police: "If one wants to get a just idea of our present condition, one must first understand that no government, no police, no order would be possible if men were not united beforehand by ties which already constitute them in a state of society." This point of view would become a major theme in not only nineteenth-century Catholic sociology, but the sociology of the main stream — including that of Émile Durkheim, who was very far from being a Catholic believer. Lamennais wrote almost entirely as the social reformer, but in the process of articulating his reform position — such as that emblazoned on his 1830 newspaper, *L'Avenir* — he found himself exploring ever more deeply the whole problem of the individual and society.

If, he said, in effect refuting Hobbes, men were indeed products of a turbulent state of nature, engaged there in a war of all against all, then only the most despotic of political states, of leviathans, would be equal to the task of maintaining order. But a state of nature in such terms has never existed. Long before war engendered the rise of the military state, human beings lived in close kinship amid religious, familial, and local groups. Unhappily, there has been recurrent conflict throughout history between these groups and the political state. The Jacobin effort during the French Revolution to level and atomize social groups and associations, in the name of the freedom of the individual and the unity of the state, was only the latest and perhaps most annihilative of the political state's wars on the groups which lie intermediate to the individual and that state.

The essence of the problem of freedom in modern society is thus placed by Lamennais, as it would be by Tocqueville, essentially in the realm of association — family, church, local community, guild, etc. — rather than in the familiar terms of individual *vs.* state. Whether under monarchy or republic, Lamennais wrote, "where there exist only individuals there is no possible protection against arbitrary authority without freedom of association." Intermediate associations had been at their strongest, Lamennais wrote, during the great Middle Ages when the political state was weak and the ideas of individualism were not yet prominent.

As the result of the Reformation, the Enlightenment and most recently the French Revolution, "there exist today in France only individuals. All the particular centers of political influence founded on special rights and distinct interest, all the hierarchies, all the corporations, have been dissolved."

Democracy is not necessarily the answer, for without freedom of association democracy, no matter how deeply pledged to the welfare of the people, always threatens to become despotic itself; more despotic in potentiality at least than even monarchy, for in monarchy there is a distance maintained between government and people that prevents the roots of power from binding people and state into one indivisible entity. "Without freedom of association," wrote Lamennais, "no democracy could survive for two days; it would transform itself into despotism immediately." It is interesting to compare this judgment with Tocqueville's in Part I of *Democracy*, published in 1835: "There are no countries in which associations are more needed to prevent the despotism of faction or the arbitrary power of a prince than those which are democratically constituted."

Lamennais was above all the tribune of the working classes. In his *Le Livre du Peuple* (1837), he addressed the masses in France:

> You have to create in the material order a less precarious, a less difficult existence; to combat hunger, to see to it that your wives and children are assured the necessities which are lacking to none among all creatures, but only to man. Now why are you in need? Because others absorb the fruits of your labor and grow fat on them. Whence comes this wrong? From the fact that each of you, deprived in his isolation of the means of establishing and maintaining a real concurrence between capital and labor, is delivered without protection to the avidity of those who exploit you. How will you get out of this fatal dependence? By uniting, by forming associations. What one cannot do, ten can, and a thousand can do still better.

Lamennais was no more a socialist than was Tocqueville. He and Tocqueville shared a deeply pessimistic view of the real condition of the working classes under a manufacturing system. Indeed, Tocqueville thought that the greatest threat to the freedom of workers, in the long run, was the "new aristocracy" created by the manufacturing economy within democracy. Lamennais did not disagree with this belief in the slightest. Because of his incessant addressing of the workers by speech and tract, he was one of the most popular and influential voices of social democracy in France. But he was not a socialist, and he spent a good deal of his reformist labors in warning the workers against socialist doctrine. He was repelled by the socialist insistence upon collectivism, upon communal ownership of property. "All questions of freedom reduce themselves in practice to questions of property." If by socialist, he wrote in 1848 when, with Tocqueville, he worked on the side of the revolution in that year, "one means the doctrines of such men as Saint-Simon and Fourier . . . which are based on the negation of property and the family, the answer is no; I am not a socialist." In his *Recollections* Tocqueville makes evident that of all the groups struggling for power in the Revolution of 1848 the socialists and even the social democrats were among the most dangerous, by virtue of their "disease of envy" and also naïve belief that the plight of the impoverished can ever be remedied by legislation.

For Lamennais the largest importance of private property flowed from the reinforcing effect it had upon the unity and stability of the family. "The principle which constitutes the family by regulating the union of man and wife is a vital law of humanity," he wrote. "It is the entire order of duties and rights without which no society would endure." He cited bitterly the doctrine of those socialists who, taking their inspiration from the Jacobins during the Revolution of '89, declared that the child belongs first to the state and only then to the family of procreation. But for Lamennais the family has an imprescriptible right over its own. No external authority, not even that of the state, can rightfully interfere under any pretext in the affairs of the family group "without violating its indefeasible liberties." To the family must go the absolute right over the kind and source of education for its children. Pluralism in education was as important to Lamennais as was pluralism in the society at large. There must be diversity of the educational establishment and an end to the monopoly of education held by the state since the Revolution. He distinguishes sharply between *éducation* and *enseignment*, the first entailing moral as well as mental development and thus crucially involving the family; the second meaning instruction alone, proceeding from a curriculum.

The family is, for Lamennais, the molecule of society, the smallest unit into which society at large may be reduced. The family is society writ small; the microcosm. His strongest criticism of the Enlightenment and the Jacobin legislation in the Revolution proceeds from what he saw as their attitudes toward the family, ranging from indifference to extreme hostility. Both Enlightenment and Revolution premised the individual as the analytical unit of society and as the autonomous holder of rights, that is, natural rights. But, wrote Lamennais, the individual is a metaphysical fallacy. The individual, compared with society, is transient, brief: "the shadow of a dream." Above all individualism — including its doctrines of natural rights, its false axiom of equality, and its sandheap-conception of the state and society — is the inexorable step toward political despotism.

*　　*　　*

By way of conclusion I want to suggest explicitly that there is not merely an intellectual affinity between Lamennais and Tocqueville but an intellectual linkage in time. By the time Tocqueville came of age in the 1820s, Lamennais was famous, at first chiefly among conservative Catholics for his epochal *Essai sur l'Indifference* with its demand for the complete freedom of the Roman Catholic Church from each of the national states in Europe which followed Erastian and Gallican ideas of the Church's necessary bondage. But, as I have noted, it was the destiny of Lamennais to steadily widen his message, to address not only the bondage of the Church but what he saw as the bondage of other forms of association ranging from the family to the school, the local community, above all the naturally free associations intermediate between individual and state, at once vessels of socialization for individuals and buffers against the power of the state.

The sources of Tocqueville's fundamental ideas, especially those of the two parts of *Democracy in America*, but also of *The Old Regime and the French Revolution*, have yet to be systematically and copiously explored. Andre Jardin's recent, deservedly praised *Tocqueville: A Biography* (1988) is weakest on the roots of Tocqueville's thought. He does, however, cite Lamennais three times, not so much as source as but as important influence upon the milieu in which Tocqueville wrote. Professor Robert Paxton of Columbia, in a review of Jardin's biography published in *The New York Review of Books* (2 March 1989), also suggests briefly the possible pertinence of Lamennais to an understanding of Tocqueville.

Up to the present moment it is the Enlightenment, I regret to say, that is most often cited as the primary source: the Enlightenment of the *philosophes*, including even Rousseau. But it is hard to imagine a greater contrast between bodies of ideas than that between the Enlightenment — with the partial exception here of Montesquieu — and the central ideas and themes of Tocqueville's two classics, *Democracy* and *The Old Regime*. True, the Enlighteners wrote a great deal about freedom, and so of course did Lamennais and Tocqueville. But whereas Rousseau and his contemporaries saw the chief threats to individual freedom to life in church, guild, patriarchal family, and other intermediate associations, and saw the democratic state based upon the general will as the sovereign hope for emancipation from these ancient groups, it was the merit of Lamennais and then Tocqueville to see the real problem of freedom in very different, almost diametrically opposite terms.

We will look in vain to Rousseau for any recognition of the values of decentralization, political pluralism, and of the intermediate associations of society. The idea of separation of powers was repugnant to Rousseau, as was any thought of strong social interdependences which didn't spring from the state alone. Rousseau is the political monist *par excellence*. Both Lamennais and Tocqueville exemplify — indeed are architects of — the plural order, the kind of polity within which individual freedoms are reinforced by the freedom of associations: religious, social, economic, and other.

Lamennais's pluralism is rooted in the liberal Catholicism which he founded in the 1820s as an answer to both the conservatism and the egalitarian individualism of his age. So is his passion for political decentralization and for freedom of association. He distrusted the kind of democracy that the legatees of the Enlightenment were preaching, the kind that had briefly flared up during the Revolution and the Terror and which remained a powerful threat to freedom. Allowing for the signal differences between Lamennais and Tocqueville, the conclusion is unavoidable, I believe, that Tocqueville's indebtedness to the movement that produced the liberal and social Catholic traditions of the nineteenth century is hardly less than Lamennais's own.

A Strategy for Freedom

by Otto von Habsburg

A realistic picture of worldwide developments shows that we are in a crucial period of changes. These changes affect practically every field of human activity, not the least in the realms of geopolitics and public affairs. Suddenly a world which has been more-or-less immobilized since the fateful agreement of February 1945 is visited by an earthquake which is shaking the established structures.

Politically, the period extending from 1945 to approximately 1983 can be called the Yalta Order. Of course, in those four decades there were changes, revolutions, and especially cataclysmic events on the African continent. Nevertheless, the global balance of forces was not fundamentally affected. This applies especially to the two main superpowers, America and Russia, as well as to their relations with Europe and the Far East. The fact that, suddenly, global stability is again upset, must be analyzed.

We had already seen one worldwide movement, namely the abortive uprising of the Left in 1968. It was quite instructive. Exactly the same phenomena—absurd programs, strange, slogans, and dirty behavior—appeared simultaneously in Paris and in Peking, in London and in Chicago. The timing and irrationality of the uprising were such that comprehension and dialogue were almost inconceivable. An outstanding Chinese scholar spoke in this context of the revolutionaries of 1968 being in the throes of a mental plague comparable to the murderous epidemics in the Middle Ages. It came as unexpectedly as it vanished, overnight. The present movement, however, despite some similarities, seems more deeply rooted in certain initial facts, almost without exception global in scope.

Probably the most significant phenomenon is the end of space in its pristine sense. In the past, distances played a near-decisive role, especially in wartime. As the potentialities for action on the part of contending powers were limited by the capabilities first of their ships, later of their aircraft, there existed havens in the world where people could find refuge from war. Furthermore, there were certain powers, notably the United States, which in two world wars enjoyed the privilege of being able to hit their enemies, while the latter had no means to strike back. The "arsenal of democracy," as the U.S.A. was called in the Second World War, was thus invulnerable. All this changed with the advent of nuclear weapons, especially after the development of intercontinental ballistic missiles. From then on, as Louis Armand has stated, everybody could be seen and killed anywhere in the world. Safety vanished as the possibility of spreading terror everywhere became a new element of global significance.

A direct consequence of this event was the fact that the old notion of military bases lost much of its past meaning. Every corner of the world can be reached by missiles launched from submarines. Simultaneously, the concept of alliances between big powers and small countries has been reassessed. In the past, when a big power came to help a smaller partner (say, Great Britain coming to the aid of Belgium), the risk which the former incurred in case of defeat was limited. It could lose a colony, perhaps a province, a dynasty could fall, but certainly the very existence of the nation was never at stake. Now this is no longer so. With weapons of mass destruction, risks have become unlimited. Consequently, if a major nuclear power goes to the help of a weaker ally, its own survival becomes the issue. The consequence is obvious: today a superpower can no longer fulfill its treaty obligations. It can still conclude treaties, but these, as General de Gaulle quite rightly realized, can no longer be truly military. The superpower must stop short of direct nuclear involvement on the battlefield. In other words, it will only use its ultimate weapon for the defense of its own national territory.

Parallel to the development of intercontinental ballistic missiles came the explosion in the means of information. In the past, even as late as in the days of Josef Stalin, a totalitarian power had ample means in order, if needed, to cut off its nation entirely from all news of the world, so that the people could learn only what their government wanted to tell them. This monopoly of information was first breached by the revolution of the transistor. After this development, information on world affairs reached nations which had been closed to knowledge of the outside world in the past. This played a major role during the years of decolonization.

With the development of television and its lightning-like transmission of information, the full impact of each world event could be felt everywhere at the same time. In the past, people were mostly untouched by what happened far away from home, since they learned of these news items only after a cooling-off delay. But today a bomb which explodes in Basra or Noumea is immediately seen and heard by everybody in his own room. Consequently, news items are not only spreading within seconds, they are also carrying a message, especially when transmitted "live." Furthermore, each event has global repercussions. This changes the world outlook of many people, especially so since usually they are not given the whole picture of any given event, but only the highlights.

This new development is raising everywhere the problem of what one might call the "cultural power" of the mass media, which is now a politically decisive element. It has, furthermore, the privilege of being able to influence public opinion without incurring any responsibility, and to criticize everything without being criticized in turn. It is a power without control. Politicians who run afoul of it are punished by defeat in elections, but people who misuse the mass media incur virtually no risk.

Today this cultural power is at least as decisive as the judicial, the legislative, or the executive branches of government were in the past. Thus the present system of checks and balances no longer functions adequately, for there is neither check nor balance to the cultural power of the mass media. This imbalance applies both in regard to individual states and to global politics.

The new dimension has one advantage: totalitarian powers can no longer act as they did before. There was much praise for Gorbachev's *glasnost*, his slogan of more transparence. In fact, the Russian dictator only acknowledged something that was beyond his control. He admitted that he did not possess the power of Stalin and that, consequently, the Soviet defense against undesirable news would no longer entail the jamming of broadcasts, but only the manipulation of available information.

A significant fact worth highlighting in this context is the importance of words as a political weapon, a concept which has not been adequately understood by the West. The Communists, on the other hand, were past masters at changing the meaning of words to their advantage, thus preparing a spiritual battleground on which they held all the privileged positions. Already today, in many countries one speaks a Marxist language without knowing it. A typical case is the practice of making "justice" and "equality" synonymous, which is at present universally accepted. With that blurring of language accomplished, plans for enforced equality, itself often the greatest violation of human rights, are effected. There are other, similar cases of language manipulation—such as, for instance, the newspeak term "underprivileged," which conveys a subtle message.

Other factors in our times are the new technologies and the speeding-up of the economic process. The basic elements of the economy are no longer raw materials, but brain power and flexibility. Computers have accelerated work considerably and have dramatically reduced the time-span which existed previously between the invention and its practical implementation. Slow and plodding manual or intellectual work is a thing of the past. The computer accomplishes in one second what previously took many hours to resolve.

Our economy is also afflicted by the fact that finances have become international. This is especially the case since the oil shock of 1973, when there was created an unprecedented situation in which enormous funds could be held by countries unable to invest them on their own territory. Kuwait, for instance, which in 1990 had holdings of over 300 billion U.S. dollars, has no natural wealth: neither water nor raw materials, but only oil under the sand which is being pumped mostly by foreign interests. By this fact capital has become infinitely mobile, since it is no longer invested in long-range projects but moves around, from country to country, from bank to bank, disrupting the international financial system. The impact is multiplied by the acceleration of relations between the various stock exchanges. In the past, economic events took some time to send their shockwaves around the world. There were pauses for reflection. Now this is no longer the case. We have in the world a 24-hour stock exchange, in which the processing by computer multiplies the effect of any upward or downward trend. This, too, increases instability.

Overshadowing these developments are the spiritual challenges of our times. People are today more insecure than ever. Modern developments raise more questions than they solve. Each new advance creates unprecedented problems. People who had been taught to believe in endless material progress are beginning to ask themselves questions as they perceive the limits of the miracle. Hence the growing demand for spiritual answers, which the established churches all too often fail to deliver. They have, under the influence of the materialistic nineteenth century, increasingly turned to worldly affairs and forgotten their primarily spiritual mission. They try to conform to what they consider the "spirit of the times." They thus infringe on the domain of the state—an area in which they are as incompetent as was Caesar when he dabbled in theology. As a result, sects are beginning to dwell where originally the established religions held sway. These strange communities will not be exorcized by hysterical denunciation; they will vanish only when the old churches reassume their real task.

Regardless of these temporary weaknesses, we are approaching a religious era. Materialism is on the way out. The quest for spiritual values is more widespread than has been generally assumed. This can be observed particularly in the scientific community. In the nineteenth century, the crushing majority of scientists were agnostics. Those who were not did not dare to proclaim their religious faith. This is no longer so. A leading thinker recently remarked that at the present level of knowledge a genuine and responsible scientist could end only two ways: by suicide or by becoming deeply religious. While in our day crowds are still leaving the churches, swept by the materialistic wave, science is reentering the House of God by the back door. Cultural and religious influence spreads from the top to the bottom. Thus in the past science destroyed the roots of religion while the people still clung to their religious tradition; now the reverse has set in. When real intellectuals return to God, that will affect the great masses. It is not exaggerated to say that, barring a worldwide catastrophe, we are on the eve of a real spiritual revolution.

All of these developments affect every regional and world power simultaneously. Nevertheless, the consequences and the impact are different on each of them. This is particularly evident when comparing the socialist countries and those following the principles of a market economy. The latter, being flexible, have been able to adapt themselves; furthermore, in their liberal atmosphere spiritual forces, while challenged by materialism, have been able to remain alive. Socialism on the other hand, has remained paralyzed in the crucial times of change. If today we witness the end of the Marxist system all over the world, it is because while capitalism was able to adjust to the new conditions, socialism has been unable to do so. The desperate efforts of Mikhail Gorbachev, the *perestroika*, changed nothing, for the notions of socialism and new technologies are incompatible. The crisis of the Soviet Union showed how much it was out of step with modern times. Its lack of flexibility was the beginning of *rigor mortis*.

This technical imbalance, while arousing hopes of solving the problems created in Yalta, is nevertheless not absolutely decisive. There are the factors of willpower and military morale, which also play a role in world affairs. One day I spoke with an outstanding black African statesman who said, concerning Russia: "When I walk in the jungle and meet a gorilla, this is always dangerous; though if the gorilla is bleeding, it is generally mortal." Even now, in the days of Boris Yeltsin and Yevgeny Shaposhnikov, Russia is the wounded gorilla.

This not only applies to the fact that the former Soviet Union has lost touch with the world economy, be it in agriculture or in information. Russia remains today the last great colonial power in a time of global decolonization. The French were already established in western Africa when the Russians first crossed the Urals to conquer Asiatic territory. Today the Russians amount to less than 50% of the toal population of the former U.S.S.R., but still retain a high percentage of all the leading positions in the commonwealth states, be it in the army, the party, or the economy. This is a situation which cannot last — the more so since, due to differences in birth rates, the Russian minority becomes smaller every day. The western part of the U.S.S.R. resembles democratic Europe, in that coffins outnumber cradles. In the Asiatic republics of the Soviet Union, the colonial area, birth rates are on the level of developing countries. This is a situation which, long range, cannot endure. Decolonization is coming to the intermediary structure replacing the U.S.S.R. as it came to other countries in the world. One should note in this connection that already the neighbors of what used to be the U.S.S.R., who all have claims against Moscow, are beginning to show the will to challenge the status quo. The Japanese attitude on the southern Kuriles is significant in this regard.

These facts, which I have summarized only briefly, are bound to affect our present situation. Of course, with the development of modern weaponry, old-style military conflicts become unlikely. They may still take place in the form of a last desperate plunge, or as the consequence of a major error. Nevertheless, the danger of major conflicts is now relatively small.

The place of direct military action is taken—we saw it clearly in the last years of the Cold War—by the growing utilization of disinformation and political warfare. Here totalitarian forces still perceive promising areas, since the West is badly prepared. This is due not only to the fact that our political horizon is rather narrow, hemmed in by election dates, but by the lack of an all-embracing worldview. Too few people see the world as a unit, with interaction in every part. It is this false perspective which leads to the glaring errors of our times—as, for instance, the belief that peace can be achieved by disarmament. History proves that this is not the case. Weapons are neutral, neither good nor bad. Their moral qualification comes from the people who handle them. Lasting peace has only been possible once political tensions have disappeared. When people are no longer afraid, they scrap weapons they no longer need. Indeed, our recent disarmament conferences have shown that the big powers are ready to discard only those weapons which, in their balance-books, have already been reduced to zero.

An illusion similar to that of peace through disarmament is that of achieving a lasting peace by freezing the present order. True détente is unthinkable as long as the present Yalta borders are maintained. It is only conceivable when people are truly satisfied with the situation as it exists. But when the Western powers accept mere words and take them for facts, they will always be easily outmaneuvered. They need a strategy in conformity with present conditions to find a way toward genuine global peace.

When looking at the world from this perspective, one realizes that the only technique to achieve peace is the one that was elaborated at the Congress of Vienna to end the terror of the French Revolution and the Napoleonic Wars. It was the greatness of the peacemakers of that time that they realized that to create a genuine understanding between nations, one had to ban fear by including the vanquished in the peaceful agreement, and to set down universal principles applicable to all nations. This would create an element of stability in international life.

Seen thus, Vienna was the exact opposite of Yalta. The former gave us a long period of peace; the latter gave us the Cold War. The vanquished powers were excluded from the negotiations, and even the smaller allies of the victorious great powers were not admitted, including such countries as France. This brought the dramatic protest of General de Gaulle when the data of the Yalta Agreement were revealed.

Thus, we must strive not for a revolution of terror but a world revolution of freedom. We are on the best road to achieve this. Today our freedom is already attracting the people of Eastern and Central Europe; and it will continue to do so, especially if our ideals are backed by real strength. Our firmest weapon will be a universal principle which will permit objective and applicable solutions; a principle, unfortunately forgotten in Helsinki. Hence the weakness of the Agreement. Helsinki was supposed to safeguard all borders for all times. This is absurd, as shown by the explosion of Yugoslavia. The only lasting solution is to be found through the free self-determination of nations, which was promised to humanity in two world wars and thereafter cynically cast aside. Today it is a genuine idée-force, which has a tremendous international impact. I myself could note this in my discussions with Russian and Communist leaders. They are in trouble when confronted with the idea of self-determination, because it destroys—if they refuse to apply it—all their fake structures of a pseudo-democracy. Self-determination will be the principle which can serve as a basis for international peace. In a period of democracy a democratic approach is needed.

We must stand on these grounds clearly and without wavering. A strategy of freedom can only be based on realism and on principles. We must maintain these values and apply self-determination, not only to the people of those countries who were vanquished, but also of those who won.

The problem with which today the former Soviet Union confronts the world can only be resolved by granting self-determination to each and every nation. This may be easier today than in the past. The great continental unifications, such as the European Community, will permit this principle to be applied within a common framework. There never was a time when the possibility of peace in freedom has been greater than today. Success depends now on Western realism and the determination not to bow to opportunistic considerations. In politics, as in international affairs, it is not our task to be popular; it is to be credible.

"While in New York I ran into the extensive book The Conservative Mind *by Russell Kirk. I chose it to read on the ship going back to Europe, and when I laid it down after my arrival in Geneva, I had no doubt about several things: that I had just read in substance and form the most interesting book I had met with in a long time, that I had been touched by the noblest American tradition, and that I had seldom experienced in a livelier manner what an impersonal, spiritual comradeship can mean. Here, so it seemed to me, I had found the true voice of that America I had always wished; but no less clear to me was the fact that this America has much to say to us Europeans, has something to say that is more than a trans-Atlantic parallel and comforting confirmation of our convictions, that the community of the patrimony of both worlds is great enough to bring about a real convergence of thought. There are few Americans from whom we can learn so much as from this American."*

— *Wilhelm Roepke, from a translation of his review of* The Conservative Mind *in* Universitas *(Stuttgart), December 1958.*

*   *   *

"Neglect of history has long been an American failing. When that blind spot is coupled with ignorance of the special nature of our own institutions the result is a sort of vacuum in the political part of the brain. Any high-sounding notion fashionable at the moment is accepted without question. The victim is ready to be herded along any path of delusion the opinion-molders choose.

"Delusion is the first fruit of ignorance. The cure for delusion is accurate knowledge. We need to understand our own system as it worked yesterday, as it works today, and as it may be made to work tomorrow. We need information acute enough to cut through the self-serving doubletalk of the politicians of both parties. . . .

"Solutions [to the many problems that face the next generation], if they are to be found at all, will come from the application of our American tradition of somehow managing to balance off the claims of personal liberty against the imperatives of efficient mass organization. For this task we need all the verve, all the refusal to accept things as they are, all the brains the new generation has to offer."

— *John Dos Passos, in his foreword to* The American Cause, *by Russell Kirk, 2nd edition, 1966.*

"For Kirk, as for Burke and Eliot, religion, and particularly Christianity, is the key to restoring the harmony of a properly ordered society, since religion is indispensable to a revitalized and restored moral imagination. 'At heart, all social questions are exercises in ethics; and ethics, in turn, depend upon religious faith.' In short, 'Political problems, at bottom, are religious and moral problems.' Kirk goes on to explain:

> Politics moves upward into ethics, and ethics ascends to theology. The true conservative, in the tradition of Burke . . . is a theist, for he sees this world as a place of trial, governed by a power beyond human ability to comprehend adequately; he is convinced that earthly perfection is a delusion and in our time, quite possibly, a notion employed by the power of Evil to crush Good by the instrument of a pseudo-good.

And here Kirk especially underlines 'the power of religious understanding—lacking which there can exist no order in the soul and no order in the state.'

"With regard to the pertinence of Christianity, Kirk writes: 'The foundation of our civil social order, like that of Burke's Britain, is not an ideology, some "armed doctrine": rather, it is the Christian religion.' Why is Christianity the indispensable component? The answer lies in the symbol of the Incarnation: 'Incarnation, the Logos made flesh, gives us the possibility of conquering past and future. If we do not know the divine, we are driven by the diabolical impulses of the underworld.' Elsewhere Kirk contends, 'What Platonism could not provide, Christian belief did: an incarnate model of the way that man should live, and a mode of participating in the life eternal.' 'The Incarnation has made it possible for us to enter into an abiding order of the soul, and so not to perish as beasts perish.' 'Christian teaching . . . did enable many people to order their souls, and so to improve the order of the commonwealth.' Kirk reflects, 'I trust that none of us shall become political Christians; but I hope that we shall not be afraid to infuse Christian faith into politics.' "

—John P. East, from his essay
"Russell Kirk as a Political
Theorist" in Modern Age,
Winter 1984.

"Although some consider cheerful conservatism a contradiction in terms, it is Kirk's very conservatism that gives him hope, for, as Edmund Burke reminds us, the goodness of one person, the courage of one man, the strength of one individual can turn the course of history and renew an entire civilization. As supporters of free enterprise, believers in democracy, and guardians of the Judaeo-Christian principles on which America was founded, we are committed to the idea that one person — even fighting against seemingly impossible odds — can change the world. . . . [We] would do well to remember T. S. Eliot's words that Kirk quotes with approval: '. . . there is no such thing as a Lost Cause because there is no such thing as a Gained Cause. We fight because we know that our defeat and dismay may be the preface to our successors' victory.' The Sage of Mecosta concludes, 'In every period, some will endeavor to pull down the permanent things, and others will defend them manfully.' Russell Kirk has cast his lot with those manning the barricades, and he invites us to be his comrades in arms."

— *Edwin J. Feulner, Jr.*
in his foreword to the
Heritage Foundation's
1992 President's
Essay.

*   *   *

"Lord, we ask your blessing on your disciple, your devotee in the honest pursuit of truth. Bless and protect Russell Kirk, his family, his colleagues in that honorable search. Reward him for what he has foresworn as distraction and compromise, comfort him in his studying, nourish the romantic spirit we love in him and never let him forget a story. Supply him with a few more ghosts.

"Bless and prosper a great gentleman, a man of lordly honor who has ever reminded us that the life of the spirit, the clear light of truth, and the dignity of honest conviction outrank the spirit of any age. Thank you, Lord, for him. Amen."

— *Monsignor Eugene V. Clark, from*
his remarks at a testimonial
dinner for Russell Kirk at the
Mayflower Hotel, Washington, D.C.,
October 1, 1981.

A Russell Kirk Bibliography

Books Now in Print

John Randolph of Roanoke: A Study in American Politics. Third edition. Indianapolis, IN: Liberty Press, 1978.

The Conservative Mind, from Burke to Eliot. Seventh edition. Washington, DC: Regnery Gateway, 1986.

Prospects for Conservatives. Fourth edition. Washington, DC: Regnery Gateway, 1989.

Academic Freedom: An Essay in Definition. Reprint of 1955 edition. Westport, CT: Greenwood Press.

Beyond the Dreams of Avarice: Essays of a Social Critic. Second edition. Peru, IL: Sherwood Sugden & Co., 1991.

The American Cause. Reprint of 1957 edition. Westport, CT: Greenwood Press.

The Intemperate Professor and Other Cultural Splenetics. Second edition. Peru, IL: Sherwood Sugden & Co., 1988.

Edmund Burke: A Genius Reconsidered. Second edition. Peru, IL: Sherwood Sugden & Co., 1988.

Enemies of the Permanent Things: Observations of Abnormity in Literature and Politics. Third edition. Peru, IL: Sherwood Sugden & Co., 1988.

Eliot and His Age: T. S. Eliot's Moral Imagination in the Twentieth Century. Third edition. Peru, IL: Sherwood Sugden & Co., 1988.

The Roots of American Order. Third edition. Washington, DC: Regnery Gateway, 1992.

Watchers at the Strait Gate. Sauk City, WI: Arkham House, 1984.

Work and Prosperity. Pensacola, FL: A Beka Book, 1988.

Lord of the Hollow Dark. Second edition. Front Royal, VA: Christendom Press, 1989.

America's British Culture. New Brunswick, NJ: Transaction Publishers, 1993.

The Politics of Prudence. Bryn Mawr, PA: Intercollegiate Studies Institute, 1993.

Volumes Edited by Kirk

The Portable Conservative Reader. New York: Viking Penguin, 1984.
The Library of Conservative Thought, by Transaction Publishers
(a selection):

> *Collected Letters of John Randolph of Roanoke to Dr. John Brocken-
> brough, 1812–1833* (edited by Kenneth P. Shorey; foreword
> by Kirk).
>
> *A Critical Examination of Socialism,* by W. H. Mallock (intro-
> duction by Kirk).
>
> *Burke Street,* by George Scott-Moncrieff (introduction by Kirk).
>
> *The Case for Conservatism,* by Francis Graham Wilson (introduc-
> tion by Kirk).
>
> *Orestes Brownson: Selected Political Essays,* by Orestes Brownson
> (introduction by Kirk).
>
> *Regionalism and Nationalism in the United States: The Attack on Levia-
> than,* by Donald Davidson (introduction by Kirk).
>
> *Edmund Burke: Appraisals and Applications* (edited by Daniel E.
> Ritchie; foreword by Kirk).
>
> *Edmund Burke: The Enlightenment and Revolution,* by Peter J. Stan-
> lis (introduction by Kirk).
>
> *The Social Crisis of Our Time,* by Wilhelm Roepke (foreword by
> Kirk).
>
> *We the People: The Economic Origins of the Constitution,* by Forrest
> McDonald (foreword by Kirk).
>
> *The Essential Calhoun,* by John C. Calhoun (edited by Clyde N.
> Wilson; foreword by Kirk).
>
> *A Historian and His World: A Life of Christopher Dawson,* by Chris-
> tina Scott (introduction by Kirk).

Dr. Kirk has written forewords or introductions to a score of serious
books by other authors and has contributed essays to some twenty-five
anthologies. He has been a prolific contributor to such works of
reference as *The Encyclopaedia Britannica, Collier's Encyclopedia, The
World Book Encyclopedia, The Encyclopedia of Southern History, The Dictionary of American Biography, The Dictionary of Political Science, Handbook
of World History, Literature Criticism from 1400 to 1800,* and others.

Books Out of Print at Present

St. Andrews. London: B. T. Batsford, 1954.

The Intelligent Woman's Guide to Conservatism. New York: Devin Adair, 1957.

Old House of Fear. New York: Fleet, 1962.

Confessions of a Bohemian Tory. New York: Fleet, 1963.

The Surly Sullen Bell. New York: Fleet, 1965.

A Creature of the Twilight. New York: Fleet, 1966.

The Political Principles of Robert A. Taft (with James McClellan). New York: Fleet, 1967.

Decadence and Renewal in the Higher Learning. South Bend, IN: Gateway Editions, 1978.

The Princess of All Lands. Sauk City, WI: Arkham House, 1979.

Reclaiming a Patrimony. Washington, DC: Heritage Foundation, 1982.

The Wise Men Know What Wicked Things Are Written on the Sky. Washington, DC: Regnery Gateway, 1987.

The Conservative Constitution. Washington, DC: Regnery Gateway, 1990.

*　　　*　　　*

Bibliography of Kirk's Writings

Russell Kirk: A Bibliography, compiled by Charles Brown. Mount Pleasant, MI: Clarke Historical Library, 1981.

Additional information about Dr. Kirk may be found in *Contemporary Authors, Who's Who in the World, Who's Who in America, Who's Who in the Midwest, International Scholars Directory, The Directory of American Scholars*, and other biographical directories. Chapters about his life and writings may also be found in Henry Regnery's *Memoirs of a Dissident Publisher* (1979) and John East's *The American Conservative Movement* (1986).

This book was typeset
by
Craig W. O'Dell
in 11-point Baskerville on 13 points of lead.
[John Baskerville, English type-designer, b.1706, d.1775.]
DATASET, BLOOMINGTON, ILLINOIS